THE CIVIL WAR
LOVE LETTER QUILT

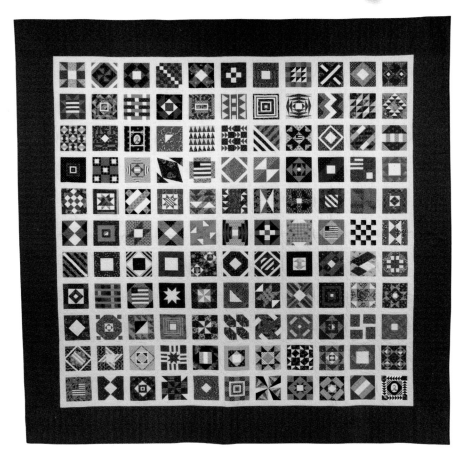

Rosemary Youngs

©2007 Rosemary Youngs
Published by

kp **krause publications**
An Imprint of F+W Publications

700 East State Street • Iola, WI 54990-0001
715-445-2214 • 888-457-2873
www.krausebooks.com

Our toll-free number to place an order or obtain a free catalog is (800) 258-0929.

The patterns are for personal use only, but they may be photocopied.

The following registered trademark terms and companies appear in this publication:

Library of Congress Catalog Number: 2006935648
ISBN 978-089689-487-7

Designed by Marilyn McGrane
Edited by Susan Sliwicki

Printed in China

Dedication

It is with a heart full of love that I dedicate this book to my husband, Tom; my children, Stacey, Johnnathan, Amy and Jeffrey; and my first grandchildren, Hailey Marie and Sophia Grace, and all of those who will follow.

Acknowledgments

Thank you so much to my dear family: my husband Tom; my children: Stacey and her husband, Micah; Johnnathan; Amy and her husband, Matthew; and Jeffrey; as well as my granddaughters, Hailey Marie and Sophia Grace, for all their love and support.

Thank you to my quilting group — Gay Bomers, Barbara David, Natalie Randall, Margo Spencer, Christine Yeager, Norma Zawistowski and Susan Zomberg — who spent Mondays listening to my ideas and testing out the new block design. Thank you for working with the patterns to make a Civil War quilt for this book. Thank you also to Carol Schultz, Dagmar Kessler and Mary Ellen Zeitz for their willingness to make projects for this book.

To my very supportive friends who don't quilt — Pat Kuieck, Marilyn Kozminski, Susan Olthof and Nancy Wagner — thank you for your rare and wonderful friendships. You are truly a blessing in my life.

Thank you to the Attic Window Girls — Pat Anisko, Audrey Berkenpas, Virginia Bergmans, Barbara David, Roberta Decker, Annette Hampton, Megan Harding, Sally Johnson, Bonnie Major, Suzanne Schultz, Sue Steinhauer and Norma Zawistowski — for their inspiration on Tuesday mornings. Each of these women worked to appliqué a special block for the Civil War Soldiers Quilt.

Thank you to my special pen pals — Maureen Baly, Judy Day and JoAnn Fuhler — who inspire me weekly with their letters and who were willing to do a project for this book,

To Tammy Finkler, for her beautiful machine quilting expertise and her willingness to fit our quilting projects into her schedule.

To all of the quilters who have inspired me along my journey, whether I met you at Attic Window, Beaver Island, Grand Quilt, Paducah, Shipshewana or the West Michigan Quilt Guild.

Thank you to the team at Krause Publications for their confidence and encouragement during the writing of this book, especially to my acquisition editor, Candy Wiza, and my editor, Susan Sliwicki.

I am indebted to the families, historical societies, libraries, universities and all of those who helped me with my research. Thank you also to all of those who have treasured the Civil War letters of their ancestors and have preserved their stories.

For my special friends, especially my women's Bible study at Trinity Reformed Church, thank you for your friendships, your encouragement, your prayers and your belief in me.

Most importantly, I want to thank God for the wonderful opportunities and the people I have met through writing, and for always taking the pieces of my life, stitching them together and making something beautiful.

Table of Contents

Introduction

The Civil War began on April 12, 1861, and it touched the life of almost every person living in the United States during that time. More than 600,000 lives were lost, and the battles led to the economic destruction of homes, farms and industries.

Soldiers wrote letters to home from the battlefields, camps, hospitals and even prisons. The letters in this book provide a firsthand account of what the soldiers experienced during the Civil War. The letters are in the soldiers' own words, although some simple grammar and spelling errors are corrected. In some cases, only partial letters are featured.

RUTHERFORD B. HAYES

Hayes joined the 23rd Regiment of Ohio and wrote letters home to his wife and children from the battlefields. In 1877, he became the 19th president of the United States of America. His Civil War letters and photographs are used with permission from the Rutherford B. Hayes Presidential Center. Thank you to Nan Card, curator of manuscripts.

AMHERST B. CHENEY

Cheney enlisted in the Michigan 21st Infantry at the age of 20. He wrote his letters home to a friend, who ended up marrying his brother. Later in life, Cheney was elected to serve in the House of Representatives. His Civil War letters and photographs are used with permission from the Sparta Township Historical Commission. Thank you to Gail Klein.

NEWTON ROBERT SCOTT

Scott joined the 36th Infantry of Ohio volunteers at the age of 20. He wrote letters home to a childhood friend, Hannah, whom he married after the war was over. His Civil War letters and photographs are used with permission from the family of Marjorie Hannah Dalby. Thank you to William S. Proudfoot, Hannah Cones Newton's great-grandson.

SAMUEL MATSON FOX

Fox enlisted with the 6th New Jersey volunteers. He wrote his letters home to his brothers. Fox never returned home; he died of an unknown illness in September 1862. His Civil War letters and photographs are used with permission from David H. Fox, the great-grandson of Samuel's brother, Charles H. Fox, recipient of the letters.

ANDREW L. GATEWOOD

Gatewood wrote letters home to his parents when he began to take classes at the Virginia Military Institute just prior to the start of the war. He later wrote his letters to home from the battlefields. His Civil War letters and photographs are used with permission from the Virginia Military Institute Archives. Thank you to Diane B. Jacob, head of archiving and records management.

DAVID COON

In 1864, at the age of 42, Coon left his wife and seven children to join the 36th Regiment of Wisconsin volunteers. He wrote his letters home to his wife and children. Coon never returned home from the war; he died at the Andersonville prison. His Civil War letters are used with permission from the Wisconsin Historical Society. Thank you to Harold

L. Miller, reference archivist. The photographs are used with permission courtesy of David Coon, great-great-great grandson of David Coon.

DAVID READ EVANS WINN

Winn mustered into service with the 4th Georgia Regiment and wrote his letters home to his wife and two sons. He was killed in action in the battle of Gettysburg. His Civil War letters and photographs are used with permission from the David Read Evans Winn Papers, Special Collections and Archives, Robert W. Woodruff Library, Emory University. Thank you to the Coordinator for Research Services, Naomi L. Nelson and to Kathy Shoemaker, Special Collections and Archives Division Assistant.

SAMUEL CLEMENT ZINSER

Zinser enlisted with the 47th Illinois Infantry. He wrote letters home to his girlfriend, whom he married after the war. His Civil War letters and photographs are used with permission from the Special Collections Center, Bradley University Library. Thank you to Charles J. Frey, special collections librarian. Thank you also to Carol Dorward and the Zinser House in Washington, Illinois for helping me with biographical information.

RICHARD H. ADAMS JR.

Adams was mustered into the 5th Alabama Infantry Regiment. His letters to home were written from the various prisons where he was held. His Civil War letters and photographs are used with permission from the Virginia Military Institute Archives. Thank you to Diane B. Jacob, head of the archives and records management.

ROBERT W. BENNETT

This short story shares details about Bennett, his family Bible and his comrades' escape from prison. It was written by Megan Harding, whose husband, David, is a great-great grandson. The photographs are used with permission from Paul and Norma Harding; Paul is Martha's (Robert W. Bennett's) great-great-grandson.

DAVID BAILEY FREEMAN

This short story shares how Freeman headed to Camp Felton, became a marker for the cavalry and enlisted with the 6th Georgia Cavalry Company D — all at the tender age of 10. The story and photographs are used courtesy of Alan C. Freeman; David was his second great-granduncle.

How to Use This Book

As you have fun piecing together these quilt blocks, enjoy this historical journey through the lives of these Civil War soldiers. Whether you decide to design a simple project or an intricate one or opt to create one of the projects in the book, my wish for you is that you will create a family treasure and have the chance to connect with the Civil War soldiers through their letters.

This book is divided into three sections. The first section covers the general instructions, techniques, fabrics and supplies that are needed. The second section contains a brief introduction to each Civil War soldier and a selection of his Civil War letters; in all 121 letters and 121 patterns are featured. The letters and blocks are followed by ideas for smaller projects and a gallery of quilts.

Fabrics, Tools and Supplies

Fabrics

Choosing fabrics is one of my favorite aspects of quilt making. The possibilities for this quilt are endless. Choosing background fabric is a very important part in the overall effect of your finished project; I suggest using a solid color or a small-scale print. Small-scale prints will be more effective than large-scale prints because the block size is only 6". For the blocks, you may wish to use Civil War reproduction fabrics, solid colors, 1930s reproduction fabrics or a variety of fabrics from your stash.

Thread

I use 100 percent cotton, 50-weight thread in my sewing machine to piece the blocks. It resists shrinking and is available in a variety of colors. For hand quilting, I recommend a strong, 100 percent cotton thread.

Scissors

I keep two different pairs of scissors on hand: one for fabric and one for paper.

Rotary cutters, rulers and mat

I keep two rotary cutters on hand: one to cut fabrics and the other to cut through the fabric once it is sewn to the foundation paper.

Sewing machine needle

It is very important to use a size 14 sewing machine needle if you are foundation piecing the blocks together, because it makes it much easier to rip off the foundation paper.

Foundation paper

Use a lightweight paper that is both easy to tear away and easy to trace on. Try different paper; some choices could include newsprint, computer paper or even tracing paper. Select paper that can easily be run through a copy machine.

Iron and ironing board

You will use an iron and ironing board when you are preparing appliqués. Typically, you will use the iron on a no-steam setting

PIECING THE BLOCKS

This book contains all 121 patterns to make the Civil War Love Letter Quilt. Trace the patterns to make the templates, which can be used in either hand or machine piecing. The more accurate you are when tracing your templates, the easier your blocks will fit together.

Pieced Block Templates

I prefer to use freezer paper because you can easily see through it to trace the templates, and because the templates can be used several times.

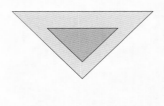 

1. Place freezer paper over the drawing of the block in your book. Trace all of the shapes onto the freezer paper; add a ¼" seam allowance on all sides. To create more exact, clear lines, use a pencil with a thin lead. Number the pieces to keep them in order.
2. Iron the freezer paper on to the right side of your fabric. Remember to set your iron to a no-steam setting.
3. Cut out all of shapes, and assemble them as shown on the pattern.

Foundation piecing

Foundation piecing is an easy technique to piece your blocks together. In this method, fabric is sewn to the paper foundation following a numerical sequence.

1. Decide how many units the pattern will be divided into.
2. Trace the pattern onto the foundation paper; use a ruler and thin-lead pencil. Copy all of the lines of each unit, and add a ¼" seam allowance around each unit.

3. Number the foundation paper in the order that the pieces should be sewn together. The more blocks you finish, the easier this will become.
4. Position the fabrics right sides together on the unmarked side of the foundation.
5. Stitch on the sewing line between the numbers using a very small stitch; 1.5 will work on most machines.
6. Continue stitching all of the pieces in numeric order until the block or unit is completed. Trim the fabric so that it is even with the outside line of the foundation. If you have more than one unit for a block, match the units and stitch them together.
7. Keep the foundation paper in place for now; it will help to stabilize the blocks when you sew them together with the lattice.

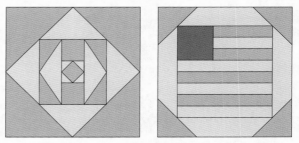

Some blocks can be pieced together as a whole unit.

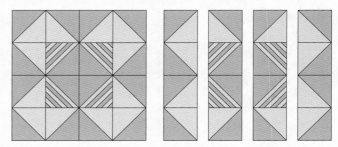

Some blocks need to be pieced together in separate units and then stitched together to make a whole unit.

Assembling the Quilt

Materials

· 8 yd. fabric (background, lattice strips, cornerstones and small inner border)
· 3 yd. fabric (outer border)
· 1 yd. fabric (binding)
· Fat quarters of coordinating fabrics for the 121 blocks
· 9 yd. fabric (backing)

Cutting Instructions

From the background fabric, cut:
  · 220 lattice strips (2" x 6")
  · 100 cornerstones (2" x 2")
  · 2 inner border strips (2" x 81½")
  · 2 inner border strips (2" x 84½")

From the outer border fabric, cut:
  · 2 outer border strips (8½" x 84½")
  · 2 outer border strips (8½" x 100")

From the binding fabric, cut:
  · 10 strips (2" wide x the width of your fabric)

From the backing fabric, cut:
  · 3 pieces (fabric width x 3 yd.)

Assemble the Quilt Top

1. Assemble each of the 121 blocks using the background fabric and various fat quarters.

2. Assemble the blocks, lattice and cornerstones into 11 rows of 11 blocks each.

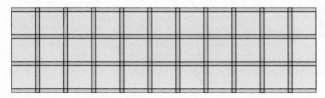

3. Stitch the rows together; match the seams of the cornerstones with the seams of the lattice strips. When all 11 rows are assembled, the project should measure 81½" x 81½".

4. Sew the 81½" inner border strips to the sides of the quilt top.
5. Sew the 84½" inner border strips to the top and bottom of the quilt top.
6. Sew the 84½" outer border strips to the sides of the quilt top.
7. Sew the 100" outer border strips to the top and bottom of the quilt top.

Add the Backing

1. Trim the selvage of each of the three pieces of backing fabric ¼" past the selvage.
2. Sew the pieces together to form a rectangle measuring approximately 108" x 120". Press the seams open.
3. Lay the backing right side down on the floor or table; secure it with tape so that it will remain flat and taut.
4. Center the batting and quilt top right side up. Thread or pin baste the top together.
5. If desired, trim some of the batting and backing off of the quilt; leave approximately 4" around each side of the quilt.
6. Quilt as desired.

Bind the Quilt

1. Sew the 10 binding strips together into one long strip.
2. Iron the binding in half, wrong sides together, along the length of the whole strip.
3. Lay the binding in the middle of one side of the finished quilt and stitch ¼" seam with your raw edges facing the edge of your quilt. Leave 3" to 4" on the end to join the bias later.
4. Stitch within ¼" of the edge of the first corner. With the needle in the down position, turn the quilt, and backstitch off the edge.
5. Fold the binding strip up, always from the corner, to make a 45-degree fold.
6. Bring the strip straight down, and line it up with the raw edge of the next side.
7. Stitch within ¼" of the next corner. Repeat until you approach your starting point.
8. As you get to the point where you first started stitching, stop and overlap both loose ends of the binding where they meet on the quilt.
9. Stitch the binding, right sides together, using ¼" seam allowance.
10. Turn the binding over to the back. Using a blind stitch, stitch on the stitching line

Rutherford B. Hayes and Lucy Webb; wedding portrait taken on December 30, 1852. Photograph courtesy of The Rutherford B. Hayes Presidential Center.

Rutherford B. Hayes

(Oct. 4, 1822 - Jan. 17, 1893)

On Oct. 4, 1822, future president Rutherford B. Hayes was born to Rutherford Hayes and Sophia (Birchard) Hayes. He spent his childhood years living and attending schools in Ohio. After graduating from Harvard Law School, he commenced practicing law in Cincinnati.

Rutherford began keeping a diary at the age of 12, which he kept through most of his life. He also composed many writings, public addresses and letters, some of which were to his wife, Lucy Webb, whom he married in 1852.

On June 27, 1861, Rutherford volunteered his services and registered to fight with the 23rd Ohio Infantry, which was commanded by William S. Rosecrans. He often wrote very positive letters to Lucy and his children from the battlefields. He always showed concern for his wife and his family throughout his letters.

Rutherford fought in major battles throughout the Civil War, including Robert E. Lee's invasion of Maryland, South Mountain, Shenandoah Valley, Cedar Creek and Winchester. He soon was commissioned a colonel in 1862, a brigadier general in 1864 and, in 1865, a major general. Rutherford was injured several times and severely wounded at the Battle of South Mountain in 1864, when he was struck by a musket ball.

In 1864, while still fighting the Civil War, Rutherford was elected to the U.S. House of Representatives for the state of Ohio. He won by a majority of the vote, even though he decided not to do any campaigning due to the war. By 1867, Rutherford was nominated to be governor of Ohio, and he served three terms until 1877, when he resigned to become the 19th president of the United States of America.

While he was president, Rutherford dealt with major events, such as the compromise of 1877, The Desert Land Act, and the Great Railroad Strike of 1877. He even started the tradition of having the Easter Egg Roll for children on the White House lawn. Rutherford made it clear that he was only going to serve one term in office, and he retired in 1881.

Rutherford and Lucy had eight children: Birchard, Webb, Rutherford, Joseph, George, Fanny, Scott and Manning. Three of their eight children died in infancy. He retired to Spiegel Grove in Fremont, Ohio, on property that was given to him by his uncle. On Jan. 17, 1893, Rutherford B. Hayes died at the age of 70.

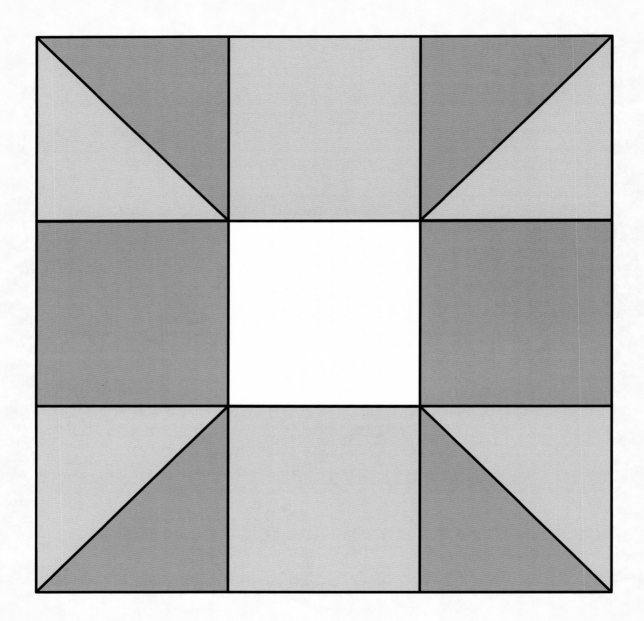

ENTHUSIASM

July 27, 1861

Dear Wife,

Our second day, from Bellaire to this place, was an exceedingly happy one. We traveled about 130 miles in Virginia, and with the exception of one deserted village of Secessionists, we were received everywhere with an enthusiasm I never saw anywhere before.

No such great crowds turned out to meet us as we saw from Indianapolis to Cincinnati assembled to see Lincoln, but everywhere, in the corn and hay fields, in the houses, in the roads, on the hills, wherever a human being saw us, we saw such honest spontaneous demonstrations of joy as we never beheld elsewhere. Old men and women, boys and children — some fervently prayed for us, some laughed and some cried; all did something which told the story. The secret of it is, the defeat at Washington and the departure of some thousands of three-months men of Ohio and Indiana led them to fear they were left to the Rebels of eastern Virginia. We were the first three-year men filling the places of those who left. It was pleasant to see we were not invading an enemy's country but defending the people among whom we came. Our men enjoyed it beyond measure. Many had never seen a mountain; none had ever seen such a reception.

They stood on top of the cars and danced and shouted with delight. We got here in the night. Gen. Rosecrans is with us. No other full regiment here. We march tomorrow up the mountains. You would enjoy such a ride as that of yesterday as much as I did. It was perfect. Now comes the hard work. Goodbye; love to all.

Affectionately,

Rutherford

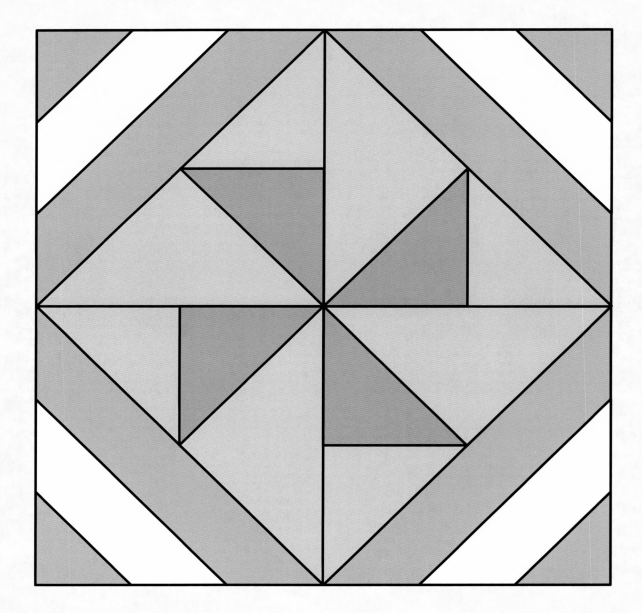

A Secession Ball

July 30, 1861

Dearest,

 We are in the loveliest spot for a camp you ever saw. No, lovelier than that; nothing in Ohio can equal it. Luckily, we are not likely to suffer in that way. We meet many good Union men; the other men are prudently quiet. Our troops behave well. We have had one of those distressing accidents that occurs so frequently in volunteer regiments. You may remember that a son of H.J. Jewett, of Zanesville, president of the Central Ohio Railroad, was, on the request of his father, appointed a first lieutenant in Capt. Canby's company. He joined us at Grafton in company with his father. He had served in a regiment of three-month men in all the affairs in Western Virginia and is very promising. A loaded gun was thrown down from a stack by a careless sentinel, discharging a Minie ball through young Jewett's foot. I was with him in a moment. It is a painful and severe wound, perhaps dangerous. There is a hope he may not be crippled. He bears it well. One of his exclamations was, "Oh, if it had only been a secession ball, I wouldn't have cared. Do you think you can save my leg?" etc., etc.

The ball, after passing through his foot, passed through three of McIlrath's tents, one full of men lying down. It cut the vest of one over his breast as he lay on his back and stirred the hair of another; finally passed clean through a knapsack and struck a man on the leg, barely making a slight bruise and dropping down. Dr. Joe has the flattened bullet now to give to Jewett.

Affectionately,

Rutherford

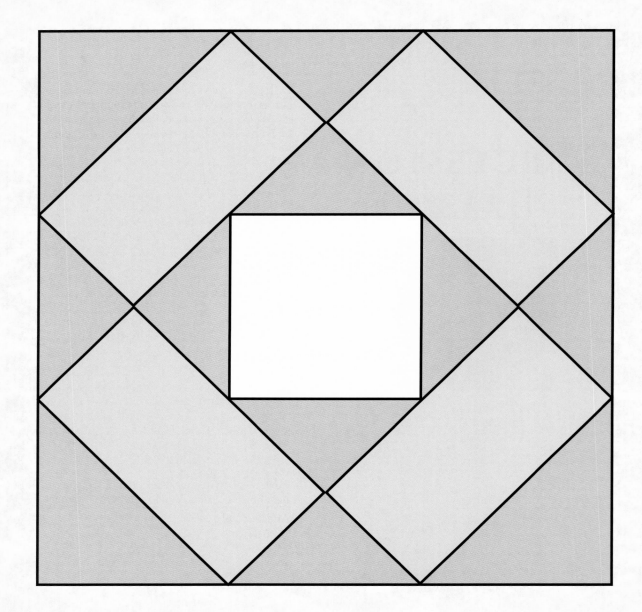

Healthful Region

Aug. 15, 1861

Dearest L,

We had four days of rain ending yesterday morning, such rain as this country of hills and mountains can stay afford. It was gloomy and uncomfortable, but no harm was done. It cleared off beautifully yesterday morning, and the weather has been most delicious since.

This is a healthful region — nobody seriously sick and almost everybody outrageously healthy. I never was better. It is a luxury to breathe. Our regiment has had diverse duties, which keep up excitement enough to prevent us from stagnating. Dr. Joe has got the hospital in good condition: a church in place of the courthouse for the merely comfortable, and a private house for the very sick.

None of our regiment are seriously ill. The sick are devolved upon us from other regiments — chiefly lung complaints developed by marching, measles or exposure. Very few, if any, taken here. We find plenty of good Union men, and most of our expeditions are aided by them. They show a good spirit in our behalf. A large part of our friends in the mountains are the well-to-do people of their neighborhoods and usually are Methodists or other orderly citizens.

Goodbye, dearest. I love you very much. Kiss the boys, and love to all. Tell Webby that during the rain the other night, dark as pitch, my horse, Webb, fell down the hill back of the camp into the river. Swam over to the opposite shore, and at daylight we saw him frisking about in great excitement trying to get back to his companion, Birch. My next horse I shall call Ruddy. Love to Grandma.

Affectionately,

Rutherford

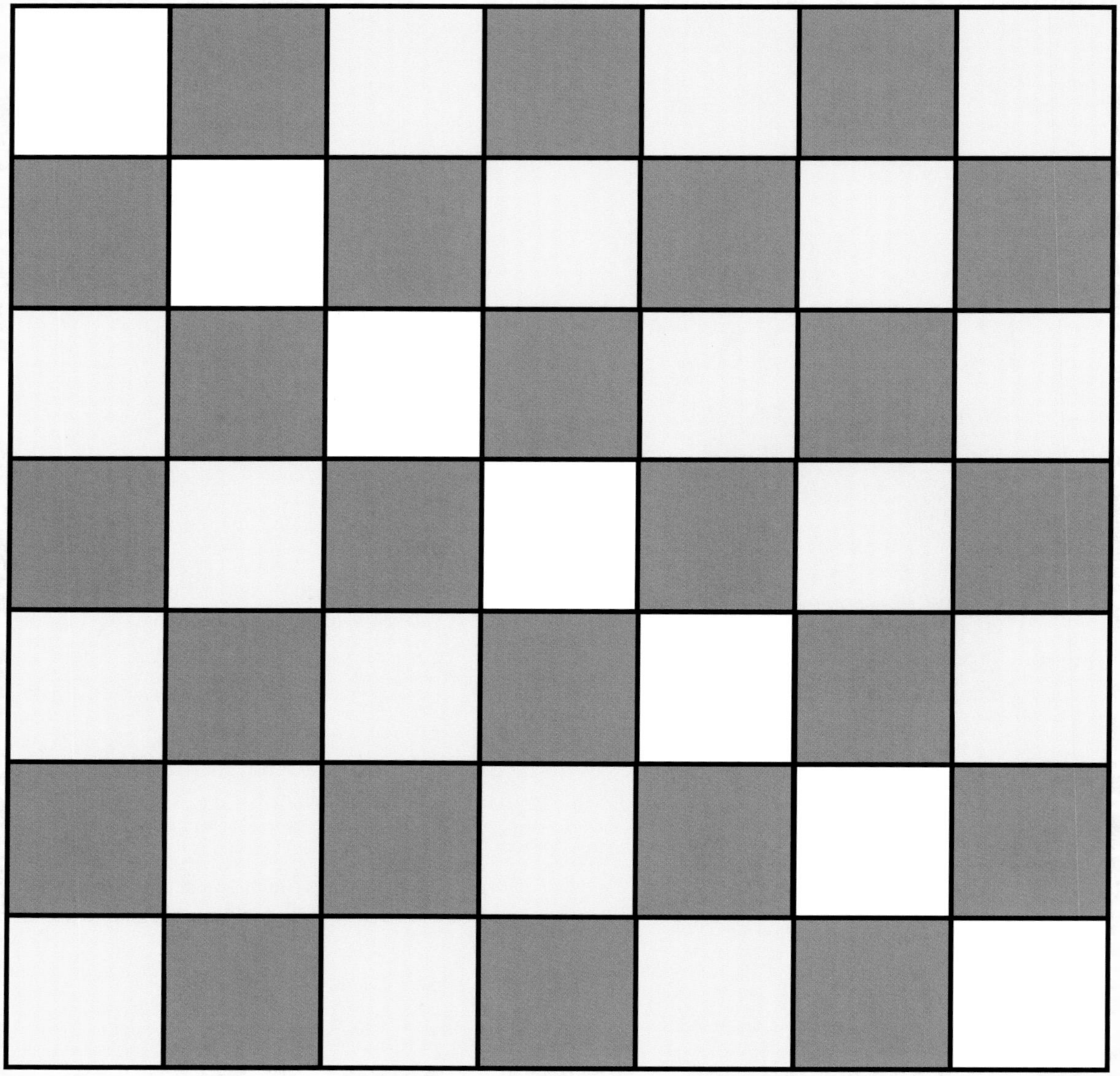

March in the Mountains

Aug. 24, 1861

Dearest,

Your letters are all directed right to Clarksburg, Va.; got one from you, one from Uncle and one from Mother with a nice Testament today. We marched from Buckhannon as I wrote you; but the rain stopped, the air was delicious, the mountain scenery beautiful.

We camped at night in the hills without tents. I looked up at the stars and moon — nothing between me and sky — and thought of you all. Today had a lovely march in the mountains, was at the camp of the enemy on Rich Mountain and on the battlefield. Reached here today. Saw Capt. Erwin and friends enough. It is pleasant. We had one-half of our regiment, one-half of McCook's German regiment and McMullen's Field Battery. Joe and I led the column. The Guthrie Grays greeted us hospitably. Men are needed here, and we were met by men who were very glad to see us for many reasons. We go to the seat of things in Cheat Mountain, perhaps tomorrow.

I love you so much. Write about the dear boys and your kindred; that's enough. Your letter about them is so good.

Affectionately,

Rutherford

P.S. My favorite horse has come out fine again (Webby first, I mean), and Webby second is coming out. Joe and I vote these two days the happiest of the war. Such air and streams and mountains and people glad to see us.

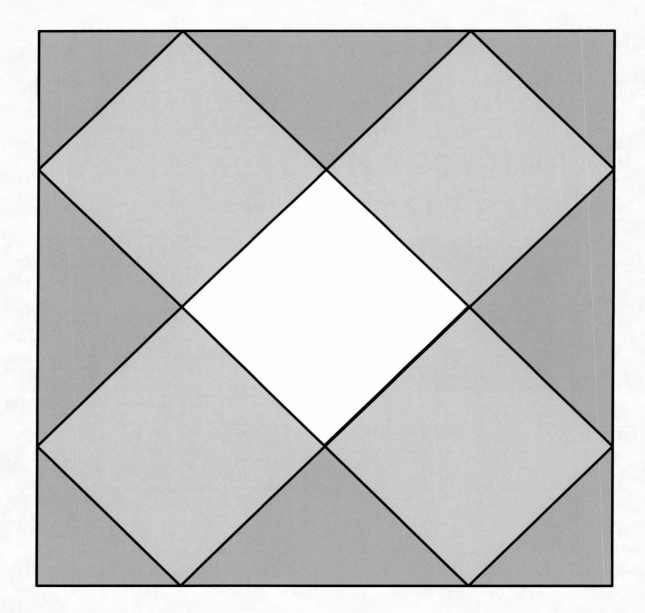

Sorrows
of War

Oct. 9, 1861

Dearest,

Capt. Zimmerman and I have just returned from a long stroll up a most romantic mountain gorge with its rushing mountain stream: a lovely October sun, bright and genial, but not at all oppressive.

We found the scattered fragments of a mill that had been swept away last winter, and following up came to the broken dam, and nearby a deserted home, hastily deserted lately: books, the cradle and child's chair, tables, clock, chairs, etc., etc. Our conjecture is they fled from the army of Floyd about the time of the Carnifax fight. We each picked up a low, well-made, split-bottom chair and clambered up a steep cliff to our camp. I now sit in the chair. We both moralized on this touching proof of the sorrows of war, and I reached my tent a little saddened to find on my lounge in my tidy comfortable quarters your good letter of Oct. 1, directed in the familiar hand of my old friend Herron. Love to him and Harriet. How happy it makes me to read this letter.

Tell Mother Webb not to give up. In the Revolution they saw darker days — far darker. We shall be a better, stronger nation than ever in any event. A great disaster would strengthen us, and a victory, we all feel, will bring us out to daylight. No, I don't leave the 23rd. I have been with them all the time except six days. I am privileged. Yesterday morning, we were in the most uncomfortable condition possible at Camp Lookout. Before night, I was in a lovely spot with most capital company at headquarters.

Rutherford

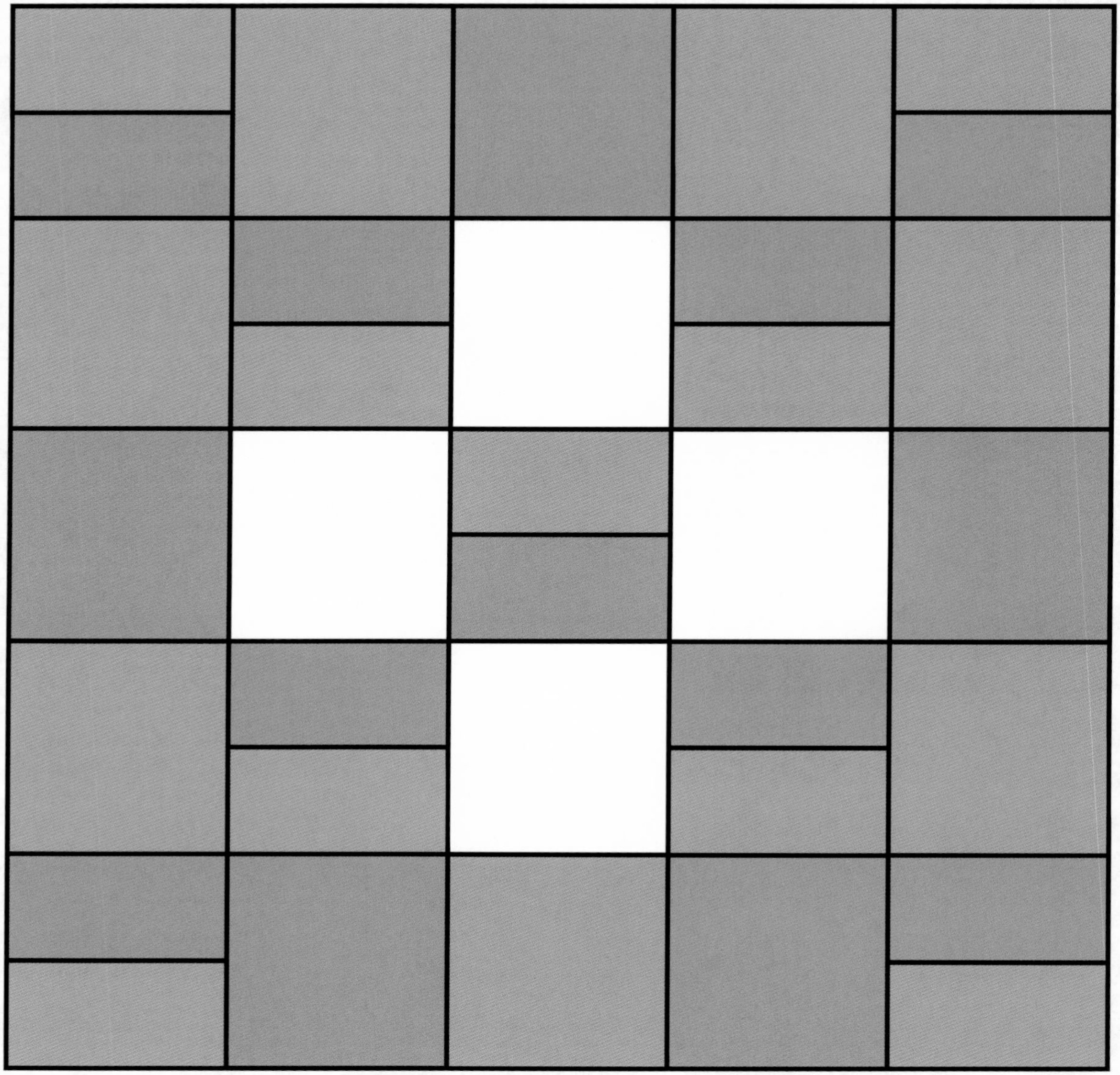

LIBERAL WITH FURLOUGH

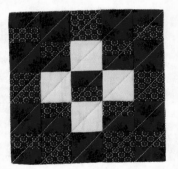

Nov. 30, 1861

Dearest,

We are now engaged in getting winter quarters fixed comfortably. There are not houses enough to lodge all the men without too much crowding. We hope soon to have elbow room. We ease it off a little by being very liberal with furloughs. We allow four men, "men of family preferred," to go from each company for 20 days. As a consequence, there must be daily some of our men going through Cincinnati. The bearer will bring probably besides this letter, the accoutrements which go with Birt's Mississippi rifle, and a couple of gold pieces, one for a present for you and one for Grandma Webb.

We are doing well. Today is bright and warm after a three-day storm of rain and sleet. I had a letter from Laura. You may send my vest, also "Lucille." All sorts of reading matter finds grabbers, but I think of nothing except any stray Atlantic or Harper's of late date. I do not wish to go home for some weeks, but if necessary, I can now go home at any time. I prefer that every other officer should go before I do. Dr. Joe is now acting as brigade surgeon, Col. Scammon as brigadier, I as colonel and Dr. Jim as temporary surgeon of the 30th. All the people hereabouts are crowding in to take the oath of allegiance — a narrow-chested, weakly, poverty-stricken, ignorant set. I don't wonder they refuse to meet our hardy fellows on fair terms. Capt. Sperry says, "They are too ignorant to have good health." Love to "all the boys," to Mother Webb, and ever so much for your own dear self.

Affectionately,

Rutherford

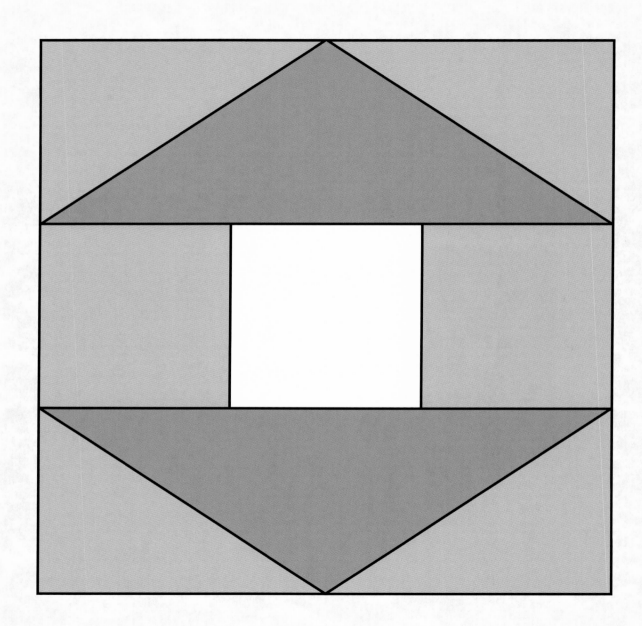

SEVERE FIGHTING

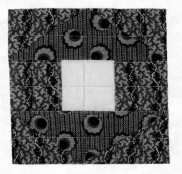

May 20, 1862

Dearest,

Here we are, "back again," 50 or 60 miles in rear of the advanced position we had taken. The short of it is, since the Rebel disasters in eastern Virginia, they have thrown by the railroad a heavy force into this region, forcing us back day by day, until we have gained a strong position, which, they are not likely, I think, to approach. I do not think there is any blame on the part of our leaders. We were strong enough to go ahead until recent events changed the plans of the enemy and made it impossible to reinforce sufficiently. I was much vexed at first, but I suspect it is all right.

We have had a great deal of severe fighting: fragmentary, in small detachments, but very severe. We have had narrow escapes. My whole command was nearly caught once; the 28th barely escaped. Gen. Cox and staff got off by the merest chance. Col. Scammon's brigade was in close quarters, etc. And yet, by good luck, we have had no serious disaster. We have lost tents and some small quartermaster stores, but nothing important. In the fighting, we have had the best of it usually. The total loss of Gen. Cox's command is perhaps 200 to 300, including killed, wounded, prisoners and missing. The enemy has suffered far more. In my fight at Giles, the enemy had 31 killed and many wounded; our total casualties and missing, about 15. We shall remain here until reinforced or new events make it possible to move.

We are connected by telegraph with you, too, so we are near again for a season.

Affectionately,

Rutherford

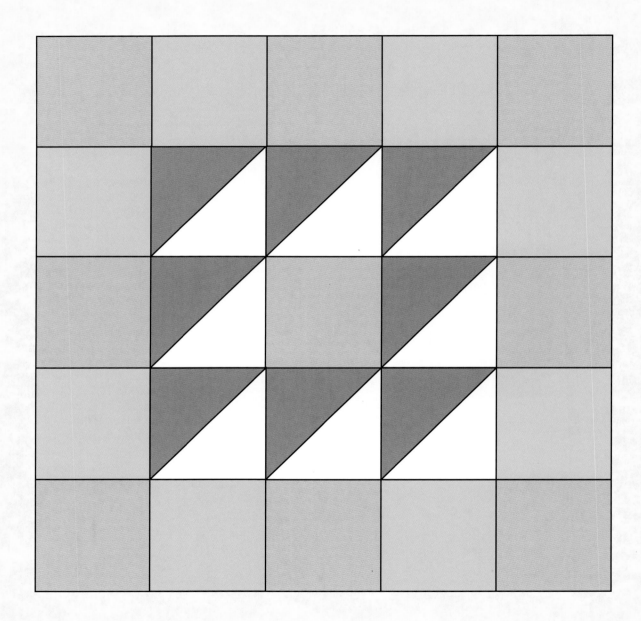

Skirmishing, Cannon Firing and Uproar

Sept. 13, 1862

Dearest,

Yesterday was an exciting but very happy day. We retook this fine town about 5:30 p.m. after a march of 14 miles and a good deal of skirmishing, cannon firing and uproar, but with little fighting. We marched in just at sundown the 23rd, a good deal of the way in front. There was no mistaking the Union feeling and joy of the people; fine ladies, pretty girls and children were in all the doors and windows, waving flags and clapping hands. Some "jumped up and down" with happiness. Joe enjoyed it and rode up the streets, bowing most gracefully. The scene as we approached across the broad bottom-lands in line of battle, with occasional cannon firing and musketry, the beautiful Blue Ridge Mountains in view, the fine town in front, was very magnificent. It is pleasant to be so greeted. The enemy had held the city just a week.

"The longest week of our lives," "We thought you were never coming," and "This is the happiest hour of our lives," were the common expressions. It was a most fatiguing day to the men. When we got the town, before the formal entry, men laid down in the road, saying they couldn't stir again. Some were pale, some red as if apologetic. Half an hour after, they were marching erect and proud, hurrahing the ladies. The enemy treat our men well, very well. We have of sick and wounded 500 or 600 prisoners taken here. Well, Lucy dearest, goodbye. Love to all. Kiss the boys.

Affectionately ever,

Rutherford

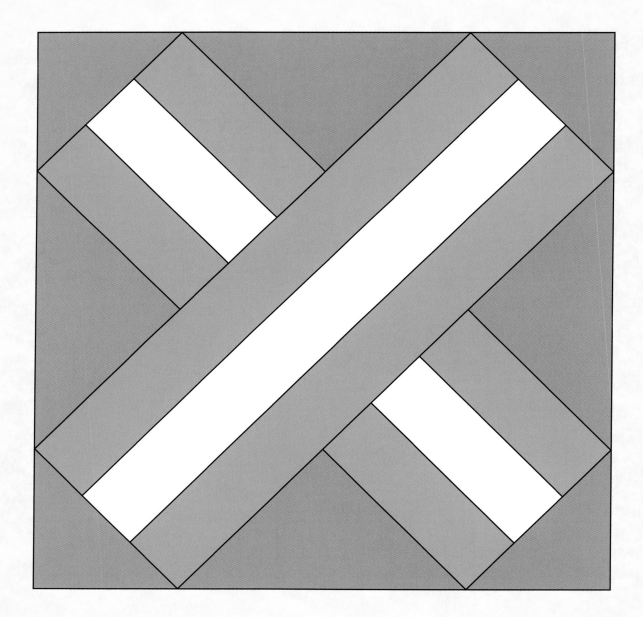

No Serious Fighting

July 22, 1863

Dearest,

Home again after an absence of two weeks, marching and hurrying all the time. The last week after Morgan has been the liveliest and jolliest campaign we ever had. We were at all the skirmishes and fighting after he reached Pomeroy. It was nothing but fun — no serious fighting at all. I think not over 10 killed and 40 wounded on our side in all of it. Unluckily, McCook, father of Robert and the rest, was mortally wounded. This hurt me, but all the rest was mere frolic.

Morgan's men were only anxious to get away. There was no fight in them when attacked by us. You will no doubt see great claims on all sides as to the merits of his captors. The cavalry, gunboats, militia and our infantry each claim the victory as their peculiar property. We can truly claim that Morgan would have crossed and escaped with his men at Pomeroy if we had not headed him there and defeated his attempt. It is not yet certain whether Morgan himself will be caught. But it is of small importance. His force, which has so long been the terror of the border, and which has kept employed all our cavalry in Kentucky, is now gone. Our victorious cavalry can now operate in the enemy's country. I thought of you often. We were quartered on steamboats; men were singing, bands playing. Our band was back and with us, and such lively times as one rarely sees. Almost everybody got quantities of trophies. I got nothing but a spur and two volumes captured from the 20th Kentucky, Capt. H. C. Breman, and now recaptured by us. Morgan's raid will always be remembered by our men as one of the happiest events of their lives. Love to the dear boys and Grandmother.

Affectionately,

Rutherford

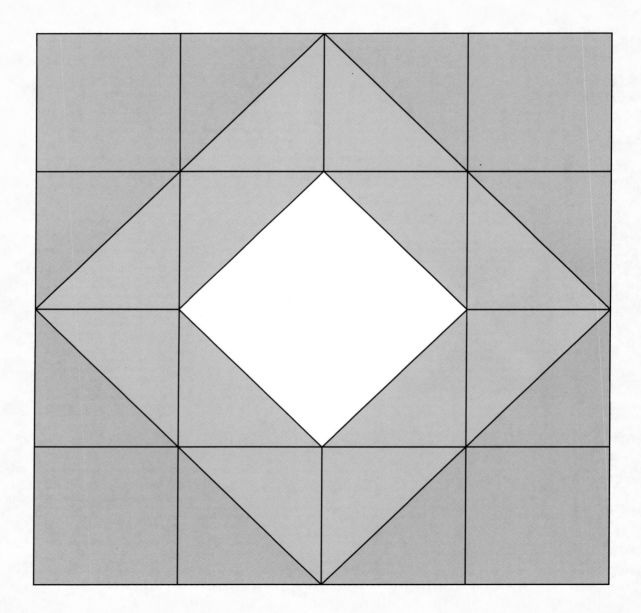

PLEASANT CAMPAIGN

May 19, 1864

Dearest,

We got safely to this point in our lines two hours ago, after 21 days of constant marching, frequent fighting, much hardship, and some starvation. This is the most completely successful and, by all odds, the pleasantest campaign I have ever had. Now it is over, I hardly know what I would change in it, except to restore life and limbs to the killed and wounded. My command in battles and on the march behaved to my entire satisfaction. None did — none could have done — better. We had a most conspicuous part in the battle at Cloyd's Mountain and were so lucky. You will see the lists of killed and wounded. We brought off 200 of our wounded in our train and left about 150. But we have good reason to think they will fare well...

This campaign in plan and execution has been perfect. We captured 10 pieces of artillery; burned the New River Bridge and the culverts and small bridges 30 in number for 20 miles from Dublin to Christiansburg; captured Gen. Jenkins and 300 officers and men; killed and wounded 300 to 500 and routed utterly his army.

One spectacle you would have enjoyed. The Rebels contested our approach to the bridge for two or three hours. At last we drove them off and set it on fire. All the troops were marched up to see it — flags and music and cheering. On a lovely afternoon, the beautiful heights of New River were covered with our regiments watching the burning bridge. It was a most animating scene. Love to all.

Affectionately ever,

Rutherford

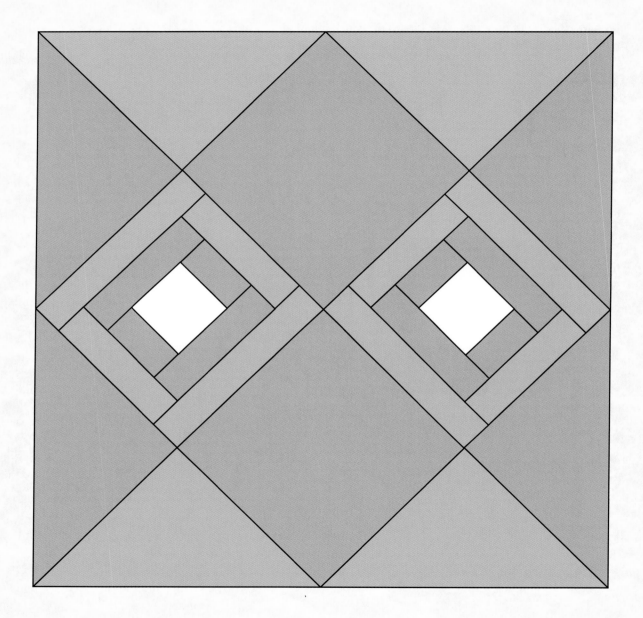

March to Winter Quarters

Nov. 13, 1864

My Darling,

You see, we have made one day's march toward civilization, and, as we hope, toward our much wished-for winter quarters. The weather has been and still is very favorable for the season — cold and windy to be sure, but very little rain. We do not know how far north we shall go, no doubt as far as some railroad and telegraphic communication. We have halted here for four days past, probably on account of reports that the Rebel Army, reinforced and reorganized, is following after us. We do not know how it is, but if they wish to try conclusions with us again, it is likely Gen. Sheridan will meet them. My first brigade went to Martinsburg a week ago. It was hoped that they would not have to come back, but the probability now is that they will return. If so, I shall assume command of them again. Gen. Duval has returned, cured of his wound.

I could perhaps keep a division, but under the circumstances, I much prefer my old brigade. It has been greatly improved by the addition of the Ninth Virginia Veterans, who now with the Fifth form the First Virginia Veterans under Lt. Col. Enochs, a splendid regiment. We are rejoiced that Capt. Hastings is improving; he is still low but decidedly improving. His sister, whom you know, and a brother are with him. Lincoln's election was so confidently expected that it does not cause so much excitement as we sometimes see, but it gives great satisfaction here. Give my love to the kind friends.

Affectionately ever yours,

Rutherford

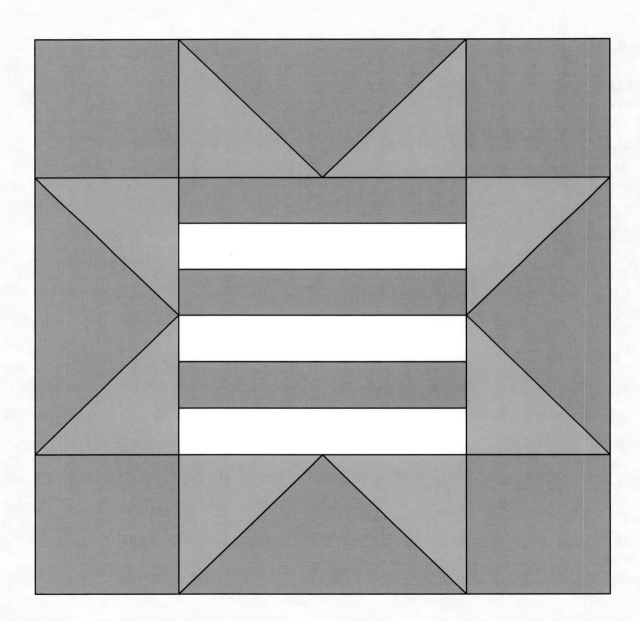

The Fall of Richmond

Dearest,

The glorious news is coming so fast that I hardly know how to think and feel about it. It is so just that Grant, who is by all odds our man of greatest merit, should get this victory. It is very gratifying, too, that Sheridan gets the lion's share of the glory of the active fighting.

The clique of showy shams in the Army of the Potomac are represented by Warren. We do not know the facts, but I suspect Warren hung back, and after the Potomac fashion, didn't take hold with zeal when he found Sheridan was to command. So, he was sent to the rear!

I am in a command of all sorts now, a good regiment of cavalry: the old Pennsylvania Ringgold Cavalry; two batteries of Ohio men, one of them Capt. Glassier's, one of the veteran West Virginia regiments; and a lot of others of less value. It was intended to send me in command of about 5,000 men, quite a little army, by mountain routes toward Lynchburg. We are still preparing for it, but I have no idea now that we shall go.

I wish to remain in service until my four years is up in June. Then I shall resign or not, as seems best. If matters don't suit me, I'll resign sooner. Now, if things remain here in status quo, would you like to come here? It is a most romantic spot. I have Capt. Nye and Lt. Turner of 36th as part of my staff, Charley Smith, Billy Crump and two other 23rd men as orderlies. We have speedy communication by rail and telegraph, and with a little more company, it would be very jolly. Love to all.

Affectionately,

Rutherford

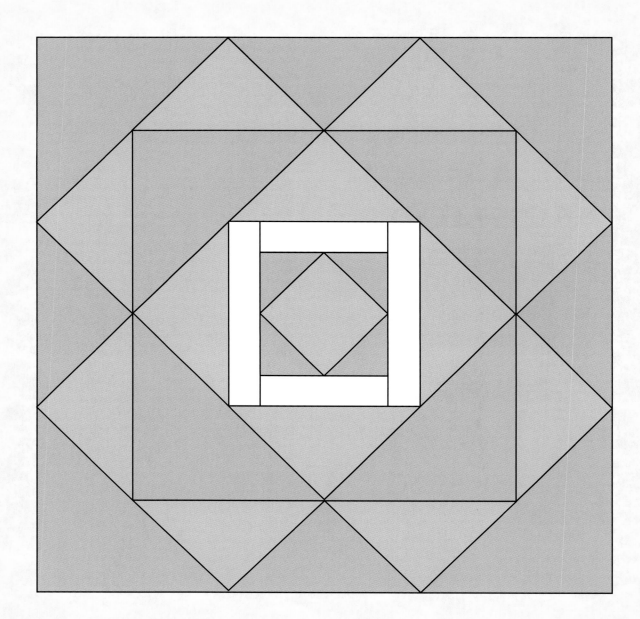

Almost Home

April 12, 1865

Dearest,

I wonder if you feel as happy as I do. The close of the war, "home again," darling and the boys and all to be together again for good! And the manner of it, too: our best general vindicated by having the greatest victory. Gen. Crook, too. Did you see, it was his immediate command that captured so much, which Sheridan telegraphs about the wagons, Armstrong guns, etc.? All most gratifying.

My expedition into the mountains will no doubt be given up, although we are still preparing. I am well satisfied with present matters personally, and think I am rather fortunate, all things considered. I decide nothing at present. I wish you to be ready to join me on very short notice. It is not likely I shall send for you, but I may do so any day if you would like to come. My notion is that an extra session of Congress soon is a likely thing to occur. That will be known in a week or two. Love to all, "so much."

As ever,

Rutherford

P. S.— My pictures being in demand, I have got another.

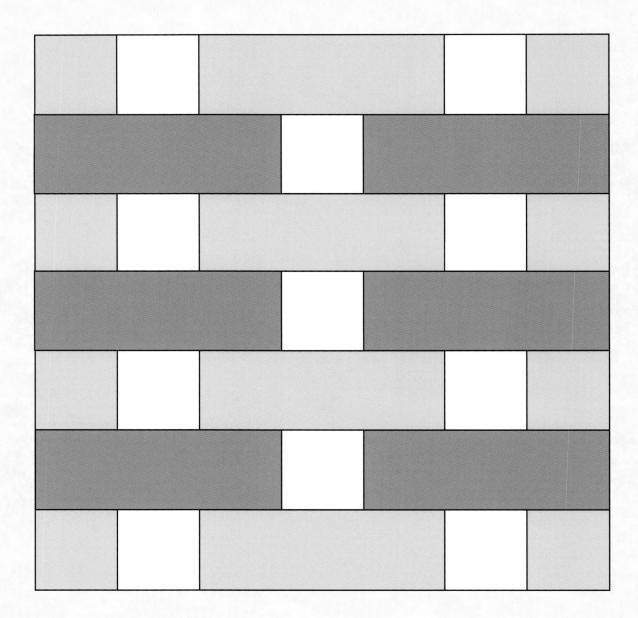

Awful Tragedy

April 16, 1865

Dearest,

When I heard first yesterday morning of the awful tragedy at Washington, I was pained and shocked to a degree I have never before experienced. I got onto the cars, then just starting, and rode down to Cumberland. The probable consequences, or rather, the possible results in their worst imaginable form, were presented to my mind one after the other, until I really began to feel that here was a calamity so extensive a state is that in no direction could be found any, the slightest, glimmer of consolation. The nation's great joy turned suddenly to a still greater sorrow! A ruler tested and proved in every way, and in every way found equal to the occasion, to be exchanged for a new man whose ill - omened beginning made the nation hang its head.

Lincoln for Johnson! The work of reconstruction requiring so much statesmanship just begun! The calamity to Mr. Lincoln; in a personal point of view, so uncalled-for a fate, so undeserved, so unprovoked! The probable effect upon the future of public men in this country, the necessity for guards; our ways to be assimilated to those of the despotisms of the Old World. As to Mr. Lincoln's name and fame and memory, all is safe. His firmness, moderation, goodness of heart; his quaint humor, his perfect honesty and directness of purpose; his logic, his modesty, his sound judgment and great wisdom; the contrast between his obscure beginnings and the greatness of his subsequent position and achievements; his tragic death, giving him almost the crown of martyrdom, elevate him to a place in history second to none other of ancient or modern times. Love to all.

Affectionately,

Rutherford

A. B. Cheney
2. m. Colark

Amherst B. Cheney. Courtesy of the
Sparta Historical Museum.

Tina (Clementine) Heath. Courtesy of the
Sparta Historical Museum.

Amherst B. Cheney

(Oct. 27, 1841 - Jan. 9, 1927)

Amherst B. Cheney was born in Ripley, Ohio, the son of A.J. Cheney and Sarah Or'way. In 1845, the Cheneys decided to move their family to Michigan, and, in 1858, they settled on a farm in the town of Sparta, Mich. It was here that Amherst enlisted in the Michigan 21st Infantry in August 1862 at the age of 20.

Clementine (Tina) Heath was born in Plymouth, Mich., in 1847, the daughter of George Washington Heath and Ann Eliza Howland. The Heaths moved to Michigan from New York. Tina was 16 years old and attending school when Amherst began to write her letters. A collection of 20 letters were found in Tina's granddaughter's steamer trunk in New York in 1999. The photographs that Tina and Amherst exchanged during the Civil War were also found with the letters.

Amherst wrote very formal letters to Tina over a two-year period; he was so pleased with every letter that she answered. He would often write, as he did on Jan. 23, 1864, "It was with great pleasure that I received your very kind and interesting letter," or on May 19, 1864, "Your interesting letter of May 1 was received a short time since and has been read repeatedly."

Amherst wrote to Tina from the battlefields of Chickamauga and Chattanooga, Tenn., along the Tennessee River, on the summit of Lookout Mountain. He wrote a letter near Savannah, Ga., as he watched the spectacle of the burning of the city. On March 19, 1865, Amherst was wounded in action at the battle of Bentonville, N.C., it was then that he made an application for a leave of absence. He spent some time recuperating at the DeCamp General Hospital in New York. While recuperating, he wrote, "I got very lonesome this morning, and in looking through my valise, I found a package of old letters, and I enjoyed myself greatly in reading them anew." Tina's letters had traveled with him through the Civil War.

Amherst was honorably discharged in June 1865 and returned home to Sparta. In 1869, he married Miss Gene Hinman and returned home to teach. He soon became interested in banking and also began a political career after being elected to the U.S. House of Representatives in 1877 and 1878. He died on Jan. 9, 1927, at the age of 85.

Tina was married to Zerah Cheney, Amherst's brother, in 1871.

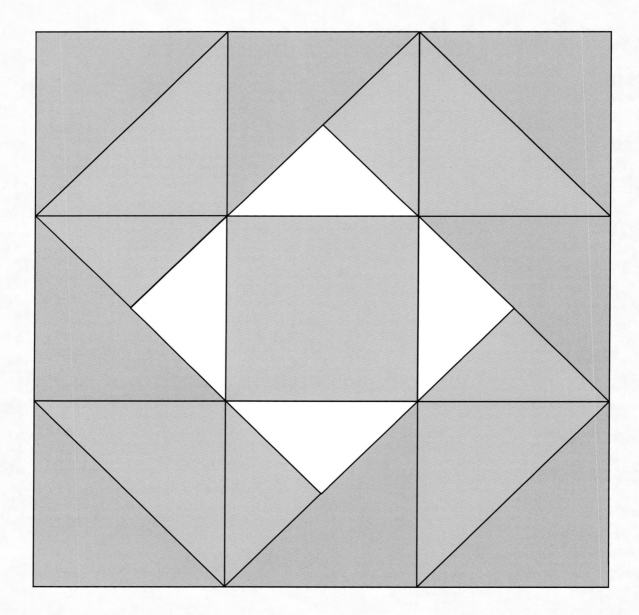

Tents of the Enemy

Nov. 4, 1863

Kind friend,

It is evening. Night has dropped her dark and impenetrable curtain over all. And I now seat myself to enjoy the pleasure of writing a few lines in answer to your kind and highly interesting letter bearing a date of Oct. 18th and received by this afternoon's mail. We are now in camp, about one-half mile in the front, or south of the city of Chattanooga, and in the extreme front of the army. The tents of the enemy are in full view, about one-and-a-half miles in advance of us. Two miles to our right, Lookout Mountain rears its rocky form. The Rebels have a battery of artillery planted upon its extreme top. They have been quite busily engaged of late, trying to shell our camp and batteries. The damage they have thus far done is very small. One shell thrown by them struck one of the hospital buildings upon the roof, passed down through it, going between the patients' beds, striking a beam, and glanced and went into the ground. No harm was done.

The position of the battery enables them to throw shot and shell in all parts of the town. Gen. Thomas is planting batteries and thinks he will be able to dislodge them. Our beloved Gen. Rosecrans has been relieved of his command and ordered to report to the adjutant general for orders. This has cast a gloom and sadness over all the troops.

You remark in your letter in a manner the weather affects people. I find a verification of your theory in myself this evening, for who could have written a gloomier and more wearisome letter than this? I defy competition in these respects and will write again when in better spirits. If you ever managed to decipher this, inform me of the fact by return mail without fail. Hoping to hear from you soon. I bid you good night.

Very respectfully yours,

Amherst B. Cheney

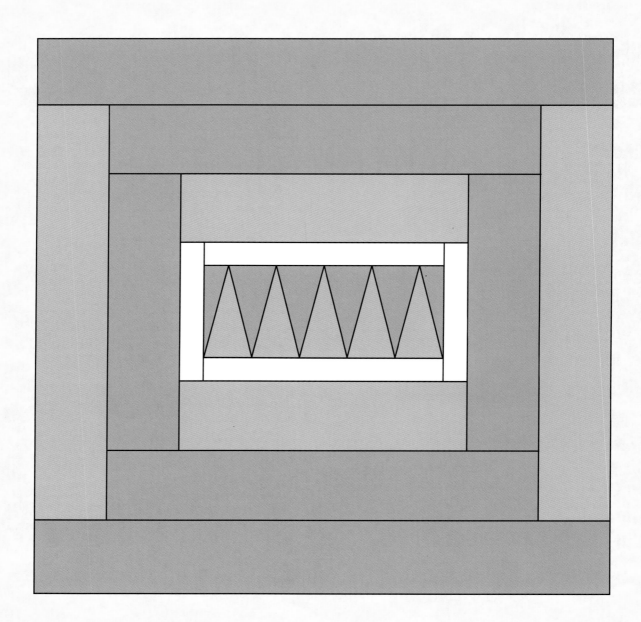

MISSIONARY RIDGE

Dec. 7, 1863

Friend Tina,

Your favor of Nov. 22nd was received with much pleasure by yesterday's mail, and I approve this, the first opportunity of answering or of trying to answer it since I wrote you last.

Many very important changes have taken place, and many decisive advantages gained. The Rebel Army, which for a time looked down upon us from the summit of Lookout Mountain and Missionary Ridge and were making demonstrations which caused many to fear for the safety of the troops in and around Chattanooga, has very suddenly disappeared and is now endeavoring to extricate itself from the perilous position the morning demonstration of Gen. "Unconditional Surrender" Grant's combined forces has placed them. The Union troops have shown an, I was going to say unequaled amount of courage in engagement, but suffice it that they fulfilled the highest expectations of their commanders. The charge that drove the enemy from Missionary Ridge was in military parlance a brilliant affair. Gen. Sheridan advanced upon their marks and ascended the ridge, taking three lines of earthworks in succession and this in a murderous fire of artillery and musketry from the top upon which the enemy's cannons were placed. The spectacle was a grand one. And although our feelings were not those of men in the line of battle expecting momentarily to be called upon to do their part of the bloody work, with all doubt of life or death before them, which obedience to that call would impose. Yet, I assure you, we were not uninterested spectators of that scene. But 'twas reason that victory for us would shorten our separation from home — and disaster lengthen — and we would not — neither would we wish to avoid a personal interest.

The weather is stormy and disagreeable at present, but not as cold as might be expected. Rations are plenty, and all are in excellent spirits. Excuse this impromptu letter. View it not with a critic's eye, but pass its imperfections by with fun.

Your friend,

A.B. Cheney

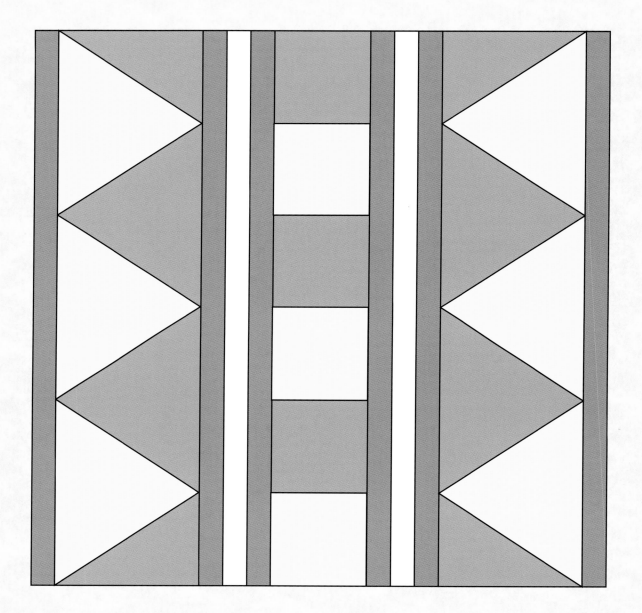

New Year's Day

Jan. 23, 1864

Friend Tina,

It was with great pleasure that I received by today's mail your very kind and interesting letter written New Year's Eve, and then while suffering physical ailment. Allow me to sympathize with you, and hope that your hand may soon get well so that you can write without its causing you so much pain.

We are on the north bank of the Tennessee River, immediately opposite in a full view of the city. About 5 miles from here and a little to the right of the city, Lookout Mountain rears its rugged sides and stands as a grim sentinel over the beautiful city. Poetically called the Hawk's Nest by the Indians, correctly did they name it. Lying in a band of a noble Tennessee, and completely surrounded by hills and mountains, it presents a picture worthy of the pencil of the artists.

Tina (please excuse the familiarity), you do not deal fairly with yourself, and very unjustly, I think. I nearly forgot to tell you how I enjoyed New Year's. Well, we have an excellent cook, and he exerted himself in getting a New Year's dinner, and the result was that we had several kinds of cake and pie. (A singular way of describing a meal to commence with dessert.) Tea and coffee, sauerkraut, mixed vegetables and a huge chicken pie. Having a better dinner than usual was all the novelty of the New Year. I honor your judgment in remaining at home in preference to endeavoring to derive pleasure fraught with winds of a cold and bitter night. And I thank you for your kindness in devoting your time in writing to me. But I am sorry that it was rendered unpleasant by that painful hand. Please don't speak so flattering of my letters, for they do not deserve it. And remember and do not trust so lightly of self, for in my humble opinion, you don't think right. Don't fail to write soon. Excuse all mistakes.

A. B. C.

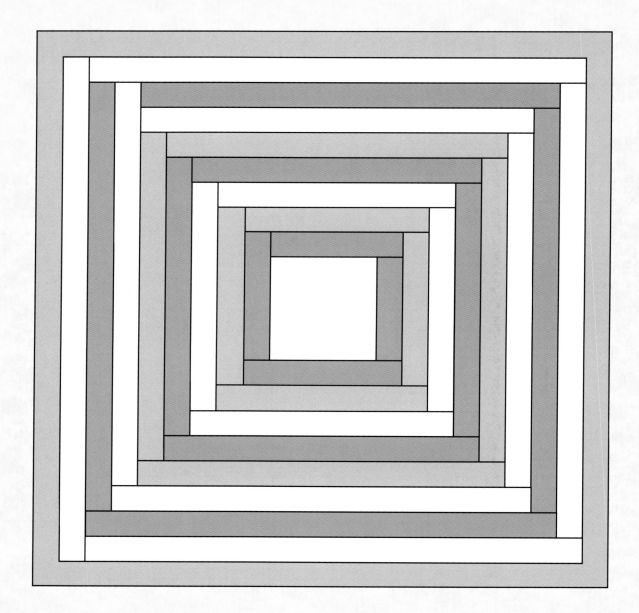

EXCHANGING PHOTOGRAPHS

April 5, 1864

Dear Friend,

Your request made in your last letter that I would send you a photograph of my humble self was inadvertently forgotten at the time of answering it, which please excuse. I now comply with your desire, although I think it will prove a poor addition to your collection of pictures. You can place it in some out-of-the-way corner of your album and among or immediately after some more ordinary and unpretending photos and others, save any sudden transition from sublimity to ridiculous.

Hoping that you will do me the favor of sending me your photo by return mail. I close hoping to hear from you again soon.

I remain yours truly,

A.B. Cheney

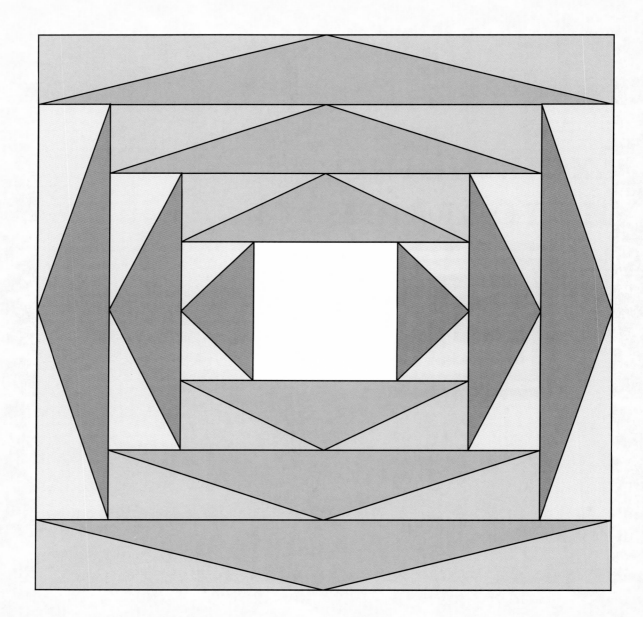

GUERRILLAS

May 19, 1864

Tina,

Your interesting letter of May 1st was received a short time since and has been read repeatedly. Day before yesterday, about 9 p.m., two of the soldiers belonging to this regiment were out about 2 miles in the country to purchase some milk for the sick. And when leaving the house of a person named Stringer (who it is said formerly belong to the Rebel Army), they were fired upon by guerrillas stationed around the outbuildings.

They succeeded in escaping unharmed and came to camp as soon as possible, when a party of about 20 men, the subscriber being one of the number, armed themselves and repaired to the spot with as much haste as possible. Quickly surrounding the house, a vigorous search was instituted, but no persons were found in the house. Meanwhile, a small distance, a man was seen to suddenly spring from behind a tree and run for the woods. He succeeded in escaping. We finally returned to camp, getting here about 1 o'clock in the morning. These guerrillas are persons that have lived upon rations furnished their families by the United States, and you can form a very correct idea of their desserts. Please excuse all the mistakes in the haste with which this has been written, and remember that now you are at school and will have lots of adventures to write about. Write soon and oblige.

Your friend,

A. B. Cheney

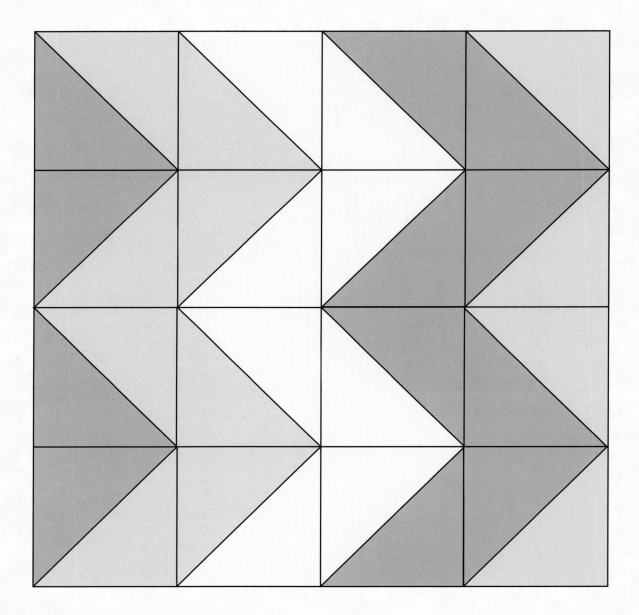

HOSPITALS

July 17, 1864

Tina,

Your interesting favor of June 19th came to hand a few days ago and received a very cordial welcome. I had been looking for it for some time. Since writing to you last, we have moved our camp from near Chattanooga to the summit of Lookout Mountain. A more desirable situation for a summer residence is seldom found. Cool breezes continually regale us; and while our less-fortunate neighbors living in the valleys below are sweltering in the burning sun, we are favored with a cool, comfortable atmosphere.

There are 80 hospitals in process of erection in this vicinity, several already completed and occupied by sick and wounded. The terrific battles already fought and being fought in the front render it necessary that extensive preparations be made to properly meet the wants of the many wounded. A situation superior to Lookout Mountain cannot be found, only one difficulty to be obviated. Water must be brought from the valley during the last of summer and the first of fall. This will be done by three large engines, which raise the water about 800 feet high. There are quite a number of buildings completed and already occupied by sick and wounded. About 2,000 are thus cared for, and many more can soon be accommodated, although I hope that there may not be many more so unfortunate as to require hospital treatment.

The blows now being struck on behalf of the Universal freedom are mighty and will have a corresponding effect. And should same Fortune continue to favor us a short time longer, I have great hopes of soon returning home with all my soldier friends.

My left eye is suffering with inflammation and prevents me from writing long at a time. Please excuse all mistakes and write as soon and often as you conveniently can.

Accept this from your friend,

A. B. Cheney

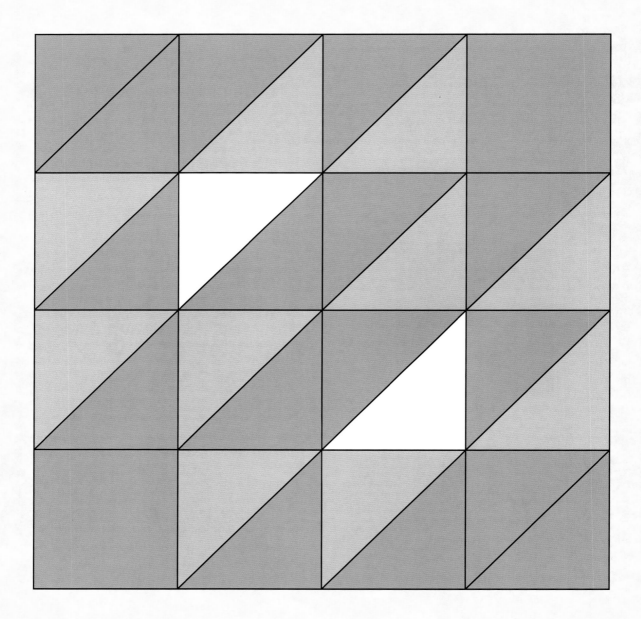

A Beautiful Picture

Aug. 16, 1864

My friend Tina,

After a delay of 24 hours, I now seat myself to write a few lines in answer to your very kind favor of the 8th. It gave me great pleasure to learn that you were enjoying yourself so well. Next to that, your carte-de-visite gave me the most satisfaction, and while looking at it, I silently honored the genius that first entertained the idea of transferring our features upon paper, thereby allowing us to gaze upon the counterparts of our friends, although far separated. I do not wish you to think me addicted to that detestable habit termed flattery, for that I abhor. But I must be allowed to tell you that it is a beautiful picture. This being nothing but the truth does not savor of false praise.

"For Flattery no excuse can find
   'Tis loathed as soon as tasted
   When offered to a well-taught mind
   And in a fool, 'tis wasted."

You speak of "writing compositions" as the bug bear of schoolgirls, and let me add of school-boys, also. I think you need not be troubled much in that respect, for should the means fail, you have but to read one of your good letters, which would be an excellent substitute for any other style of writing.

It would have given me much satisfaction to have attended the picnic of which you wrote. At such times, it appears as though people divest themselves of all perplexing cares, and with kindly feelings, enter with zest into the pleasures of the occasion. Tina, you must excuse this apology of a letter, and I promise to do better next time.

Hoping that you will soon favor me with another of your kind letters, I remain yours truly.

Yours,

A. B. C.

DELAYED MAIL

Nov. 12, 1864

My friend Tina,

I presume that you long ago concluded that I had never received your last, or that I did not intend to answer it, although either conclusion is incorrect. Still, you could not think otherwise under the circumstances. It has been six weeks since I received it, and no ordinary circumstances could possibly excuse one for such long-continued delay.

We are now camped in a pleasant grove of little pines, about one-half mile south of Cartersville, and expect to march in the morning. I have not heard from home in a long time, but hope to hear soon. I do not know when I shall have the opportunity of mailing this, but will send the first opportunity.

Yesterday, we held our election and again pledged ourselves to continue to those principles which we left our homes to defend. May God in his goodness smile upon the efforts of those trying to preserve the temple of Liberty inviolate. The successes, which have of late attended the Union arms, have filled every boy at heart with joy, while they have created dismay and trepidation among their enemies. May we continued to defeat and foil their every attempt until peace again greets us with all her blessings. Should I not have an opportunity of mailing this soon, I will write a postscript. Write as often as convenient.

Yours truly,

Amherst B. Cheney

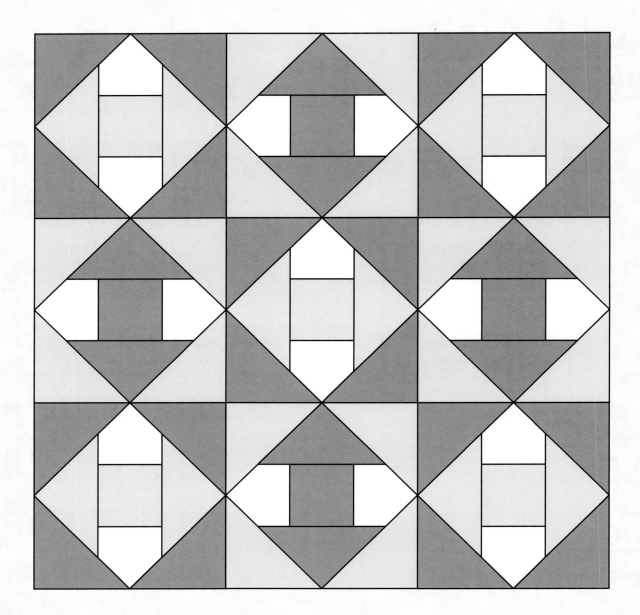

Burning of the City Gate

Dec. 20, 1864

Tina,

In accordance with my promise contained in the enclosed letter written at Cartersville over one month ago, I now add a postscript, which will probably trouble you some to read, as it is written while sitting upon the ground with no other desk than my lap.

As I suspected when writing the enclosed letter, we marched on the morning of the 13th Nov. and traveled southward, destroying the railroad as we went, thereby cutting communications with friends, and with no prospect of again hearing from them in many long weary days. Arriving at Atlanta, we halted one day, during which we beheld a truly grand and awful spectacle, the burning of the "City Gate." Just before dark, the clouds of smoke in the direction of the principle portion of the city gave warning that the work of destruction had begun. As the flames increased, enveloping block after block, the wind came up and added anger to the already fiercely burning pile. And then ensued a scene which it is impossible to describe. Huge volumes of fire were continually ascending high in the heavens, brilliantly lighting up the country for miles around. The roar of bursting shells, falling walls and exploding mines, together with the descending shower of ashes and embers, which fell for a great distance around, all combined to render the scene terribly grand terrific. I cannot describe the feelings with which the army witnessed this dreadful conflagration. The thought that such extreme measures were absolutely necessary was truly painful. Yet none could deny that was the only course to be pursued.

We have seen the "Cotton of the Cane" of Georgia, it swamps and piney woods, its rice fields and Negro quarters. The army has subsisted upon the products of the country. Cattle, sheep, fowl, potatoes, rice, sugar, molasses and everything else that could be used to advantage was appropriated to the benefit of the United States. About 3,000 Negroes joined the army during the march and are on their way to Port Royal to obtain employment and school for their children. We received a large mail from home yesterday, but no letter from you. I have lost your address and shalt direct this to Sparta.

Write as often as convenient, and receive the kindest wishes of your friend,

A.B. Cheney

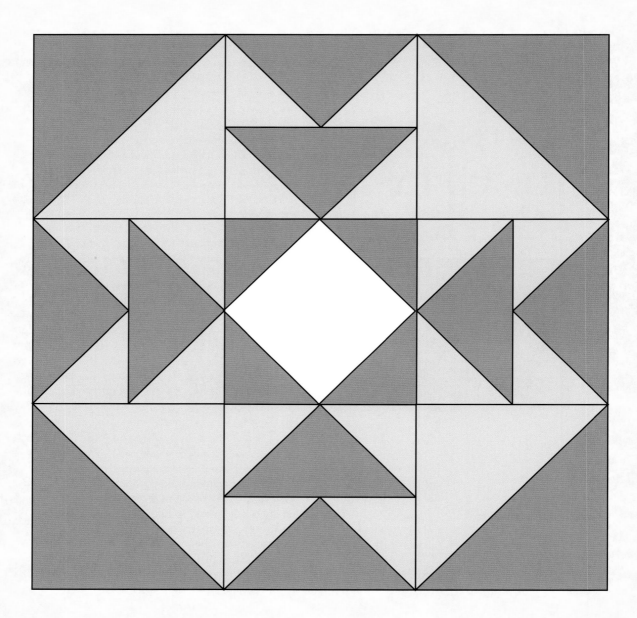

Benefits of the Sick and Wounded

April 10, 1865

My friend Tina,

Circumstances of a nature far different from those surrounding me when I last wrote you now allow me the pleasurable opportunity of penning you a short letter acquainting you with my present address thereby giving me hope of being favored soon with another of your ever-interesting and welcome letters.

After a tiresome and tedious journey by railroad and steamboat, we arrived at this place day before yesterday, and we are now enjoying those comforts so readily and abundantly contributed by the earnest men and noble women of the nation for the benefit of the sick and wounded. I have never before had an opportunity of personally acquainting myself with the manner or extent of the provisions made for the care of the disabled, and I am pleasurably surprised at the perfect arrangements made by the medical department ably seconded by the people for those who are so unfortunate as to require the care of a patient. The glorious news that came from the South yesterday in reference to the capture of Lee and his army by Grant has had a good effect upon us all and has hastened the cure of us all. Surely the end of the rebellion draweth near. Every loyal heart has reason to rejoice at the unparalleled success of the Union arms.

The hospital of which I am an inmate is pleasantly situated in the harbor. From my window, I can look out upon Long Island Sound. In the distance, the numerous vessels constantly passing to and fro formed a pleasing and ever-varying scene. The batteries and forts in the vicinity of the city are firing a salute, the cause of which we have not learned. It certainly must be good news for which a person can reasonably wait a short time. The shadows of night are slowly gathering around, and the ward master has not lighted up and I will close this uninteresting letter, hoping to hear from you soon.

I remain your friend,

Am. B. Cheney

APPLICATION FOR LEAVE

April 28, 1865

My kind friend Tina,

Your very interesting and patriotic letter of the 18th came to hand several days since, but I have not had a good opportunity of answering it until the present time. I shall not be able to write a fitting answer now, but will do as well as possible. I am very glad that you did not wait for an answer to your previous letter, for it has not made its appearance. It probably went to the Regiment. I wrote you a short note while at Goldsboro, soon after being wounded, but I scarce remember what I wrote — not a great deal at most. I was wounded at the battle of Bentonville on the 19th day of March. My wounds were two in number, in right arm and chest — neither very severe. I have made an application for a leave of absence, and should it come around all right, I shall start for Michigan on Monday next or as soon as it returns.

It has been a very quiet and almost dismal time here for the last week owing to the inhuman assassination of the great and good man Abraham Lincoln. A nation truly mourns. N.Y. City has been draped in the emblems of grief. With very few exceptions the citizens have united paying tribute to the memory of the Commander-in-Chief. Never has there been such a concourse of citizens collected in the city as came forth to escort the hearse and to get a last look at Honest Abe.

The kind ladies of the city visit the island almost daily and gladden the hearts of the sick and wounded with their kind words of cheer and by distributing those articles of luxury so highly valued by the sick. A Mrs. Chapman and a Miss Prime are the ones who visit the pavilion in which I am. May they live long to enjoy the blessing so justly showered upon them by hundreds of disabled soldiers. Like angels of mercy, they smooth the pillow of the dying; and as the words of kindness and consolation fall upon the ear of the almost-dying invalid, they infuse new energy into the wasted frame more beneficial than ought found in the Materia Medica. May God bless the ladies, the soldier's friend.

As I am not sure this will reach you ere you go home; I will not write more at present. Hoping to visit all my friends soon. I close this poor excuse of a letter, and I guess you will conclude that I had better not say anything about your writing after you have perused this.

Yours,

A. B. Cheney

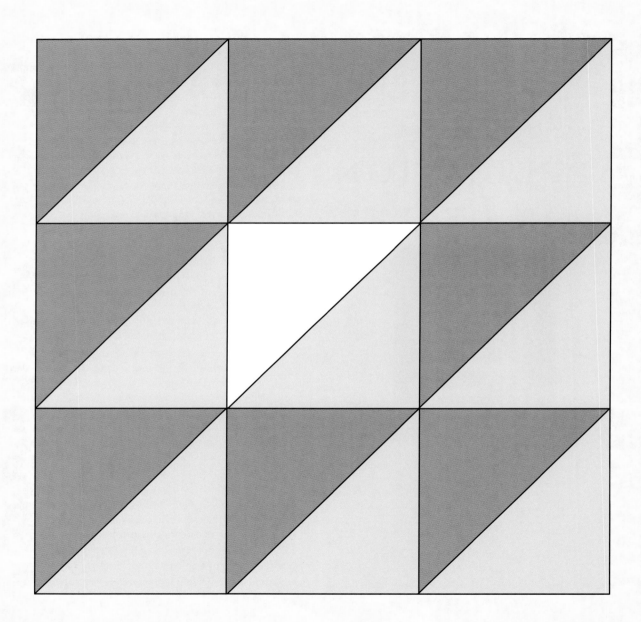

Back Home

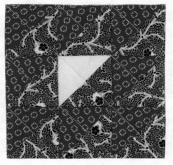

Dec. 14, 1865

My friend Tina,

Your pleasant letter of the 7th just was gladly received last Friday, and I was ever so much pleased to learn that you had returned. I wondered many times if you are going to stay at Detroit all winter, and perhaps for years. I had the presumption to write a letter intended for you about two weeks since, but not knowing under what circumstances it might be received, as well as remembering that when I saw you last, we arranged that you should acquaint me with your return. I deemed it a better way to wait until you came back. Zerah is at Ann Arbor, but I expect he will be home on a visit before long, perhaps during the holidays. When he does return, be it soon or far in the future, I will give him your kind invitation, and I doubt not he will be pleased to take advantage of the opportunity.

I am somewhat disappointed to find that you cannot make Mother that contemplated visit. But when we cannot control circumstances, we ought to submit to circumstances with as much grace as our dispositions and feelings will allow. I shall take this first opportunity of visiting you. The people here are making quite extensive preparations for Christmas. Each of the churches intend having a Christmas tree, the Methodists on Christmas eve, the Baptists on Christmas night. A good time is anticipated.

If you have no other arrangements made, and if it would be pleasant for you, I should be very pleased to come out Christmas afternoon and bring you out and either take you home after the evening exercises or on the next day, if you could stay no longer. You must excuse this hastily written note, and please send me a line by return mail. To the line, you may attach as many more as you can find time an inclination to, and be assured they will be carefully and attentively read, while I shall always entertain the highest respect and esteem for my kind friend, Tina.

Goodbye for today only,

A.

*Robert Newton Scott. Courtesy of the family of
Marjorie Hannah Dalby.*

*Hannah Cone Scott. Courtesy of the family of
Marjorie Hannah Dalby.*

Newton Robert Scott

(April 4, 1841 - March 2, 1925)

Newton Robert Scott was born in Pullman County, Ind., on April 4, 1841; he had four brothers and one sister. His parents, Mary and Hullum Scott, moved to Iowa in 1856, when Newton was 15.

It was in Iowa at the age of 21 that Newton enlisted in the 36th Infantry of the Iowa Volunteers. He wrote his Civil War letters to Hannah Marguerite Cone, who was born in Saugamon, Ill., on Dec. 5, 1841, one of 12 children. Her parents, Ezra Parker Cone and Mary Jones, moved to Iowa when Hannah was 2 years old. She was 21 years old when she began to receive her letters from Newton. Hannah was a childhood friend who had lived in the Scotts' neighborhood in Albia, Iowa.

Newton served three years in the war. He would often write to Hannah and tell her about the conditions of the soldiers, including her brother, William Cone, who also served in the 36th Iowa Infantry, because so many of them were familiar to her. Newton was always so pleased with her letters and enjoyed hearing about the activities that were going on at home, except for one letter that he received on Feb. 26, 1865, when Hannah had to tell Newton that his sweetheart, Hattie Kester, had married another.

Newton Robert Scott's collection consisted of 13 letters that were written home to Hannah and three that were written home to his parents. The letters were written mostly from Arkansas, in such places as Helena, Little Rock and Yazoo City. His unit captured Little Rock and fought in the battle of Marks Mills; 65 men from his unit were killed in battles, and 238 men died from different diseases.

Finally, in August 1865, Newton Robert Scott was mustered out. He returned home and married Hannah Cone in 1867. They remained in Iowa for the rest of their lives, and they had nine children. Newton spent his life working as a railway mail clerk. He died at the age of 83 on March 2, 1925; Hannah died at the age of 69 on March 7, 1911.

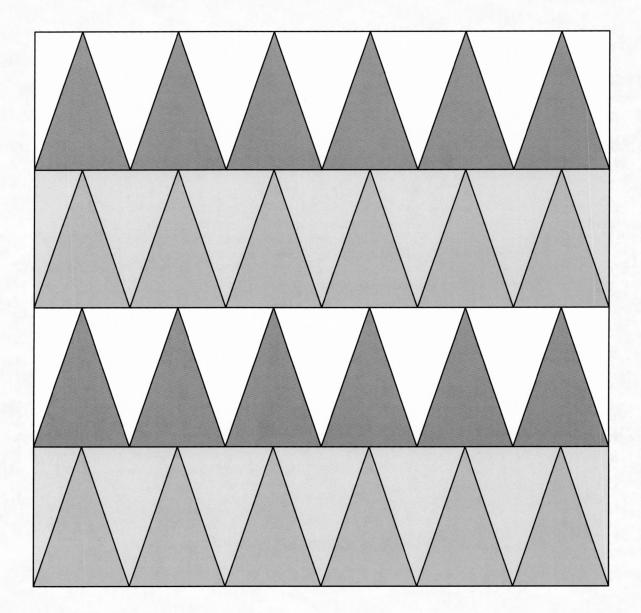

CONDITIONS

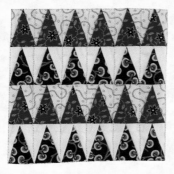

Dear Miss,

I will inform you that I am well at this time and that our company is all well, except two or three persons. Our mess is all well at the present, and I hope that when this reaches you that it may find you and friends well. Yours of the 19th is received.

I was glad to hear from you and that you were well, but I had about given up getting any answer from you. But, better late than never for indeed, Miss Han, I do love to get news from home, for it looks as if that is all the consolation that we soldiers have, for we are away from home, and we have to do as best we can. It is and has been very cold and disagreeable today. We cook and eat outdoors, and we run to the table and eat but nearly freeze our fingers while eating. We have one stove in our barracks, which does a great deal of good, but one stove is a small makeshift for 80 or 90 men. It is very cold standing guard, especially at nights, but if we are spared to get through the war and return to our homes, all will be well.

If you were in Keokuk and saw the number of sick and disabled soldiers, it would make your heart ache. They are dying every day. But enough of the hard side of a soldier's life; I would tell you the good side if I knew it, but don't think that I am homesick or disheartened, for such is not the case, for I am only telling you a few simple facts of the soldier's campaign. Indeed, I wish never to return home permanently until this wicked and Godforsaken rebellion is destroyed. If we had our choices, of course, we would be at home, for we are not in the army for fun nor money, and furthermore, we wish never to fill a coward's grave.

Dear Miss, we have no fears but that we will ever have the goodwill of those kind friends left at home. Success to the Union armies, and ere long, may we all be permitted to return to our homes and live quiet and peaceable lives. Give my love and respects to all friends, and reserve a share for yourself. Please write soon, and tell all to remember and write to the soldiers, for it gives them great pleasure to hear from home.

In friendship, love and truth, I am truly yours,

Newton Scott

TRAVELS

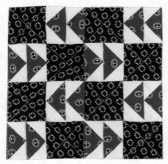

To Miss Hannah Cone,

I will inform you with pleasure that I am well at the present time, and I hope that when this reaches you that it may find you well. I can tell you that the boys are generally well at the present and in very good spirits. I suppose that you have heard the particulars of our travels from Keokuk to this place through Will's letters, hence, you will please pardon me for giving it but a brief notice.

We left Keokuk on the 24th and came down the river, stopping every now and then at the little towns by the way. I can tell that those little towns on the Missouri side of the river are hard-looking places — little, dirty cabins with nothing to sell hardly but whiskey, and the people look to suit the places, but enough of that. We arrived at St. Louis about 2 o'clock on the morning of the 26th. We were most all sound asleep. Next morning at daylight, we went up on deck, and we conspired that we have never seen before. The steam boats were down on the river wharf as far as we could see. But again about 3 o'clock in the afternoon, we received orders to put on our harness and march to this place!

Company A was the first to march off the boat. We formed and marched up through the little village of St. Louis to this place, and we found a very nice place here that are good quarters for us. We get plenty to eat, and suffice it to say that we are doing very well.

We expect to leave here in a day or two to go; we know not where but suppose to Helena, Ark. I can tell you that we found several boys here that we knew via Philander Wilson, George House, Y. Lee, Albert Miles and others. I am sorry to tell you that we left H.W. Reikel and Y.M. Osburn in the hospital at Keokuk, but I hope that they will follow us very soon and also that we left six or eight others there.

Well, Miss Han, I will tell you that I and Will have written about a dozen letters since we left home and received but two or three letters. This is the second one that I have written to you and received no answer.

Love and truth, I am very respectfully yours,

Newton Scott

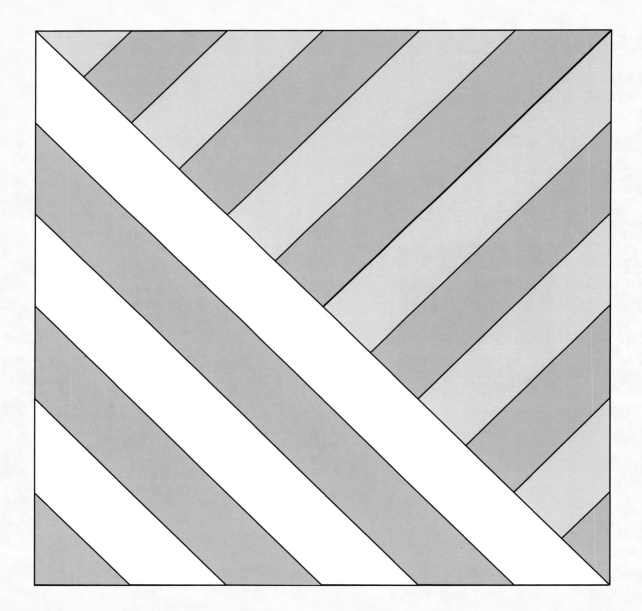

STEAMBOAT

March 9, 1863

Dear friend Han,

I will inform you with pleasure that I am well at the present, and I hope that when this reaches you that it may find you well. I received your letter of Feb. 8 on the second day of this month, and I have delayed answering it, which I hope you will excuse me for, and I will promise to do better in the future.

I was very glad to hear from you and that you were well. The boys are generally well. I believe at the present I will inform you that we left Helena on the 24th of February, and we have been on the boat ever since. We were six days coming 18 miles through the Yazoo Pass, one of the most crooked and narrowest channels that a steamboat ever went before, but we have got through with about 25 boats altogether. We have some six or eight gunboats with us, and we are now penetrating into the very Heart of Dixie since we started. We have taken over $100,000 worth of cottons and taken what beef and chickens that we needed. We have seen no armed Rebels yet, but we are expecting to be fired at every day by guerrillas. I know not where we are going for certain, but think that we will fight our way to Vicksburg. I expect that we will have our first fight at Yazoo City, below the mouth of the Tallahassee River. I expect ere this reaches you to be in a fight, but that you know it is what we all came to war for. We have got to fight before we can come home.

If you see Amanda, please tell her where I am and that I know not how soon that I will write home. I may not write until I see the end of our expedition, though tell her I will, if necessary at anytime. Tell her that I have written two letters home since I started. Well, Han, I believe that I have written all of any importance at the present; I can't say how soon this letter will get back to Helena. Please write soon; my love and respects to all, and reserve a share for yourself. Please excuse my bad writing for I have a poor way of writing.

Direct as before, very respectfully yours in friendship, love and truth,

Newton Scott

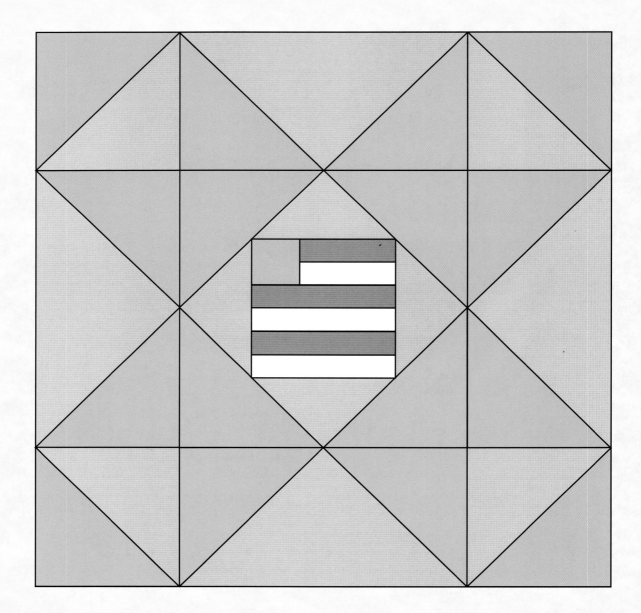

SICKNESS

April 9, 1863

Dear Miss Han. M. Cone,

I will inform you with pleasure that I am well at the present, and I hope that when this reaches you that it may find you well. I have received no letter from you since about the 1st of March. I wrote you an answer on the 9th of March and received no answer yet, and I have concluded to write one letter for spite. Well Han, I don't know that I have much of interest to write at the present, but I will write a little and tell you how the boys are getting along since I wrote you last. We have had considerable sickness in our company. E.F. Knight has been very sick but is getting well now. Dorsey Makin is very sick at the present. He took sick on or about the 15th of March and has been gradually sinking ever since. He is not expected to live. I have been waiting on him ever since the 24th of March. We carried him from the boat yesterday evening to his relatives here, and I and Will P. are staying with him. I think that he cannot last but a few days longer. The rest of acquaintances are generally well, I believe, at this time.

We left Fort Greenwood on the 4th and arrived here on yesterday. We will go into camp here, but I know not how long we will remain here. I think it is doubtful whether we would stay here very long. I have not room to tell you anything about our expedition, for it would take about 20 sheets of paper to tell all, but suffice it to say that we had a pretty hard time and suffered considerably with sickness and done but little damage, only in the destruction of cotton and property. I have seen a great many large buildings and fencing burned and any amount of other property taken. We got several messes of good chicken while we were gone. We respected Rebel property but little, and wherever they fired on our boats, we landed and burnt every thing that would burn.

Respectfully yours,

Newton Scott

White-Headed Boy

Dear Friend,

I will inform you with pleasure that I am well at the present, and I hope that when this reaches you that it may find you well. I received your letter written May 18th today. I was glad to hear from you and that you were well.

Our regiment is about 300 strong at present and will soon be full, and then I expect that we will go south to Vicksburg, Port Hudson or New Orleans. I would love to be at home with my friends, but so long as this war lasts and I remain in good health, I expect to stay in the service, and if it should end soon, I may stay longer, but the future can only tell coming events.

Well, Han, I will inform you that I and Will had our pictures taken and sent one each to you and Manda by Lt. Walker. I suppose that you have received them ere this time, and when you write again, please tell me if I look anything like the little white-headed boy that used to visit Miss Hattie Kester. Well, Han, you must excuse my foolishness, for you know that I always will gab.

I saw Will P. yesterday; he was well. We are camped about 1½ miles from the 36th Iowa. I pay them a visit every day or two. I will tell you that the weather is getting pretty warm down here now, and you may be sure that I stay in the shade as much possible. Well, Han, I believe that I have written all worth writing at the present. We have no news from Vicksburg or below of interest at the present more than you have heard. Now, Han, having sent you my picture, I will make one request of you, and that is I wish you and Amanda to have your pictures taken both on one plate, if you can get good ones that way, and if not, have them taken single and sent to me. I wrote to Manda; Amanda will pay the expense. I will close for the present. Please give my love to all and reserve a share for yourself. I will give you my address on another piece of paper, and please write soon.

In friendship love and truth, I am very respectfully yours,

Newton Scott

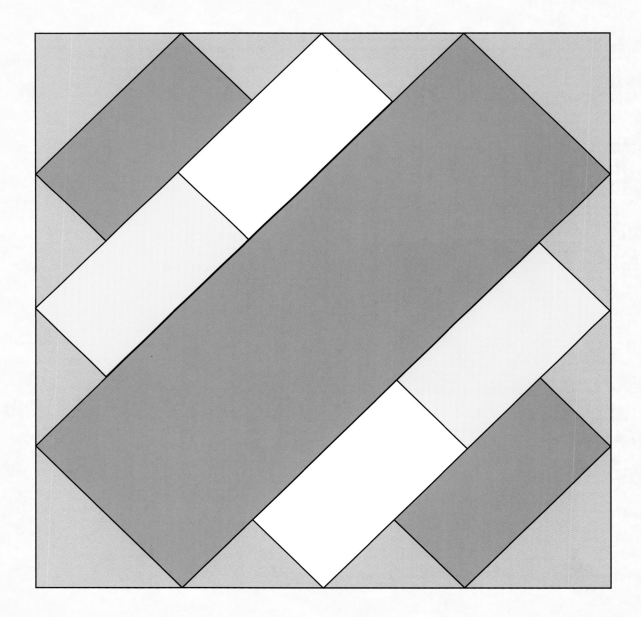

SINGLE THRASHING

Dear Friend,

I will inform you with pleasure that I am well at the present, and I hope that when this reaches you that it may find you well. I received your letter of the 27th on the morning of the 21st that you sent by Dr. Ivens. We were starting out on the second day; Scout and I received a letter after I had started. I was glad to hear from you again.

I will tell you that we were out 18 miles in the country and found plenty of apples, peaches and berries. I received the pictures that you and Amanda sent me and I was glad to see the second choice. Again, I think the pictures are very good ones, and I also received the butter and berries that mother sent me. Will P. is well; he is gone after his cans that you sent to him by Dr. Ivens.

I am very much overjoyed over our late victories at Vicksburg, Helena and Port Hudson and other places. I suppose that you have heard the particulars of our fight at Helena while you all was having such good times up at Albia on the 4th. We were shooting Rebels, and the bullets came whistling around our heads thick as hail, but by the goodwill of providence, we repulsed the Rebels with great slaughter. I was over a part of the battle ground the next morn and saw the dead Rebels scattered over the ground. At one place where the Rebels charged and took one of our batteries, I stood and counted 35 dead Rebels in about 15 paces of ground square. Our loss in killed, wounded and prisoners was less than 200, and the Rebels' loss was over 2,500. We gave them one of the most-single thrashings that they ever got from the Yankees. Well, Han, I believe that I have written all for the present. Please write soon and write all news and particulars. Give my love to all, and reserve a share for yourself.

In friendship, love and truth, I am as ever, respectfully yours,

Newton Scott

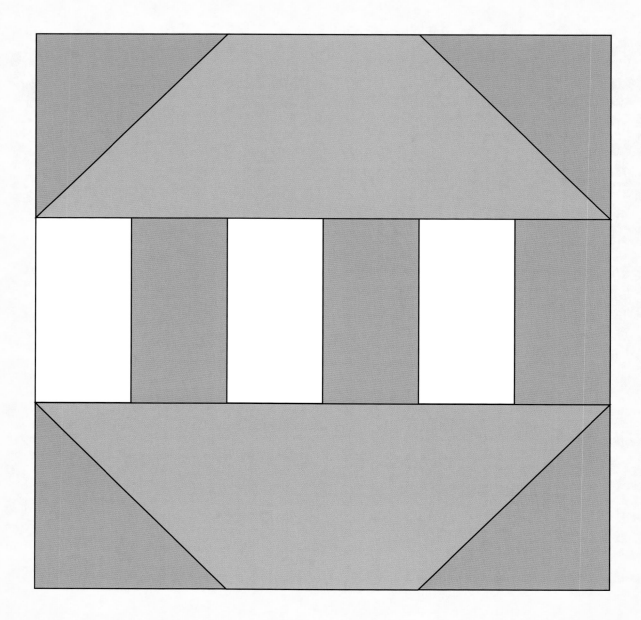

PRETTY LONG MARCH

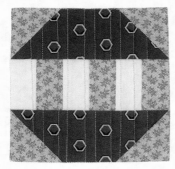

Aug. 11, 1863

Dear Friend,

I will inform you with pleasure that I am well at the present, and I hope that when this reaches you that it may find you well. I have received no letter from you since the one you sent by Dr. Ivens, but I hope that I will receive a letter soon. Will P. is well, and the boys are generally well, I believe, at this time.

I will inform you that we will leave Helena today at 3 o'clock on a march through Arkansas. I suppose that we will go to Little Rock and likely to Texas. We are going to have a pretty long march, and the weather is very warm down here. I do not know the number of troops that will leave Helena with us but suppose about 5,000, and we will join Gen. Davidson about 25 miles from here. He has some 7,000 cavalry; suffice it to say that old Price has to leave Arkansas or give us battle. I expect that we will have a fight with him at Little Rock or near that place. If we do, we will do the very best that we can for him. After we leave here, I expect that it will be some time ere we receive any mail. I have no idea how soon that the mail will reach us, and we will seldom have the opportunity of sending any letters back, but suffice it to say that I will write as often as I can, and I wish you to write soon and direct as before. Well, Han, I have nothing of much interest to write to you at present, but I will try and do better next time. Will P. is going to drive a team; he will not get to write home before we start. Everything is excitement in camp at present. They are pulling down the tents, and I have to quit writing to help them. I will close for the present. My love to all, and reserve a share for yourself.

In haste, yours truly,

Newton Scott

REBEL SPY HUNG

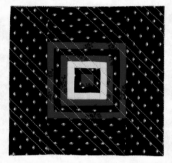

Jan. 19, 1864

Most respected friend Han,

It is with much pleasure that I take the present opportunity of writing you a few lines in answer to yours of the 28th, which was received a few days ago with pleasure. Well, Han, I will tell you that I saw a Rebel spy hung here on the 8th. He was caught going out past our picket guards and was arrested and examined and papers of importance to the Rebels found in his possession. He was brought back and court marshaled and sentenced to be hung dead by the neck on the 8th. He was executed in the presence of some good persons. His name was David O. Dodd.

Well, Han, you stated that you had a pretty dry Christmas up home. Well, indeed I hope that you had a merry time on New Year's Day. Well, let me tell you that we had a pretty dry time here on Christmas and New Year's Day. No roasted turkey for dinner nor visitors to see us, but we stayed at our camps thinking of home and of old times and hoping for happier days to come. Suffice it to say that those two noted days were as other days in the army of Arkansas. Well Han, I have my paper nearly filled, and I have not written half that I could if I had room, but I cannot tell you all with my pen, for if I did, I would load down the mail. Well, I must close for this time. Please write soon, and write all the news and particulars, and please excuse this ill-composed letter and my poor writing, and I will try and do better in the future.

From your friend and well wishes,

Newton Scott

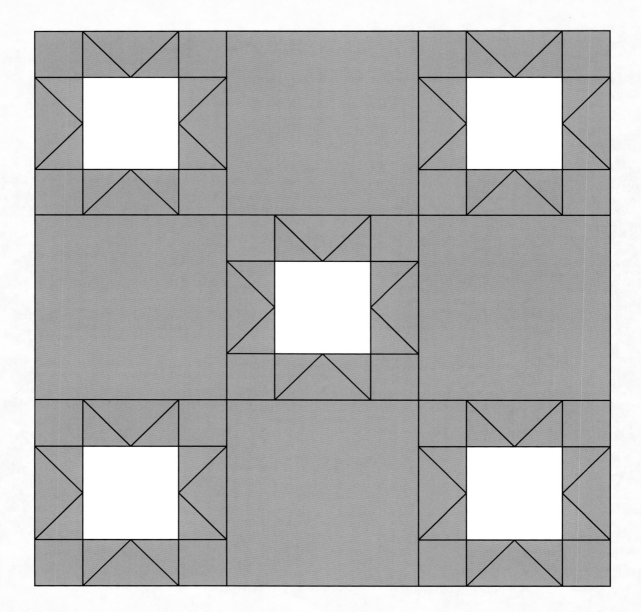

BRAVE BOYS OF THE 6TH IOWA

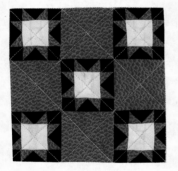

Feb. 14, 1864

Dear Friend,

Your long looked-for letter of the 25th is received at last. I was very glad to hear from you again, for it has been some time before since I received any letter from you. This leaves me well, and also, the boys are generally well. I was glad to hear that you were anticipating a good time on the arrival of Company E of the 6th Iowa, and indeed I hope the boys, one and all of them, and the girls will have a merry time while on there short visit home, for if anybody deserves a good time and honor, it is the Brave Boys of the old 6th Iowa. All honor to them, but I don't think it right for them to re-enlist and serve three years longer and let those cowardly copperheads stay at home and spit their treason at the poor, worn-out soldiers. What do they care whether the soldiers live or not? Away, away, with all such fiends, but again, I think the war will close by the time our term of service expires, and I hope that those veterans will not have to serve their three years. But the future only can decide when it will close.

You said that you wished Company A would come home this spring or summer. Well, you may be sure that I would love to come home to enjoy some fun, but then you know that 30 days is the longest period that furloughs are given, and that would be a very short time to remain home, and hence I will be content to wait, and if I live to see the close of the war or expiration of our time of service. Oh, indeed, I would love to be at home and enjoy the pleasure of friends and cut around with some of the girls again, but I wish to come knowing that I can remain at home if I choose, and if I live and have my health, I expect to come home that way. I think it the duty of every able-bodied man if necessary to help defend his country. But I think three years is sufficiently long for one man to serve while they all take their turns. But those old troops re-enlisting will soon put an end to the rebellion, certainly for they will know that they cannot conquer well-drilled and well-tried soldiers, and their army is deserting daily and coming over to our army, and a great many of them are enlisting in our army.

Newton Scott

PEOPLE AND PEACHES

July 22nd, 1864

Dear Friend,

Your letter of the 8th is received with pleasure. I was glad to hear from you all and that you had gained your health again. This leaves me in moderate health only. I resumed duty on the 13th and have been on guard several times since, and I'm doing very well, and I hope when this reaches you that it will find you well and enjoying yourself.

I saw Will P. on yesterday. He was very well and hearty. The boys of Company A are mostly well, except some of the recruits. Well, Han, you stated that you wished me and Will could get a furlough home. Well, indeed, we would love to come home, you may be sure, but it is almost impossible for a well man to get a furlough when sick men cannot get them when it would save many dear lives. I have no idea of getting home until the expiration of my time of service. If permitted to live, then I expect to return home and see the people and eat peaches. We could get home this winter coming by re-enlisting as veterans for three years longer, but I am not wanting to get home that bad yet a while. I did think when I left home that the war would not last over 15 months, but now I would not be surprised if it lasts five years, though it may close soon, and I hope it will. But I am pretty certain it will not close ere our time of service is out. Well, I have no news of interest to write at this time. The weather is very warm here, and there is considerable sickness among soldiers, citizens and refugees, and many dying off. There is not much fighting going on in this department, but considerable bushwhacking up and down the White River and along the railroad, but it doesn't amount to much as yet. Well, I believe that I have told you all for the present. Please write soon and give all the news and particulars and what-for times you are having up in Iowa, and if my luck is still living and on pleading terms. After my best wishes and respects to you, believe me.

Very truly yours,

Newton Scott

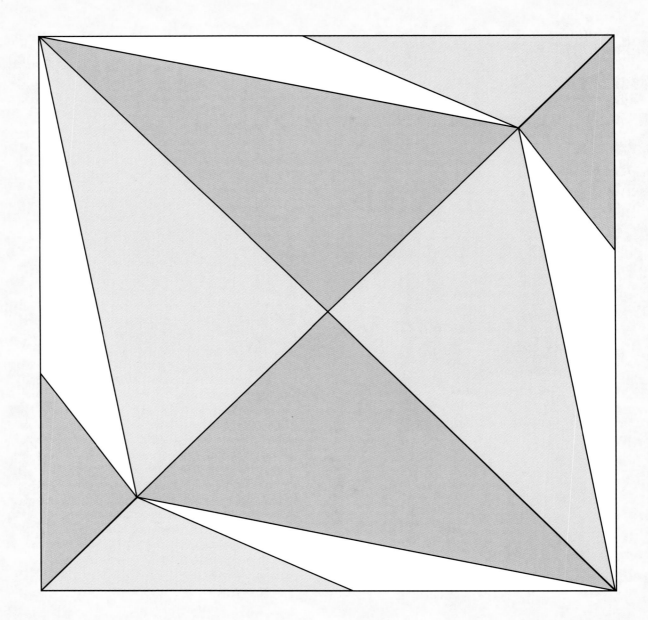

PLEASURES OF SWEET HOME

Nov. 3, 1864

Dear Friend,

Yours of the 16th is received with pleasure. I was very glad to hear from you and that you were well. This leaves me well at the present and hope that when this reaches you that it may find you well.

The boys of Company A are mostly well at this time. Your brother was well on yesterday. He was up to see us, he is still on detach service in the city. I'm sorry to inform you that Zellek H. Collins of our company died here at Regimental Hospital on the 1st from the disease typhoid fever. Friend Harvey was a good soldier and a social comrade, and we will regret his lost very much.

I had almost given up getting a letter from you, and I think that we are getting very careless in writing to each other, so let's do better in the future. Friend Han, you stated in your letter of the 16th that you often looked over to my old home and thought of the many happy hours that yourself and I with two others had enjoyed. You stated that Miss Samatha Gillespy was going to get married soon. Please tell me in your next letter the lucky man's name that has married Miss Samantha, and also please, oh please, tell me if my Hattie is married yet, for I know that she is tired of single life ere this time.

Well, Han, I will tell you that we have just 11 months from tomorrow to serve for Uncle Sam, and if our health and lives are spared, we expect to visit our friends after that time and enjoy the many pleasures of friends and the pleasures of sweet home. I expect to return to old Monroe County again if I am spared to live and have my health after my 11 months is served for Uncle Sam. And I hope and think that the war will be over by that time. I think that the election or re-election of President Lincoln will do much toward the closing of the war. I will vote for Old Abe without a doubt.

But I must close, for it is 8 o'clock at night and the drum is beating for roll call and I must go. Please write soon and give all the news and particulars, and you will please excuse my long letter and the composed letter and the poorly written remarks, and I will try to do better in the future. Please write soon, without delay.

Very respectfully yours,

Newton Scott

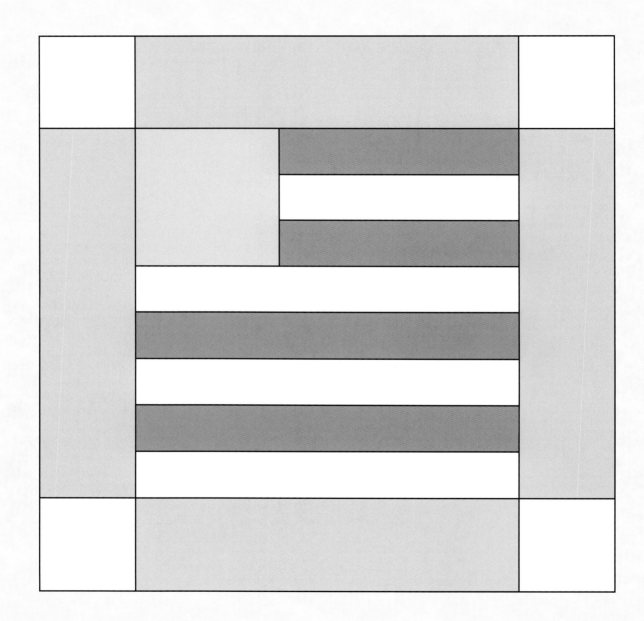

A Consoling Thought

March 13, 1865

Miss H.M. Cone,

Your very welcome letter of the 26th is received, and I hasten to reply. I was very glad to hear from you once again and that you were still on the land and amongst the living but sorry to hear that you were unwell. Hope that you are well ere this time. But I expect that you have been losing so much sleep attending those oyster suppers and the very many weddings that have transpired up in your country of late, which has likely caused your ill health to some extent. But, Han, you must excuse me for writing as I do, for you know that when I was home in my young days, I most always was at home with my Mother and only went visiting my darling once, twice and sometimes thrice a week, but will promise my mother to do better in the future if I am spared to return home again. But in reference to your cousin Perry and Mr. Hunter getting married, I and Will think that they might as well have postponed their wedding a few days while I and he returned home. But then, we will rest contented with the consoling thought that if we should ever get married, no one can cheat us out of being present; if so, we will forfeit the ghost. But I must stop my foolishness or you will think me crazy.

I must close as my sheet is full, and I hope you will excuse my long letter, but indeed, Han, I could fill another sheet and not be tired. My health is tolerably good; also, Will is well. Please write soon and give all the news to direct to St. Charles, Ark.

Respectfully yours,

Newton Scott

SAD
BEREAVEMENT

May 24, 1865

Miss H. M. Cone,

Yours of the 13th is received; I was glad to hear from you and that you were well. I had almost given up ever receiving another letter from you, but better late than never. This leaves me well at this time. Also, the boys are generally in pretty good health at this time. I hope that when this reaches you that it may find you enjoying the best of health.

Well you stated in your letter that many changes had taken place up in Monroe here of late, and the most heartbreaking of all is my Darling has long ago forsaken me and married and left me to mourn my life away, or in other words, do the best I can during my future life. Yes, indeed, I thank you very much for your sympathy toward me in my sad bereavement. (Hope I will survive the sudden shock). I wish for better success in the future. Well, you stated in your letter that you thought the time not far distant when we would return home. Indeed I hope not, but I don't think that we will get home for two or three months yet, but hope we will get home sooner. Though it is the general opinion here that we will get home by the 20th of July, if not sooner, and I hope we may have no news of much interest to write from here at this time.

Everything is quiet here except that the Rebs still continue to come in and surrender themselves and take the oath. There is no Rebs of any consequence north of the Arkansas River and west of the Mississippi River now, having all or nearly all come into our forces and taken the oath. Well, I believe that I have written all for this time. Would be very glad to see you and have a long talk with you. I could tell you much more if present than I can write, and hope now soon we will get home to enjoy the comforts of civil life and the many pleasures of good friends. Will say to you that I don't understand your meaning when you said that for your reason for not writing sooner you could not write but would tell me when I came home, but hope it was for no error of myself. But I can't insist on knowing, as you said you would tell me when I came home. Well, I will close for today.

Please write soon and tell me all the news and particulars, and hoping to hear from you soon again, believe me as ever, yours, very respectfully,

Newton Scott

Samuel Matson Fox. Photograph courtesy of David H. Fox.

Samuel Matson Fox

(Feb. 27, 1840 - September 1862)

Samuel Matson Fox was one of six children born to Adaline Porter Dearth and Samuel Madison Fox, who were married in 1836. He was the second-oldest of four brothers and two sisters living in Trenton, N.J. His parents died when the children were young, so they all became orphans and were raised by family members.

Samuel enlisted with the 6th New Jersey Volunteers in the fall of 1861 at the age of 21. He became a drummer. He enlisted with his younger brother, Edward, who was 19. The following year, his brother, George, who is unemployed and cannot find work, joins the regiment, also as a drummer. Drummers did not carry rifles, and Samuel did not have to participate in all of the fighting.

Samuel's letters were written home to his brother and other family members. A total of 17 letters were found in a cardboard box, together with the letters that his brothers George and Edward wrote. In his first letter home in November 1861, Samuel sent Joe $2 to save or to put to good use. He sent George $10 and told him to buy his little brother, Joe, some boots. He would also send money home for his other brothers' and sisters' care. He always signed his letters, "your affectionate brother."

Samuel wrote his letters from the battlefields; he would write home that cannons were firing all the time, and it made it lively at camp. Some of the letters that Samuel wrote home also included patriotic drawings. One drawing included two crossed-staff American flags with the motto "I will protect you all, 6th New Jersey Volunteers." Another letter included a drawing of a shield with stars and stripes and the motto "The Jerseys Forever."

Samuel wrote his last letter home from Harrison Landing, Va., on Aug. 12, 1862. He never made it home from the war. On Sept. 6, 1862 Edward wrote a letter home stating that Samuel was not feeling very well. It was on Oct. 1, 1862, that Edward wrote home to say how lonesome he has been since the death of his brother, whom he used to see every day. "We used to talk about home, and we loved each other as ever any brothers did. George and I stayed with him from the time he was taken sick until he died, both day and night."

Samuel's brother, Edward, received a medical discharge in 1863, and George finally returned home in 1865.

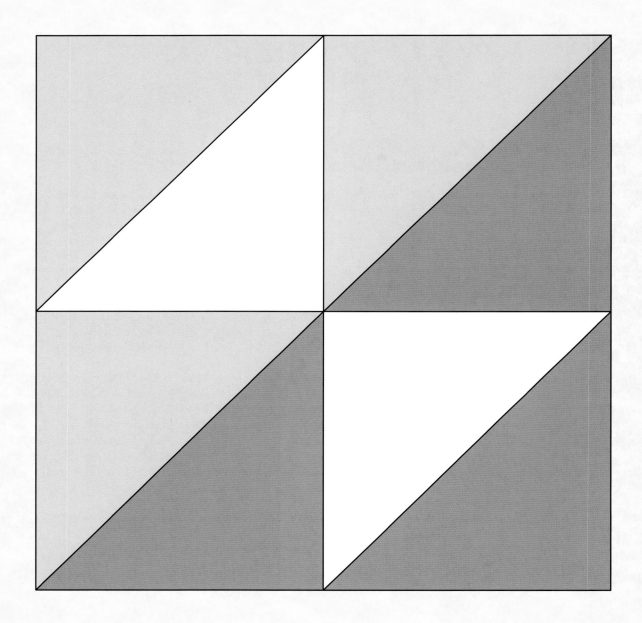

JERSEY BOYS

Nov. 17, 1861

Dear Brother,

I now take the opportunity of sending you a few more lines, hoping to find you all well. I received a letter from George and Joe; was sorry to hear that Joe was unwell. Charley, tell Joe if he is sick much, he need not go to school this winter and can recite his lessons at home. Also say to Mrs. Casey if she thinks best for Joe to stay from school this winter, I am perfectly willing. He shall quit, as I know he is not healthy and think it best to look to his health while he is young. I take all responsibility on myself, so she can act for me.

I sent Joe $2 for to save or put to a good use. I sent George $10 and told him to get Joe boots. Eddy's regiment will be paid next week, I expect. I don't think we will go to South Carolina by the looks of things, but I will always write to some of you so you can always know where I am. Charley, it is very cold here now, and we are all anxious to get in barracks or go down south farther, but I think the Jersey Boys can stand much as any of them, and by next spring I think we will be in Trenton. Charley, tell George if he has not sent my undershirts to get Joe to look for my buckskin gloves. I think they are in my old overcoat, and send them, too, for we can't get in Washington to buy anything. Charley, you must excuse me for not writing more than I do as it is hard to find news for all, but I will do the best. Can you show Joe the letter and give him the money? We don't get much, so a great deal can't be expected. I sent the remainder of my money to Annie. I shall have to close by sending my love to all our folks. Eddy joins in the same, hoping to find you all well as Eddy and myself are at present. I bid you adieu.

I remain your affectionate brother,

Samuel M. Fox

P. S. Tell Joe to write again soon, and you and George to let me know if you get this letter. Give my best wishes to all inquiring friends.

DRUMMER

Dec. 3, 1861

Dear Brother,

I received your letter, also Joe's and Mr. Jones' today. Since I wrote to Trenton last, we have moved to Bum Point, Madowama Creek and expect to move to Budd's Point in a day or so, opposite the Rebels' batteries on the Potomac. We came in steamboats all the way but 13 miles, walking the rest, and had a gay time of it. We waded through water up to our waist and mud to our knees but are now in our tents.

Tell Joe and all I was glad to hear from them and happy to hear they were well as I am at present. I can't write much now as I have not much time on account of the mail leaving. You want me to tell you about getting a job drumming here. I think you can get a job either in the 5th or 6th. We are one drummer short, but Eddy has been trying to get transferred to our regiment. Now it is as I said, I expect you can get in one or the other, but you must know first you will see some pretty hard times marching. But, I don't want to discourage you; all I can say is stay home if possible. If not, you can come and see; you take the boat from Washington to this place (G. Street Wharf, Washington, is were we started from.)

I wrote to Annie to not write until I sent word and to let you all know, but I get the mail just the same now. Some of you write to her and let her know. Tell Joe and Charley I will write as I can, and tell Joe to let me know if his hen laid that egg in his next letter. I will write to Joe in a few days. You need not think strange when I don't write, as we march some time before we know it. I will now have to close. Eddy is not here yet.

From your affectionate brother,

Samuel M. Fox

P.S. Direct as before to Washington D.C.; all the boys on their best respect to you. Give my love to Joe and Charley and show them this letter. We have only stock here for a day or so to wait for the 5th and 7th. We will move two miles further and then encamp.

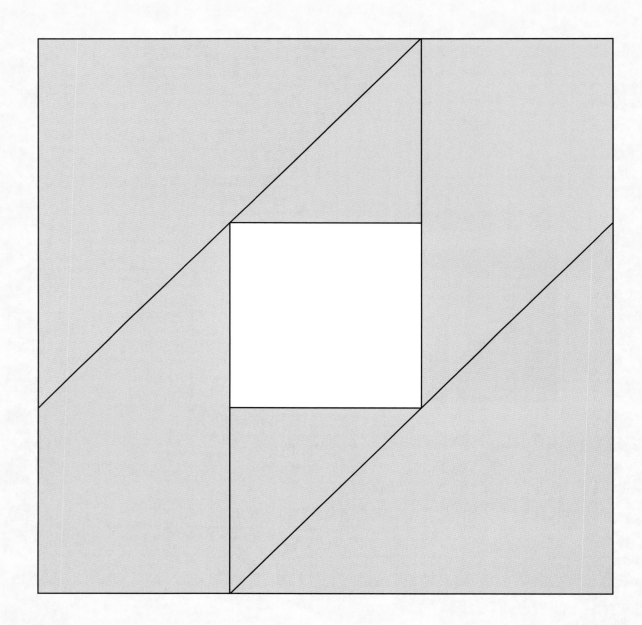

64-Pound Shell

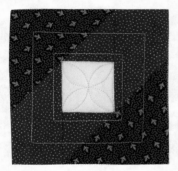

Dec. 15, 1861

Dear Brother,

It is with pleasure I send you these lines on this beautiful Sabbath day. Charley, there is nothing new occurred here since I wrote last. Our vessels continue to run the Rebel's blockade. We heard very heavy firing all day yesterday in the direction of Bull Run. Our gunboats are firing on a Rebel battery a little way above us.

You may have seen in the papers about a deserter coming over to Gen. Hooker's headquarters from the Rebels. He told our men there was over 200 men who wanted to desert in this regiment. Eddy showed me your letter to him, and I have just got one from Joe. Tell Joe I will answer his letter soon; also, I will see Eddy about the money. I was glad to hear George had got some work and hope he may have it steady. I felt very sorry to hear of the death of Mrs. Jones' child, which was such a nice little babe.

We have had it very cold here nights and have got a small stove in our tent, which makes it very warm and we enjoy it very much. Our boys just brought in a shell which the Rebels fired over in our battery which did not burst; it weighs 64 pounds. They say our boats were firing in the woods to see if there also were any more batteries. Then when a new battery fired on them, one ball hitting one of our boats, the Harriet Lane they ran up and fired shots, every one bursting in their battery, silencing them right away. We have a battery on our side which is also firing today. Charley, we hear cannon firing all the time here, which makes it lively in camp. Our officers say we will be home in time to draw the first pay after we get ours on New Year here. I hope it may be so, not because I am tired of soldiering, but to see our Glorious Union once more at peace. I will have come to a close by sending my love to all our folks. Eddy joins in the same.

I remain your loving brother,

Samuel M. Fox

P.S. I expect a letter from Annie soon, as I have written to her. Tell Joe I will let him know what to do with my shirts when I write to him. Tell him I got the feathers and am going to show them to Eddy. I have just had some good things which Aunt Sarah sent Eddy and me from Philadelphia. Eddy wrote to her, and she answered him and sent off some apple cakes, candies and dried beef, which we enjoy very well.

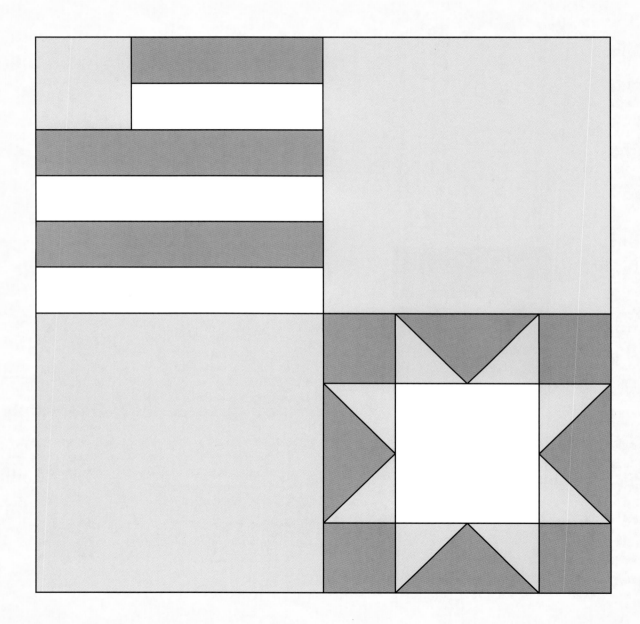

DRESS PARADE

Jan. 1, 1862

Dear Brother,

I have just got an opportunity to answer your letter, which I was happy to get. Charley, I have had a letter from Annie. She said you had wrote to her, and she was answering your letter. I got a letter from Joe saying he and Mrs. Jones were going to send my box on Tuesday, and I expect it is on its way while I am writing. Tell Joe I had better wait until I get my box before I write to him. We don't get them for a week after they get to Washington sometimes, as our quartermaster has to get them in Washington and bring them to us by the boat. He generally waits until quite a number are there before bringing them.

Charley, I expect you will be quite a housekeeper when Mr. and Mrs. Nickelson get back. I often cook something extra down here, and I think we will have to see who can beat whom when I get back. I showed your letter to Eddy but have not seen him for a day or two, as we have been busy. I will see him tonight and show Joe's letter to him. I see him every day on dress parade but don't get a chance to speak to him then.

The bands arrived here on Monday for the 5th, 7th and 8th Regiments, but our band can beat them all. We are all laying in our tents, singing today, as we have New Years for a holiday. The Rebels are quite still across the river now. They fired a gun at 12 o'clock last night for New Years; our men also fired several. I have three more letters to write today and will have to draw a close, although this is not a very happy New Years Day to the American people, but we must all offer an earnest prayer to God for a speedy settlement of this rebellion. So wishing you may all have good health, I will close, hoping to hear from you soon as convenient.

I remain your affectionate brother,

Samuel M. Fox

P.S. Give my love to all our folks and tell them to accept the wish of a Happy New Year, not leaving yourself out. Eddy and myself are in good health and wish you the same good luck.

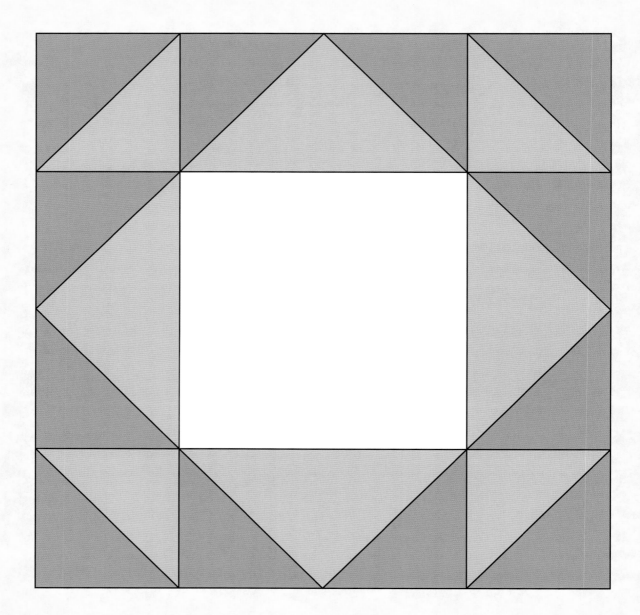

TREAT FROM HOME

Jan. 20, 1862

Dear Brother,

I received your letter of the 12th and was happy to hear from you. It has been snowing and raining together here for near two weeks and has not cleared up yet. You would not believe how muddy it is down here in Dixie, but we have gotten used to it now and don't care much whether it clears off or not.

I would like to hear from grandmother; you must let me know how she is in your next letter. I am expecting an answer from Joe, as I wrote to him after I received my box. Charley, I had a fine time over the nice things in it. Eddy helped me to devour the contents, and we both felt a little homesick after having such a treat from home. George wrote to me saying he was out of work and wanted to come here as a drummer. I answered his letter and expect he will come if George can't get anything to do. It will be better for him here than doing nothing. I opposed him coming once but said nothing against it this time as I don't believe we will have to move from here until we come home, and I expect to eat my Fourth of July dinner in Trenton and hope I won't be disappointed. If George does come, Charley, tell him to get me a small screwdriver from Mr. Jones. He will know what size; I want it for two small screws on my drum, also a small pair of pliers.

We expect to be paid off this week; if we do, I will send you and Joe both something. I was over to see Eddy the other day. He has it very nice in his tent, and Capt. Gould thinks the world of him. I like Gould much better that Capt. Ewing, and we are glad Ed is with him. Eddie is very partial with an old colored man who cooks for this captain and often has something extra for his meals. I have nothing in the way of war news to send. The Rebels often fire at us but have not done us any damage yet. I think they will have to do their best soon, as their time is short. With these few lines I will have to come to a close hoping my letter may find you all in good health as it leaves Eddy and myself.

I will conclude by remaining your affectionate brother,

Samuel M. Fox

P.S. Give my love and Eddy's to all our folks. Stand by the flag that is an honor to all who respect it.

Mr. Rabbit

Feb. 2, 1862

Dear Brother,

I received your letter and was happy to hear you were all well. Eddy and I have been out taking a walk today along the Potomac. We had an opera glass and had a fine view of the Rebels' batteries. We saw the baggage wagons very plain going up the hills over in Dixie. We had two more with us, and when we came back, we had a great time trying to shoot a rabbit. One of our party fired three times and missed Mr. Rabbit. Eddy fired next and missed also. We had a sword along; one of our fifers crawled behind the stump and made a dive at bun and penned him in his hole were he sat. We all made a charge on him then, thinking we had him for certain, but in reaching out, Mr. Rabbit give a spring and left us in double-quick time. This is the first fight we have had down here, and we gave in. We were defeated on account of having a poor commander.

It has cleared off at last down here, and we welcome the beautiful sun on Saturday afternoon, as we would welcome our dear friends at home. We began to think the sun only shone here at certain parts of the year, but we feel like soldiers again, nothing to complain of, and when I'm situated, I feel as happy as the happiest. I suppose you and Joe have received your money. Before this I sent you $1 and Eddy sent $4 to Joe. The boots I bought made a hole in my money, and I want to save all I possibly can, so I could not spare any more. I feel rather glad George has enlisted, as he can save more by being here than home, however, we will see now how the three Foxes make out in the saving list. I feel confident of being home to spend my Fourth of July with you and Joe. Be good and see how your brother Sam has made out by going a-soldiering. I will have to close now hoping my letter may find you all in good health.

Your affectionate brother,

Samuel M. Fox

P.S. Write soon, Charley. You must excuse this writing, for my pen has grease on it and will hold ink. I have more and will do better next time. Give my love to George, Joe, grandmother and Aunt Mary's folks, and take out a portion for yourself.

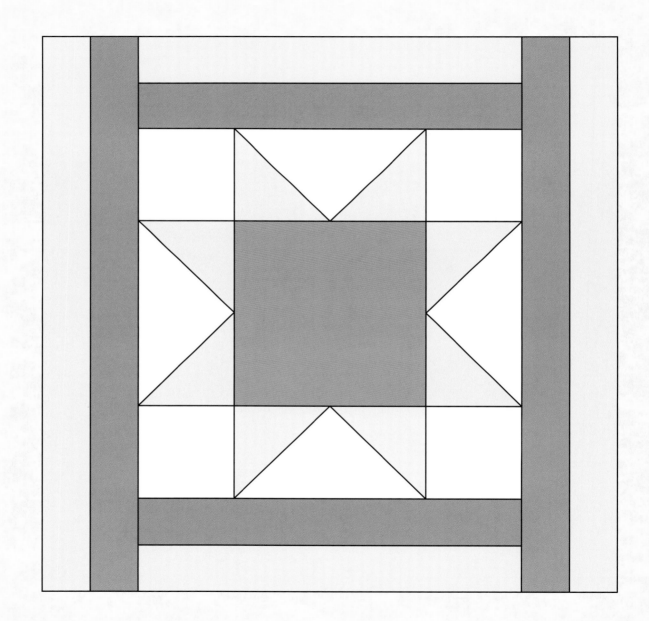

FUNERAL
PROCESSION

Feb. 15, 1862

Dear Brother,

I received your well-written letter of the 9th and was happy to hear from you, also to see how you improved, both in writing and composing a letter.

We have had a few days' fine weather here, but it has commenced snowing again now, which we dislike very much. Charley, our division surgeon died with the heart disease on Monday and was taken to the landing on Thursday to be conveyed to his home. His name was Dr. Bell. It was the most splendid funeral procession I ever seen. All the staff officers in our division attended, and all on horses. Charley, you can imagine what a beautiful sight it was to see 100 officers on horses. All fine-looking men and horses, it was a sight I would not have missed seeing for a great deal.

We are all in good spirits here after our recent victories and all agree in saying down with rebellion. We have commenced now; let us finish it in double-quick time. We have been expecting George every day. Eddy and I were pleased to hear you had both got your money. Eddy is a little jealous of me getting so many letters; he wants you to write to him. I think it will be best to change. Write to Ed first and me next; then he will not complain. I received a letter from Anne yesterday. I will tell her to write to you and Joe. She got my money safely. All the folks are well. Annie has fine times skating. Uncle John, Mr. Grey and all go together, taking several of the girls in the neighborhood with them. I will have to close now by sending our love to you, all in good health, as my letter leaves us at present.

From your affectionate brother,

Samuel M. Fox

FORGOTTEN THE WORD DEFEAT

March 3, 1862

Dear Brother,

I now take the opportunity of answering your letter to me. I was glad to hear you were well and also happy to inform you we are all well here.

I expect you had a fine time on Washington's birthday with your military and the illumination at night. I had heard of our victory in Tennessee and of all cheering. You never heard as there was in our different encampments, and we agree with the people at home that Seccesh is near gone under. However, we must not feel disappointed to hear of a reverse, because such is to be expected, but we will now soon fix old Jeff off, because our soldiers are full of fight and have forgotten the word defeat.

George is well and is going to write to you soon, today if he gets a chance. Charley, you want to know how I am getting along with drumming, of course. I won't brag, but still I have learned quite fast and think by the time I get home, you can call me a drummer, too, without feeling ashamed, but still I shall not continue long with the drum after the war is over, as I have got enough of the plaything already. However, I will give Charley and Joe a few of my best beats and then quit. Charley, Eddy has got another little dog. We are all laughing away now at a good rate at him. I keep him in my tent, for he is black with a white breast and is full of fun. He will run after sticks and fight the snow. We have a great deal of fun with him, which we like down here. We have had another snowstorm, and it has not cleared off yet but has stopped snowing. We are so tired of wet weather here that we hardly know what to do with ourselves but lay in our tents, which we are tired of. However, we are living in hopes of seeing some fine weather soon. We have got a cannon presented by our government by the loyal Americans in England that are the Whitworth guns. Gen. Hooker tried them at the Rebel batteries the other day and threw about 10 shells in there.

Your loving brother,

S. M. Fox

P.S. We all join in sending our love to you all. Write soon.

Drummer Sam

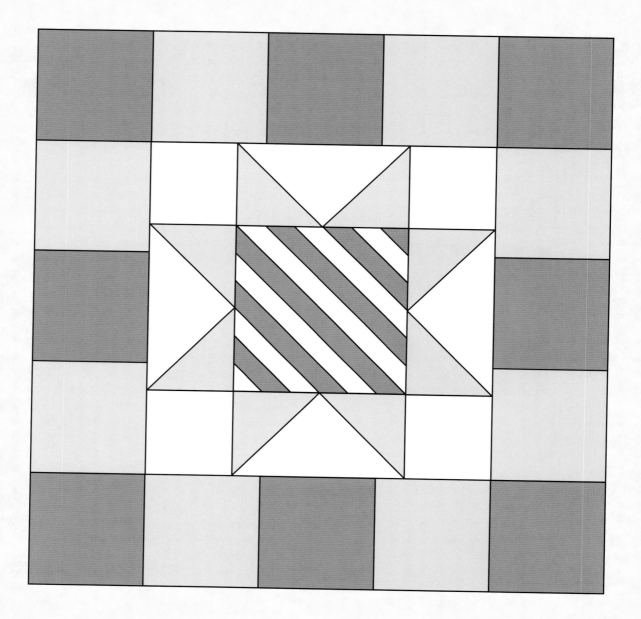

STARS AND STRIPES

March 15, 1862

Dear Brother,

I received your letter and have just got an opportunity to answer it. I suppose you have heard of the Rebels evacuating the batteries opposite us. It was a great sight. They left at night and left some cavalry behind to destroy what was left behind, which they did the next day. They blew up their magazines and burnt the steamer, George Page, and two schooners. Our gunboats, Yankee and Anacosta, ran down and threw shells in their batteries and in the woods for two hours and then landed and raised the Stars and Stripes on the flagpole.

We have seen the mean little Rebel flag on so long. The next day, the 5th New Jersey and 1st Massachusetts crossed over and destroyed all they could not, which was a large quantity of shot and shell and all the cannons we did not want. We brought our splendid cannon away they got from England, the large cannon, and took from us at Bull Run.

The next day, Companies B and D of our regiment were ordered over to advance farther on. I took a musket and went with my company. We went to a place called Dumfries and had a fine time. We got some quantity of clothes and blankets and burned many things we could not take. We were there some time when we saw 50 Rebel Cavalry on a high hill looking at us. Our company went on skirmishing after them with Capt. Ewing heading while Company D acted as reserves. We got within 200 yards of them, and they ran away like a cat would from a dog. We were busy all day after them, as they would come in sight about every hour, but our force was only 100, and we could not surround them. We blew up a house packed with shells and purchasing next day and left for home with one old Seccesh who told the Cavalry we were coming after them. I got a lot of drumheads, three nice shirts, some Seccesh letters. They left most all behind, so I think they left in a great hurry.

I will have to come to a close now as I can't tell all we took from the Secceshs. George, Eddy and I all join in sending our love and hope you are all well as we are at present.

I remain your affectionate brother,

Samuel M. Fox

THE MONITOR

Dear Brother,

Since I received your last letter, we have had a move of over 150 miles. We embarked on the large steamer, John Brooks, and our whole division went on different boats. We got off on Monday morning last and reached fortress Monroe on Tuesday, and Charley and I saw some very great sights. I saw the Monitor and the picture in Frank Leslie's paper is exactly like her. We left fortress Monroe on Tuesday afternoon and came to our place where we now are.

We have a very fine campground and have very curious tents. Perhaps you seen them home, each man carries his part of the tent, and three or four go together and they make a fine little tent. These tents were all homemade.

Charley, we are not allowed to write anything concerning our movements now, but after it is over I will tell you. George and me have been sick for the first time. We are getting better now. We have had a bad cold. Charley, you must see Joe and let him read this also. Tell me how he is getting along, and tell Johny we have not been paid off yet. Tell Aunt Mary and Uncle Ralph we all send our love to them. Tell Grandmother we all think of her and want to see her as soon as possible and I hope we may. Charley, I heard Mrs. Irvin had a young son, for gracious sakes let me know if this is so and who she is married to. We have all the oysters here we want out of the river here. Eddy is fat and hearty and likes it first rate down here, Charley. I will have to come to a close now, but you may expect a longer letter next time. I had to hurry so for the mail and had no ink. We all join in sending our love to you all and hope to find you well.

I remain your affectionate brother,

Samuel M. Fox

P.S. Tell Joe to be a good boy, as we expect to be home in two or three months and then for the presents. Hooray for our side.

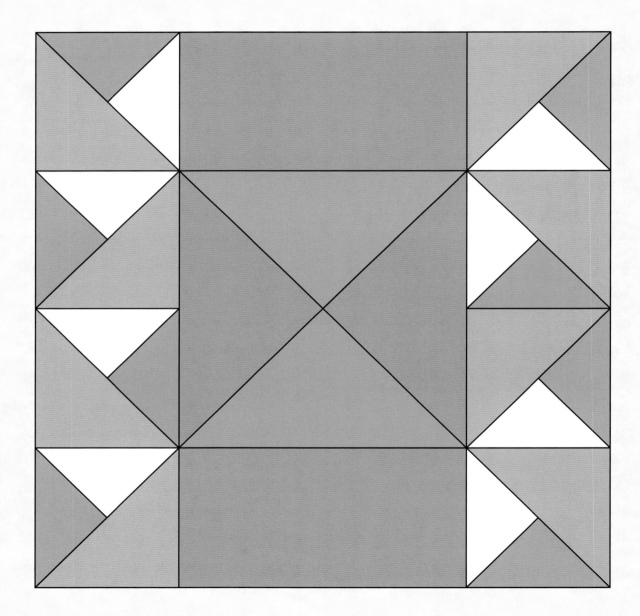

FALSE GRAVES

Dear Brother,

As I now have an opportunity of writing a few lines to you, I will try to give you some information as to where we are and how we are getting along. We are now encamped at a point called Baltimore Crossroads, 4 miles from the Chickahominy River. There is a small force of Rebels; they have burnt the bridge, and I expect we will have to build it again, and we may go on the main road.

We can't tell what we are to do, as we are ignorant of official movements. We are now 15 or 20 miles from Richmond, so you may know if we are victorious, which we feel certain we will soon see the Rebel capital. We have marched over 50 miles since we disembarked from our fleet at shipping point and have seen some pretty hard times in the mud and rain, but still, all of us are as joyful as if we were going through State Street.

We were all surprised at the Rebels evacuating Yorktown when we saw their fortifications as they surrounded the whole town and were very strong as we were going by them. We have seen a very large number of false graves containing cannons, as we have since learned they had headboards all cut very nicely, and all was done to deceive us, but our commander was too smart for them.

We were very much troubled by torpedoes placed in the ground from Yorktown to Williamsburg, but afterward, Gen. McClellan made the Rebel prisoners blow them all up. We were not troubled by them anymore. We are now encamped in a pine woods, opposite a splendid mansion surrounded by a large field of grain. We now have a fine chance of resting ourselves in the shade. You must excuse me for not writing before, as we are continually marching to different places, we being on the reserve, which causes us many cross marches under the circumstances we are placed. I think I am excusable; I shall always write to you when the opportunity permits. Hoping to hear from you soon, I will have to close, as I have a few words to say to Joe.

I remain your affectionate brother,

Samuel M. Fox

P.S. Charley, show this to Joe and tell him he must write and not forget to go to school for a while. We all join in sending our love to Mrs. Irwin, Nancy and all inquiring friends.

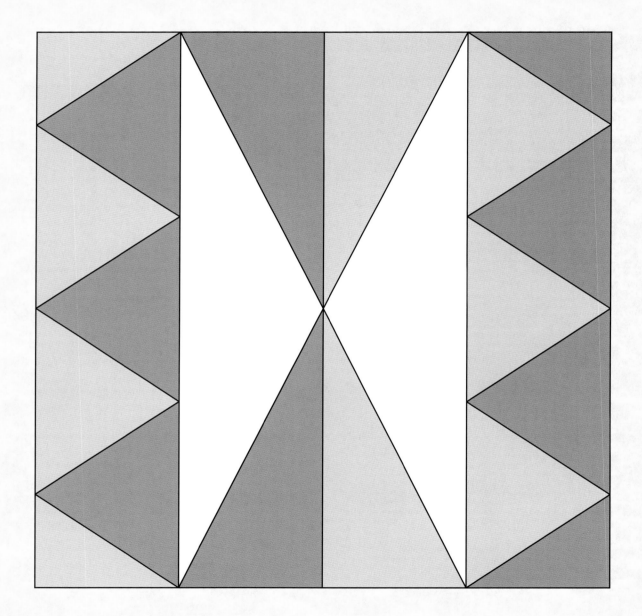

BATTLE AT WILLIAMSBURG

June 15, 1862

Dear Brother,

I received your last letter and was happy to hear you were all enjoying good health.   Charley, there has been nothing very exciting here since the last fight, which I suppose you have seen the accounts of it in the paper. It was an awful battle, and the Jersey Boys have again added an honor to their Little State as they fought at Williamsburg as bravely as soldiers ever fought. The 5th and 6th regiments got one brigade of the Rebels on the run when Gen. Hooker told us we had done enough, and we could come out and the rest could keep them going.

Our regiment has become very small by sickness and our loss in battle. The whole number of effective men in our regiment now is 375, this being more than any of the other three we have on account of this had the 2nd New York attached to our brigade. They have been lately to Norfolk and now see what soldiering really is since they have joined with us.

We are all beginning to feel like coming home and are very anxious to have another try at the Seccesh, also to take their capitol to see if it will bring us any nearer home. I think Little Mac will soon make a strike, then look out, and if we don't take Richmond, it will astonish your brother Sammy very much.

We all continue to enjoy good health and hope to be blessed so throughout this war, then our happy days will come, as I know how happy I should feel to see you all. Charley, we will do as the song says. Wait for the wagon. Charley, I send you $15 for Nancy for Joe's board, and I want you to get me 50 cents worth of 3-cent letter stamps out of the one dollar bill and keep the rest for yourself. Charley, I believe there is no more at present, so I will come to a conclusion hoping you may all continue to enjoy good health and to hear from you soon.

I remain your affectionate brother,

Samuel M. Fox

P.S. Write soon.

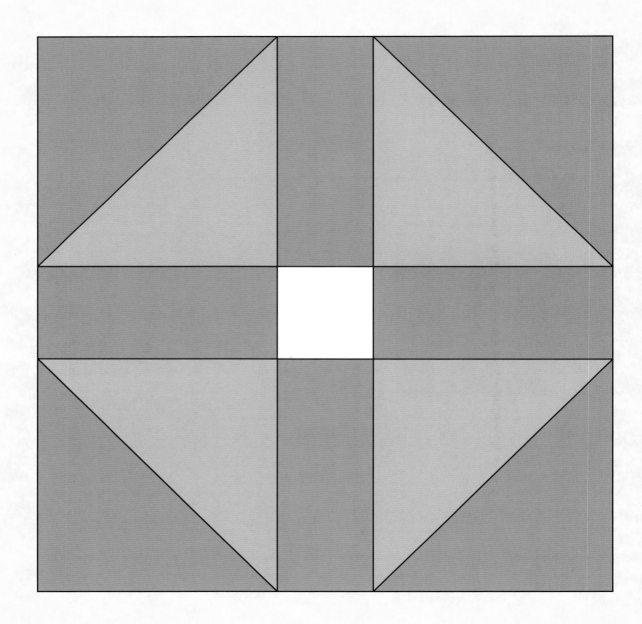

LETTERS OR PAPERS FROM HOME

July 25, 1862

Dear Brother,

I with pleasure take this opportunity of answering your last letter. I have since received the Harper's Weekly you sent me, also several Trenton papers from Uncle Ralph, all of which I return my thanks for, as we love dearly to get papers here.

Charley, I hardly know what to write about, as we are now lying in camp where there is nothing new transpiring, however, I shall endeavor to do the best I can since receiving your letter. It would be a grand sight for you to see our army here — cannon, horses and infantry all encamped close together. The militia of Trenton would look like one man among thousands here, but we have become so used to it, we hardly notice anything but the mailbag when it comes to see if we have a letter or papers from home. The express has become very intimate to us again, bringing boxes of good things from home, which we do not see down here very often. When we have money, the rascals here charge so much we can't buy without spending a month's wages for a very few things. I will give you a list of some of their prices. Cheese has been 50 cents, 75 cents and $1 per pound. It is now 40 cents a pound; sugar 30 cents per pound; butter 50 cents per pound; ginger cake 10 for 25 cents; lemon and oranges 12 cents apiece; herring 3 cents apiece; for a small loaf of baker's bread 25 cents. You can see by this we can't afford to have anything good here. We all continue to keep our health and feel thankful to God for his kindness and pray for a continuance of the same. Health is the main thing here, for when a man gets sick, it is impossible for him to get anything he can eat down here. I must draw to a close now but will try to have a better letter next time for you, hoping to find you all enjoying good health.

I will close by remaining your loving brother,

Samuel M. Fox

P.S. George, Eddie and I join in sending our love to you all. Write when you can, and accept thanks for the paper you sent.

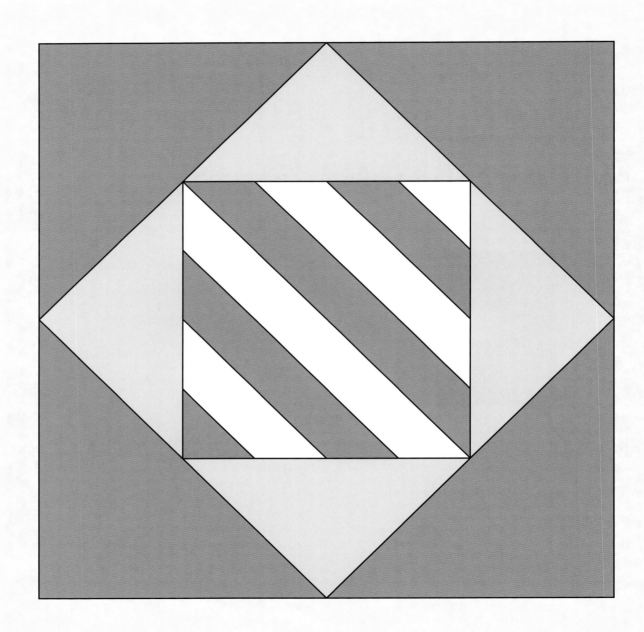

LAST LETTER HOME

Aug. 12, 1862
(Last letter that Samuel M. Fox wrote home)

Dear Brother,

I take this small opportunity of writing you a few lines and sending some money for Nancy; you can give it to her and send me a receipt for the same.

Charley, we are now all packed up to leave the Peninsula and expect to go any minute. Our knapsacks have gone ahead, accounts for my sending dirty paper and no stamp on this note, as all our things have gone with the knapsacks. We can't tell where we are to go; some say to join Pope's Army, others say fortress Monroe, and we have all kinds of rumors. In fact, none of us know; I think we will join Pope. We are anxious to go there, as the country is more healthy, besides, there is good water there.

I shall answer all letters as soon as I have a chance; tell all our folks and my friends I can't write just now, but will the first opportunity. Please write to Annie and let her know. You can write, and I think we will receive letters in five or six days. I must now draw to a close hoping to find you all well as we all are at present.

I remain your affectionate brother,

Samuel M. Fox

P.S. Charley, I enclose $20 for Nancy and one for yourself.

Cadet Andrew Gatewood on the right,
Cadet James W. Warick on the left.
Photograph courtesy of the Virginia
Military Institute Archives.

Andrew Gatewood in later
years. Photograph courtesy of
Virginia Military Institute
Archives.

Andrew C. L. Gatewood

June 30, 1843 - July 31, 1919

Andrew Cameron Lewis Gatewood was the seventh of nine children — six boys and three girls — born to Samuel Vance Gatewood and Eugena Sophia Massie. Born on June 30, 1843, he spent his childhood years living in Bath County, Va., where his parents had been married on Dec. 2, 1835.

In July 1860, Andrew entered the Virginia Military Institute in Lexington, Va., which was founded in 1839 and was the nation's first state military college. Andrew was 17 when he began studying with classes from the VMI. He wrote letters home to his parents describing the routine with classes at the institute. A typical day involved getting up at 5 o'clock in the morning, performing squad drills, studying and classes in the afternoon, more squad drills at evening, along with dress parade. He was very concerned about his grades and his standing in his class; his courses included mathematics, geography, French and English.

In his first letter home, Andrew mentioned how homesick he was. In other letters home, he would just write asking for news about his family. Twenty-eight of the letters that Andrew wrote home were found; most of the letters were written from VMI, where he served as a cadet or drillmaster. Later letters arrived home described his service with the 11th Virginia Cavalry Regiment as a second lieutenant, including a letter he wrote on Sept. 3, 1862, that described the battle of Manassas.

Andrew served with the 11th Virginia Cavalry until the end of the war. He returned home and married his childhood sweetheart, Mary Warwick, in December 1869 in Bath County, Va.; they had seven children. In 1877, he moved with his family to Pocahontas, Colo., where he spent his remaining days working as a farmer. Andrew died at the age of 76 in Pocahontas, Colo.

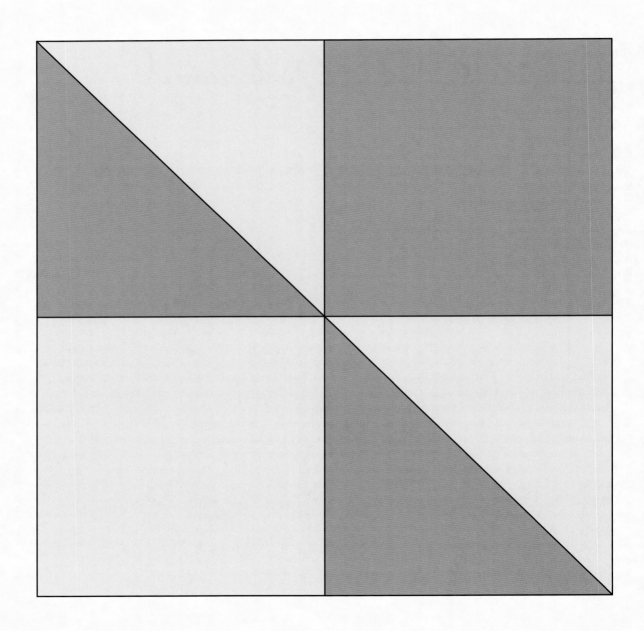

Virginia Military Institute

Aug. 4, 1860

Dear Pa and Ma,

I have written to Ma once, and now it is my time to write to you. I've not got much to tell you, but I will tell you all I know. I arrived here safe and entered the Institute on last Wednesday. I paid Col. Smith the money and took his receipt for it.

I tell you, this is a hard place. I have been initiated, and it went pretty hard with me. They whipped me with a bayonet scabbard and they spelt my name, county and state, the Virginia Military Institute and what class I was going to enter. You know what they mean by spelling you is they tie your hands together, put them over your legs or knees and then run a stick in between your legs, turn you over and then whip you with a bayonet scabbard. They call it bucking you. They give you a lick for every letter in your name, county, state, Virginia Military Institute and what class you enter. I do tell it hurts awful bad. They twist your arms nearly off, and I don't know what they don't do.

We are all in camp now. It is a hard way of living. We go to bed every night at 10 o'clock and get up at 5. They don't allow you but three minutes to dress in the morning, and then the roll is called. I was awful homesick for two or three days. I believe if I had had my money back, I would have come home, but I begin to like it better now. We have pretty good fare. Tell Wm. B. Gatewood there are four little boys here not a bit larger than he is, and they get along first rate. Give my love to Bias; tell him to be a good boy and write to me. It will soon be time for us to go, and I will have to stop. I have been pretty homesick for three or four days but am getting over it. I would like mightily to see you all, but I can't, I reckon, for some time. Excuse all mistakes as I am in a powerful hurry. Goodbye; write soon.

Your son,

A.C.L. Gatewood

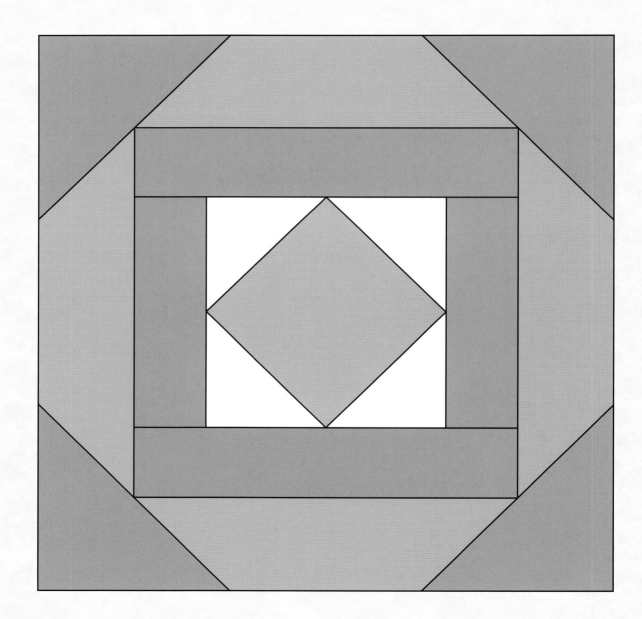

SQUAD DRILLS

Aug. 25, 1860

Dear Ma and Pa,

I received your letters yesterday by Cousin Warwick and was very glad to hear from you both and to hear that all were well. I have not got much news to write about but to let you know that I am well and hearty. I believe that I have fattened 5 or 6 pounds since I came over here. We have to take so much exercise; it agrees with me first rate.

We have to get up every morning at 5 o'clock, go to squad drill at 5½, drill an hour, come back, go to breakfast at 7, and then we go to squad drill again at 9, drill until 10, come back and study until 12, and then go to recitation, go to dinner at 1 o'clock, study until 4, go to recitation, and then go to squad drill again at 5, drill until 6, come back and go to dress parade half-past 6, go to supper at 7 o'clock and then we go to bed at 10. You can see we have not got much time to spare. I tell you it keeps me busy as a bee.

I have my pants and fatigue jackets, and I believe my coat is done, but I don't want it until I go in barracks. I am going to buy a secondhand coat. It will save my new one very much indeed. I can get one for $4 or $5, not worn much. We will all move in barracks on Friday next. I have gotten used to living in camp and like it very well now. Six of us sleep on a tent floor 7 feet square and keep two trunks in besides. Each one takes a plank. You said something about one of my roommates in your letter being so bad. James Warwick behaves himself very well here, and we get along very well. George Cameron, Marshall Francisco, Warwick and a young man from Augusta by the name of Gibbons and myself are going to room together. He is a very nice young man and very studious. I would like very well to stay here if I can, but the course of studies are a great deal harder than they used to be; they are nearly as hard again as they were last year. They are very strict here in everything. I have been on guard twice since I've been here and will be on tomorrow again. Tomorrow we have to walk eight-and-a-half hours, four in day and four at night. There are about 120 new cadets here now and about 30 or 40 to come yet, which will make in all nearly 300.

From your son,

A.C.L. Gatewood

GREATEST JOLLIFICATION

Sept. 1, 1860

My Dear Pa and Ma,

Of writing to you all, I take the opportunity tonight. We all moved into barracks this evening. We had the greatest jollification this evening you ever saw. In the first place this morning at 9 o'clock, we all marched into the arsenal and old Col. Smith gave each one a bed. Then we moved into our rooms, and at 2 o'clock this evening, all had to turn out and police camp. The greatest fun was to see all the tents fall at once, so many tents. At the first tap of the drum we loosed the tent cords. At the second tap we raised the tent poles, at the third tap all the tents fell together. It looked so nice to see so many tents all fall at once, and then a great many of the new cadets commenced dancing on the tent floors, they were all glad to get out of camp. But I got to like camping out very well. All that I disliked camp was that you could not keep anything clean and had no room for anything except for what you were compelled to have. But I like barracks first rate. We have a very good room, and more over, I have very good study roommates, none any ways wild, except Warwick, and he studies very well indeed. We all start into studying hard on Monday, and I am going to study hard as I can and try and stand well in my class. If I don't get over 10 demerits for this year, I can get a furlough for 15 days next summer. I will not get any if I can, but I tell you it is very hard to keep from getting them; they are so very strict here, but I have been getting along very well so far. We are not allowed but one trunk in each room. We have a wardrobe with four shelves on it; the other boys took the shelves and I took my trunk. We have little iron bedsteads in our room. There are 250 cadets here now. I must bring my letter to a close. Write soon. I have never received but two letters from you all since I came here and I have never received any letters from sisters since I came here. I wish some of you would write to me sometimes. I wish you would tell me where Will is and what he is doing. Tell him to write to me and give me the news. I will write soon again.

Your affectionate son,

A.C.L. Gatewood

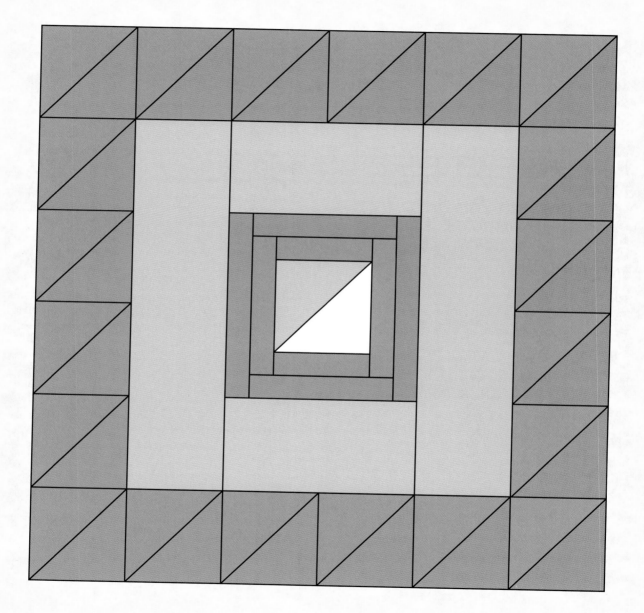

EXAMINATIONS

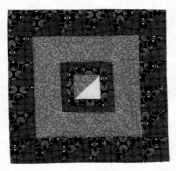

Dec. 22, 1860

My Dear Ma and Pa,

I have been looking for a letter from you all for some time but have never received a line from any of you but once since I was at home, and that was about three or four weeks ago. I am glad to tell you that I am getting along very well now and have been making a first-rate mark since I last wrote to you.

I think I can stand a very good examination. Our examination commences on the second day of January and will continue a week or two. I don't know exactly how long it will take, but it will not take less than two weeks, as there are about 250 cadets to examine in mathematics, French, Latin, geography and many other studies too numerous to mention. It will take some time to examine all the cadets in all their studies. We only get two days' holiday: one Christmas and one New Year's. The balance of the time we will have to study hard to prepare for the examination. The maximum on all the studies are 15 for the week; if you make 13.5, 13 whole ones and five-tenths for the week, you do very well, but I made 15.5 on Mathematics, which is five-tenths over the maximum. This is a first-rate mark, the best in my section. My name is up over at Col. Smith's as best in my section for last week and will be again this week.

South Carolina has seceded, and I suppose some of the other Southern States will in a few days. I have nothing new to tell you all. I wish to goodness you write to me some times to let me know if you are all dead or alive. I want Pa to write to me and let me know all about Elk and his stock. I must write to sister Susan and Mary today. I have not heard from either of them for some time. Give my love to Mr. Coffee, Bias Stofer, all the neighbors. I have not got but seven demerits and will not try to get any more. You must both write to me soon. I don't suppose I will write anymore before the examinations. I think I can stand an examination very well. South Carolina has seceded and all the others will soon. I'll end, then we will have to fight. Give my respects to all the neighbors. Write soon. I sent sister Mary my likeness; you can see by asking her for it. I suppose she has received it some time ago. Goodbye.

From your son,

A. C. L. Gatewood

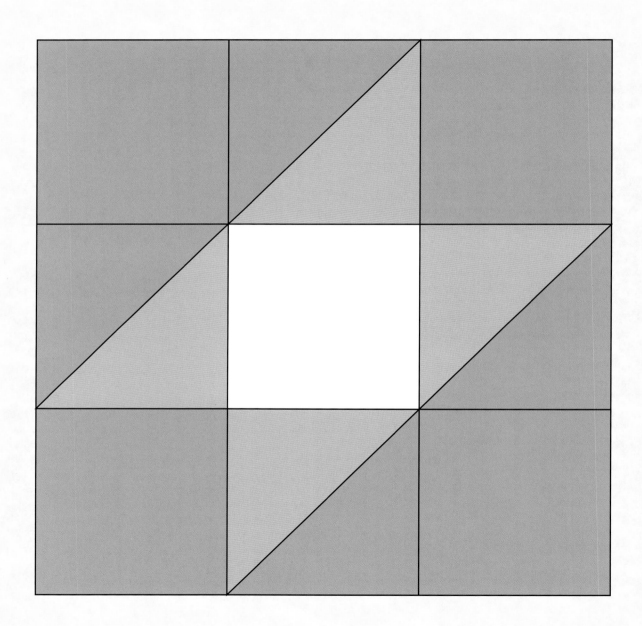

FLORIDA HAS SECEDED

Jan. 9, 1861

My Dear Ma and Pa,

I concluded I would write to you and let you know that I am through with my examination and I am glad to say that I got through very well indeed, a great deal better than I expected. I did not make as good a stand as I expected, but a very good one indeed. I expect to make a raise before July, if I don't, it will be because I can't study, which I know I do very well.

I will give you below how I stand in my class. There are 110 members in my class and I stood as follows: Mathematics 43; French 50; Geography 30; Declamation 40; Composition 24th. This considered a very good stand in such a large class, but you will see a difference at July if nothing happens and if the Union is not dissolved between now and then. I will have rather easier studies after January than before for a while. Pa just left yesterday for home. I was very glad indeed to see Pa; I wish you had come over with him to see me. I would like very much to see you and Bias. I hope I will see you all the 4th of July if nothing happens. I don't know what is the reason, but I can't get either of my sisters to write to me. I have written to both of them several times and have never received a word from either of them. I have written to both of them, and they won't write to me. I wish you would tell them when you write to them please to write to me once in a while to let me know if they are all well or how they are doing.

I suppose you all have heard that Florida has seceded. Alabama, Louisiana and Mississippi will secede tomorrow, or at least that is the opinion of the people. I am afraid we will have civil war in our midst before very long. Give my love to Wm. B. Gatewood, Mr. Coffee, Stofer and all the neighbors and darkies. Where is Aunt Sarah? Is she gone to Charlottesville, or where is she? You also must write to me often, both of you. Tell Bias to write to me. Tell Mr. Coffee to write to me. Give my love to all.

From you devoted son,

A.C.L. Gatewood

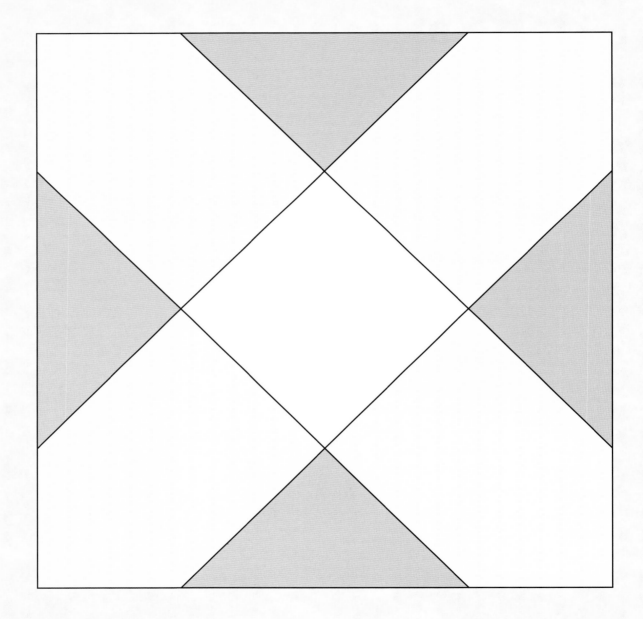

RUNAWAY SLAVE

Feb. 1, 1861

My Dear Ma and Pa,

I received your letter a few days ago and was very glad to hear from you all and to hear that you were all well and getting along very well.

I was glad to learn that you had gotten Jesse again. What in the world are you going to do with him? Will you sell him or will you keep him? I think if you keep him, he will run off from you again, and probably, if he runs off again you won't have the pleasure of getting him again. If he goes again, it is my opinion that he won't stop this side of Ohio or Pennsylvania, and so you had better make sure of him while you have got him. I think I would sell him to some Negro trader and let him try picking cotton in the South and see if he likes that better than lounging around at Mountain Grove and doing nothing. He will find out that he will soon wish he was back with Master Sammy, as he calls you. I wish you would write to me and let me know what you have done with him or what you intend to do with him.

Well, I cannot tell you anything, as I have nothing new to tell you, only I am getting along first rate since January examination. If I continue to do so from now 'til July, I will make a very good stand at July Examination, if nothing happens. I wish Virginia would come to some definite conclusion what she is going to do. I wish she would secede if she intends to do so. We are all right-side up, ready to fight or do anything else to save Virginia. If we don't leave or nothing happens, I think I stand a very good chance for a corporality next year. You need not say anything about it to anybody. But I have the recommendation of one of the best soldiers in my company. We have a splendid captain in our company, his name is Morrison. He is very popular in the corps as a cadet and as an officer. As soon as the weather breaks, we will have squad, company and battalion drill every day.

Write to me soon, both of you. My deposit has not been made yet. I don't know how soon cousin Warwick will make it. I need a little pocket money very bad now at this time. Write soon. I must write to sister Mary tonight. I wrote sister Sue the other day. Give my respects to Mr. Coffee, Stofer and the neighbors. Goodbye.

From your beloved son,

A.C.L. Gatewood

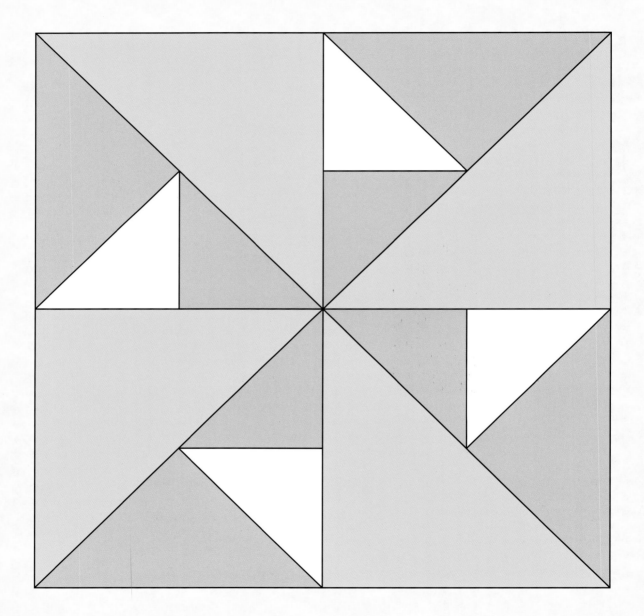

MRS. MASSIE'S PARTY

Feb. 8, 1861

My Dear Ma and Pa,

I received your letter a few days ago and was very glad to hear from you indeed. I will endeavor to answer your letter, but I have no news to tell you, not a particle. I have been away from the Institute for two weeks or more. But about two weeks ago, I was very much surprised one evening whilst I was out at drill, and when I came back, I looked on my table and found a note directed to Cadet Gatewood, and when I opened it, I found it was an invitation from Mrs. Massie inviting me to come to a party she intended giving in a few days afterward. Well, there were several other cadets invited, and we all went and had a very nice time. They seemed to be very glad indeed to see us. They treated me very kindly and asked me back to see them again. You said in your letter that Pa had gotten Jesse again, but you never said what he intended to do with him. I wish you would write to me and tell all the news and who were candidates for the convention besides Terrill, and who was the secession candidate. Are the people in Bath for secession or for Union? Dorman and Moore were elected in this county for the Convention, both Union men.

I have not got anything new to tell you this time. My deposit has not been made yet. I wish cousin Warwick would make haste and deposit it. I can't get any pocket money until my deposit is made or get it from home. I need a little money now very badly. I bought a new dress cap from a cadet the other day that was shipped for $2.50 which would have cost me in the store $4.50 and some other little necessary things, and I would like to have some money to pay for them. I was obliged to have them anyhow, and they cost a great deal less than I could get them in the store. I bought them to save money.

I want to write to sister Susan yet tonight, if I can spare the time. Give all the news when you write. Give my love to sister, Wm., B.G. and Mr. Coffee, Stofer and all the neighbors. I must write to Michael tonight; if I don't, he never will forgive me for it. I suppose he thinks I am above writing to him. Goodbye to you both.

From your son,

A.C.L. Gatewood

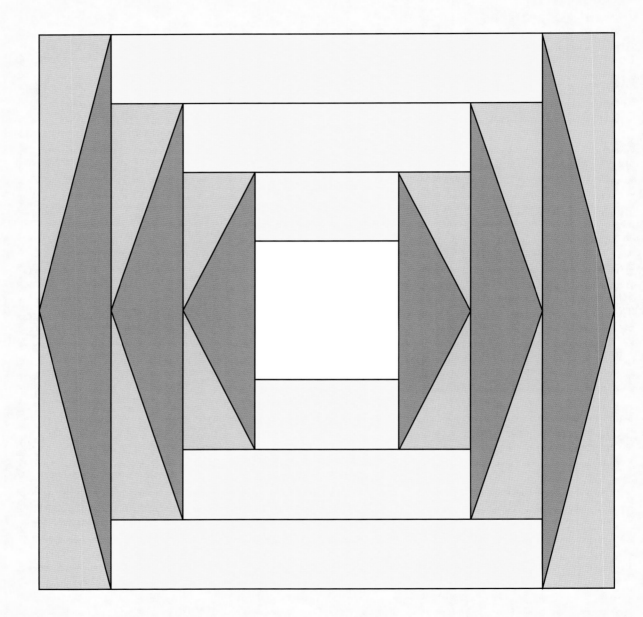

WILL VIRGINIA SECEDE?

March 10, 1861

My Dear Ma and Pa,

I received your letter a few days ago and was very glad indeed to hear from you and to hear that you were all well. I have no news to tell you, only that I am well and hearty and am getting along very well in my studies.

Lexington is very dull, indeed, at present. Well, old Abe has taken his seat. I wonder what will be done now? I suppose Virginia will either have to go North or South now; there is no choice to save the Union, so she might as well secede now as any other time. The convention in Richmond is not doing anything at all now, but they will have to do something now, and that pretty soon. I hope Virginia will secede. Well, we will all go to squad drill tomorrow. There are over 200 cadets here now. We have four companies, A, D, B, C. There are one orderly sergeant and three company sergeants in each company. They divide each company up in four squads; the orderly sergeant has first pick, and he always picks the best soldiers. My orderly sergeant picked in his squad. The orderly sergeant and captains always make the corporals out of this squad. I think I stand as good a chance for one as anybody else.

My respects to all the neighbors. If Virginia secedes, they will send us all over the state to drill recruits. I have got father's letter to write yet tonight and a long lesson for tomorrow, therefore, I have not got time to write any longer. I have written this letter very carelessly and fast. You will have to excuse me this time, and I will take more pains the next time. I am very much obliged to you both for the money you sent me. Cousin Ellen and family send their love to you all. Write to me something about your overseer; where he is from, and how he does, and where does he live, at home or up the Creek? Give me a general description of him. I must write to captain tonight. I cannot get either of my sisters to write to me. It makes me feel very badly; I suppose they have both forgotten me and forgotten that there is any such person living. I write to both of them, but they won't write me. I suppose I will have to stop writing. Give my love to both of them when you write to them. Write soon. Excuse all mistakes, as I have written this letter in 5 minutes.

Goodbye, from your son,

A.C.L. Gatewood

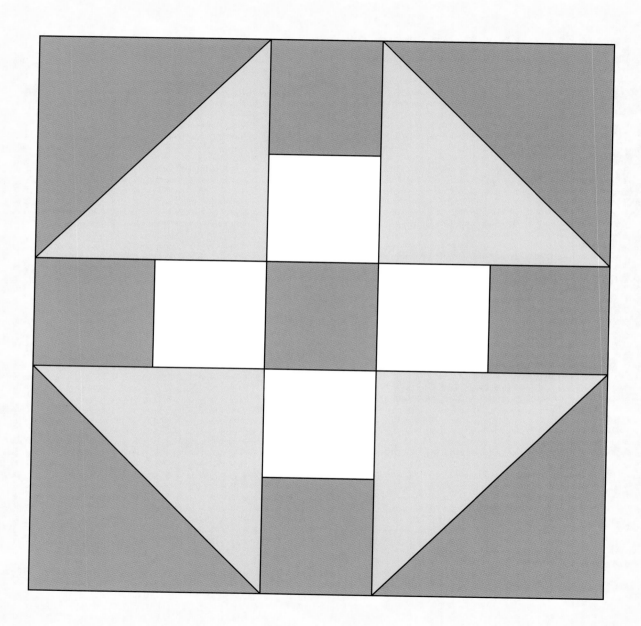

GOING TO RICHMOND

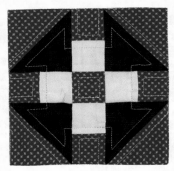

April 20, 1861

My Dear Pa and Ma,

I wrote to you not longer than last night, but I must write to you and let you know all the news. There is nothing new, I suppose, but what you have heard. But I am going to tell you both something confidential, which you must not tell anyone by any means whatever. It is something that Maj. Gilham told corps this morning. It is that we must keep ourselves in readiness. He expects a dispatch from Col. Smith tonight to bring us down to Richmond immediately. We will start to Richmond on Monday, pretty certain. But now, I don't want you all to be the least uneasy about me, because I will be in the least danger. I will write down here the words that Maj. Gilham spoke to us this morning. He says, "Young gentlemen you all are too high-bred to be food for powder. I don't intend that you shall go and fight against the Yankees at the North. I intend to take you to Richmond. You are a well-drilled corps. I want you to go and let the governor, the officers of the army, see how well you can drill, and then every one of you shall have an office. I don't know whether you will be kept in Richmond to drill recruits or sent throughout the state." He says, "I'll see that you are not brought in the battlefield as privates, if at all."

You all need not be in the least uneasy about me. I will promise you that I will behave myself like a gentleman and will try and distinguish myself. I would not have you the least uneasy for the world. I will tell you none of the cadets will be in any danger at all. For God's sake, don't be uneasy. No doubt I will be sent to Bath to drill recruits for the army. We will leave for certain before Wednesday. Maj. G. and Col. S. want to show off the battalion in Richmond. There has been from 500 to 600 men left this county for Harpers Ferry this week. I have nearly packed my knapsack ready to go. Give my love to sister Mary and brother William. Tell them not be uneasy about me. The drum is beating for tattoo. I must stop. Write soon. I will write to you when we get to Richmond. Give my love to Mr. Coffee and all. Goodbye. God be with you.

From your devoted son,

A.C.L. Gatewood

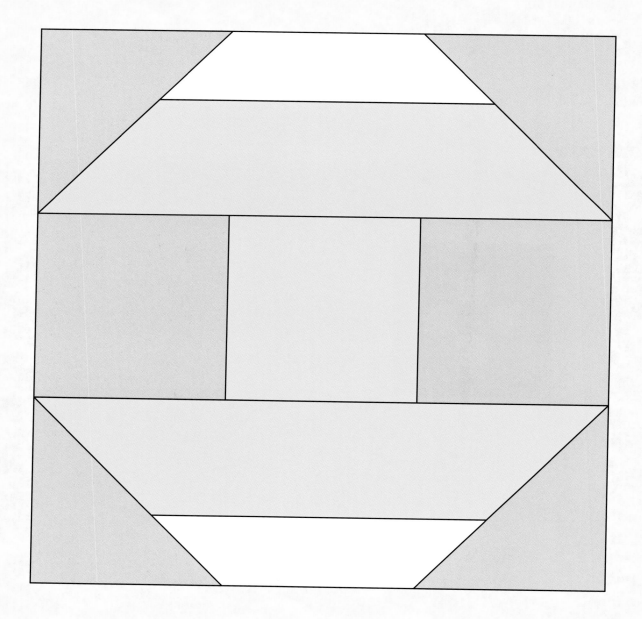

FIGHT LIKE A MAN

April 18, 1862

My Dear Parents,

I have written to you two or three times lately, on account of the great excitement now prevailing. We received a dispatch from Gov. Letcher last night at 2 o'clock, wanting Col. Smith to come to Richmond immediately. In the same dispatch we received orders to hold ourselves in readiness and to drill three times a day. We have drilled three times today. We have suspended all academics, light morning at times, except tactics, all of us are studying tactics. We don't do anything at all but study tactics and drill.

We received a dispatch this evening at 3 o'clock saying Harpers Ferry has been taken from the federal troops, Gasport Navy Yard has been taken, two million have been taken from a wrecked vessel. Virginia has seceded by a unanimous vote. Three Cheers for Virginia. We fired a salute of 15 guns cannon this evening in honor of the glorious Old Dominion. We will be sent all over the state in a few days to drill recruits for the Southern Army. I want them to send me to Bath or Pocahontas, if I can get there. I will be satisfied anywhere. You all must not be uneasy about it. I don't think I will be in any danger; if I am, I have 10 chances to one of getting back safe. I would rather die in defense of my country than any other way. I will stand up and fight like a man for our rights with as light a heart as anybody else. If we are ordered off to any point, it will be to Washington. But I think we will be distributed over the state in a few days to drill recruits for the Army. If I am ordered off anywhere to drill recruits, I will write to you and let you know where I am going. That will be fine fun for us, but if I do have drill, I am going to be very strict.

Write soon. Don't be uneasy. Give my love to Will and Mary, my respects to Mr. Coffee, Bonner and all. Excuse bad writing and also mistakes. I am in a powerful hurry. There were two cadets sent to Staunton today to drill recruits. Give my love to all. Tell Mr. Coffee to talk to that company and don't let them back out. I got a letter from Wm. Taliaferro today; all well. Write soon. I did not take any pains as I am in such a hurry. Goodbye, God be with you.

Your son,

A.C.L. Gatewood

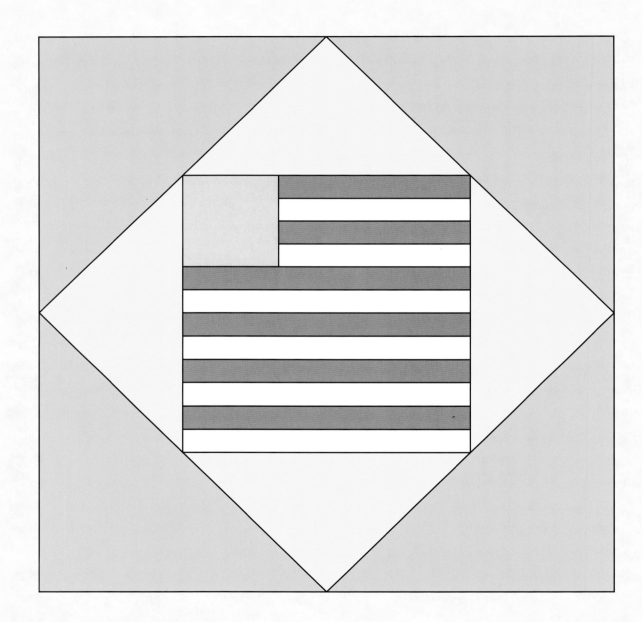

ACCEPTING THE FLAG

April 16, 1864

My Dear Ma,

I wrote to you a few days after we came over here but have not heard a word from you since. I have been looking for a letter from you every day. I have not heard a word from sister since I came over here. We have had quite a nice time since we came over here. Our regiment presented the Corps of Cadets with a very fine flag captured at Langston's Station. Col. Ball presented the flag in a very beautiful speech, and Col. Ship commandant of cadets, accepted the flag in a very appropriate speech. The Regiment then made two very good charges in front of the Institute, and then the Regiment was invited by the cadets to the Mess Hall, where there was a very nice dinner prepared for us. After dinner was over, we mounted our horse, and the cadets gave three cheers for the 11th Virginia Cavalry, and of course we returned the salutation. They then gave three cheers for the Bath Squadron.

We had a Grand Review of our brigade here yesterday by Gen. Smith. There were a great many persons present, nearly all of Rockbridge County. We also had several speeches by Judge Brockenbrough, Gen. Smith and Gen. Rosser. The latter made one of the best I ever heard. It was one of the most feeling speeches I ever heard. He was alluding to his brigade and its former commander, Gen. Ashby. He said he was proud to command such a brigade, and he hoped as long as he lived that the reputation won by its former commander would never go down. I expect you will see an account of it all in the papers before long.

I started Jesse down to Charlottesville day before yesterday with my young horse and told him to stay there and help work for sister. I have no news at all to tell you. Hope you'll write as soon as you get this and direct to Lexington, Va. I will send this letter by hand to Millboro and have it mailed there, and you'll get it sooner. Write to me soon and give me all the news. Mr. Coffee took your cloth to the factory, and Mr. Mohler says he will take it out to Bath for you as soon as it is done. Tell Grandma and Uncle Hez my love to all. All the boys are well. Write and tell me what Br. is going to do. Goodbye.

Your affectionate son,

A.C.L. Gatewood

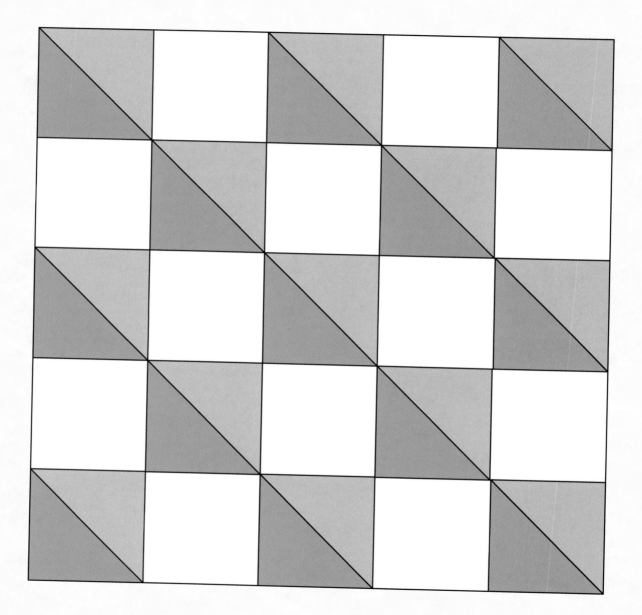

No Letters

April 27, 1864

My Dear Ma,

We arrived here yesterday evening from Lexington and are encamped at this place. I have just come from Gen. Rosser's headquarters, and he told me that he had just received a dispatch from Gen. Imboden saying that the enemy was advancing up the valley, Infantry Cavalry and Artillery, also a good many Negro troops. We are now under marching orders and may move at any time.

I have no news at all to tell you. I wrote you a letter the day before we left Lexington giving you all the news. The people in Rockbridge were sorry to see us leave; they think a great deal of Rosser's Brigade. I stopped at Cousin Ellen's and ate dinner as we came along. They were all very kind to me while I was up there. I never saw anyone improve in my life like Rose Cameron has. She looks better than I ever saw her in my life. I did not get a letter from you the whole time I was in Rockbridge. I got one this morning that has been written for a coon's age. I have not heard from sister lately, don't know how Mr. Goode is; hope he is better.

The men of this Brigade are in fine spirits and are spoiling for a fight. I don't think it will be long before you will hear from Rosser. I have no news at all. When you write, direct your letters to Waynesboro, Co. F, 11th Va .Cavalry, "Rosser's Brigade." Give my love to Grandma, Hez and Mr. D, and keep a sharp lookout for Averill's forces. We have been whipping the Yankees on all occasions of late, if we will just keep it up. When you write, give all the news and write soon. Goodbye.

From your affectionate son,

A.C.L. Gatewood

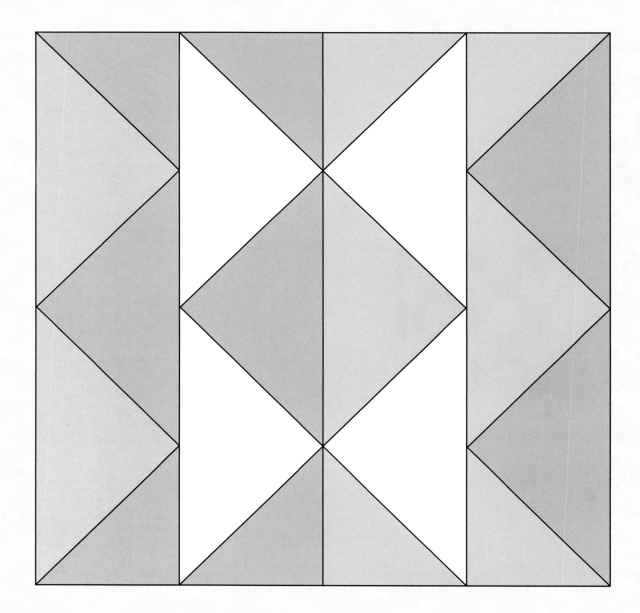

Selling The Horse

April 29, 1864

My Dear Ma,

I thought as we are going to leave here tomorrow for East Virginia, I would write you a note and let you know where we are going. Gen. Rosser received a dispatch this evening from Gen. Lee ordering him on to East Virginia. They are expecting a big battle to come off pretty soon, as they have been skirmishing down there for several days along the line.

I have sold that young bay colt, the wild one, the one that threw Anderson, to David Thomas, a member of my company, for $800. It is not a big price for him, but he is a poor man and has had such bad luck with horses that I would not ask him as much as I would anyone else. If he comes after him, you can let him have him, and if he pays you any of the money, you can just keep it for me, because I will have to pay it to Andrew Cameron. You asked me in your last letter how much I paid Andrew for the horse I bought of him. I expect it will scare you when I tell you. I gave $2,500 for him, but he offered me $3,000 for him since. But I don't intend to ride him very long and will get him fat and will get $4,000 for him. I want Dick well taken care of, and I want him to bring me $2,000 as soon as he gets fat. I wish you would tell Uncle Jimmy to salt him regularly for me and to keep him on good grass so he may improve and fatten fast.

I will stop to see sister as we go through Charlottesville. I have no news at all to tell you. I will write to you again as soon as I get to our destination. All the news. Rose Cameron and Lilla Warwick each made me a beautiful "laurel badge," which looks very pretty indeed; nearly all of the men wear the Brigade badge of three laurel leaves, a very good and appropriate badge for the Brigade that wears it, I think, because they have won their laurels, and they ought to wear them.

Give my love to Grandma, Hez, Mr. D. and the family. Tell them Henry, Archy and George are all well. Write soon. I have not gotten but one letter from you since I left home. Write often. Goodbye.

Your affectionate son,

A.C.L. Gatewood

David Coon. Photograph
courtesy of David Coon,
great- great-great-grandson
of David Coon.

Isabel A. Coon, David's second wife.
Photograph courtesy of David Coon,
great-great-great-grandson of David Coon.

David & Mary Coon — 1843

David and Mary Coon, David's first wife. Photograph courtesy of David
Coon, great-great-great-grandson of David Coon.

David Coon

Feb. 10, 1822 - Nov. 2, 1864

David Coon was born on Feb. 10, 1822, in Beekmantown, Clinton County, N.Y. On June 15, 1843, he was married to Mary A. Adams. They had five children: Alonzo, Dennis, Herbert, Emma and Hiram. In 1859, David's first wife died, and he married Isabel A. Hall. They had three children: John, Jedediah and Matthew.

It was on March 1, 1864, at the age of 42, that David left his job at the lumber mill to enlist for the war. He joined the 36th Regiment of Wisconsin Volunteers and signed up to serve 3 years. This was an immediate decision; David did not even have time to go back and say goodbye to his family. He expected to receive $165 bounty from the government, and he thought he also would be able to send his wife home more money.

He started out serving at Camp Randall helping the sick in the hospital. While he was unsure why he was sent to serve there, he felt that he could do more good there than any other place in camp. David was soon ordered to fight on the battlefields. While he served in the Army, he would write his family home at least one letter a week. He wrote a letter to his wife and also separate letters to his children. He missed his family dearly, signing his letters, "From your affectionate husband and father."

In one of his letters, he included the following poem.

Though I sit not by thy side, Still I fancy thou art nigh,

As I peruse they letter, And hasten to reply.

Me thinks that the tears, Oft to thine eyes will come,

As our little prattlers ask, "Ma, why don't pa come home?"

On Aug. 25, 1864, the 36th Regiment fought at the Battle of Reams Station in Virginia. David was taken prisoner along with most of his regiment. He was taken to the Andersonville Confederate prison at Ft. Sumter, Ga., where he later died of pneumonia on Nov. 2, 1864, at the age of 42.

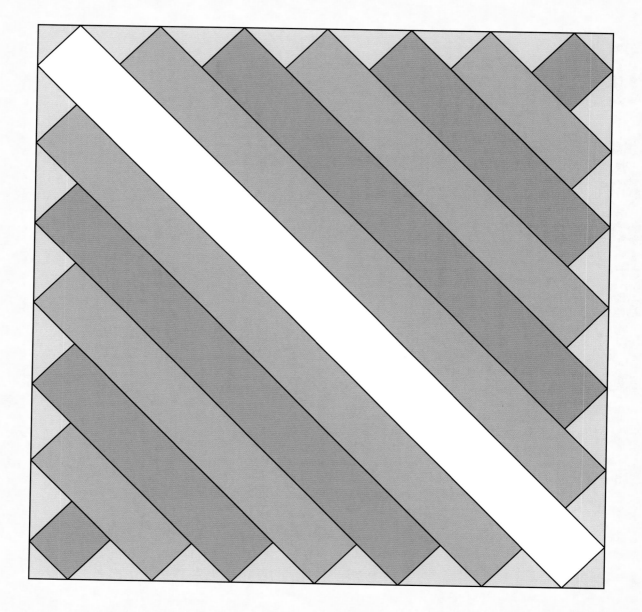

PAY AND BOUNTY

Feb. 28, 1864

Dear Wife and Children,

Well, I didn't go back to bid you goodbye. I found it necessary when I got to Berlin to come right on to this place in order to get in time to make arrangements to secure my bounty, etc. I have enlisted in the 36th Regiment, and yesterday was taken into a room with nine others and stripped naked, and passed examination so slick that there wouldn't have been any chance at all of getting clear if I had been drafted, but Orange Snell was thrown out, the last man I should have thought of.

Now about the pay and bounty. I expect $165 local bounty, which I think we had better pay for the sugar bush, 40 and all of our other debts, and you will get $5 a month from the state, and I think I can send home $5 a month more; and I hope Herbert will be able to raise your provisions and some to spare. Plant an acre of beans, and Emma must help hoe them and work in garden, etc., and do the best you can, all of you. The Government bounty I want to have salted down, so that it will keep. I got 44 brooms and sold at $2 per dozen. Poor little things.

Got the things you sent for and left them at L.A.'s. I wish you had them. I had a chance to get the brooms and myself brought down to Berlin, and did not get a chance to go to see Hiram and Dennis, and I have thought that it was best, perhaps, that I should have left the way I did, as it spared us all the pain of parting that we should have experienced had I not expected to return before my final departure. Herbert, I expect Mr. Dunlap will send for 100 buckets, and I want you to tighten the hoops and let him have as good as there is. I have been thinking that we are a good deal better off than the rest in the neighborhood that have left, in having a team and a boy old enough to use it and take care of things, and I hope you will succeed and take good care of things. I must close for this time, hoping to write again in a few days when we get a little settled. You needn't write until I write again.

Your affectionate husband and father,

D. Coon

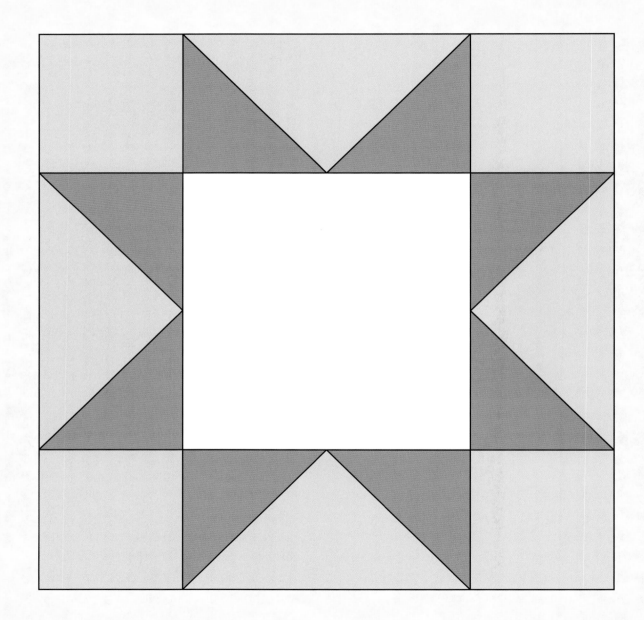

CAMP CONDITIONS

Dear Wife and Children,

I received your very welcome letter last night, and was very glad to hear from home. I am not very well, have had a very severe cold for a week or more and have had to get some medicine at the hospital. I am getting better, but my cough is very bad in the night. There has been three taken out of our company to the hospital, and another had the measles that didn't go. Our captain has the mumps. We have not yet got our clothes and are beginning to need them pretty bad, especially shirts. The campground is very muddy. I suppose you must be having some snow about these days. We had a little here last night, which has nearly gone off today.

As to our fare, I have drawn a blanket, and if we had plenty of straw I might sleep quite comfortably, but as it is, it is not quite as comfortable as camping in the sugar bush. We have now plenty that I could eat if I was well and had a good appetite. It consists of bread, beef, pork, potatoes three or four times a week, rice once or twice, beans the same, coffee, sugar, tea once in a while, etc.

As for Luman, he is here, and as near as I can judge, is making money quite fast. He is cooking for the office boys, those who do the writing and business at headquarters. He draws the regular rations for all that eat there. No men are able to eat the amount of rations that they are entitled to, so they draw what they need and the balance they are entitled to in money, which he takes and buys butter, flour, dried apples, milk, and they have their regular pies, fried cakes, and baked puddings. The men are satisfied so long as they get good living to give him all he can make over. Another thing, he has to draw and distribute traveling rations to soldiers leaving camp for the South, which consists of crackers and cheese, 1-1/2 pounds cheese to each and as many crackers as they can take in their haversacks. So in sending off a few hundred men, he will perhaps have some barrels of crackers left. He keeps one or two men to help him, which he pays 50 cents a day extra. He sent home this week a barrel of lard, that is fried meat fat for shortening, that must have weighed 300 pounds.

Yours as ever,

David Coon

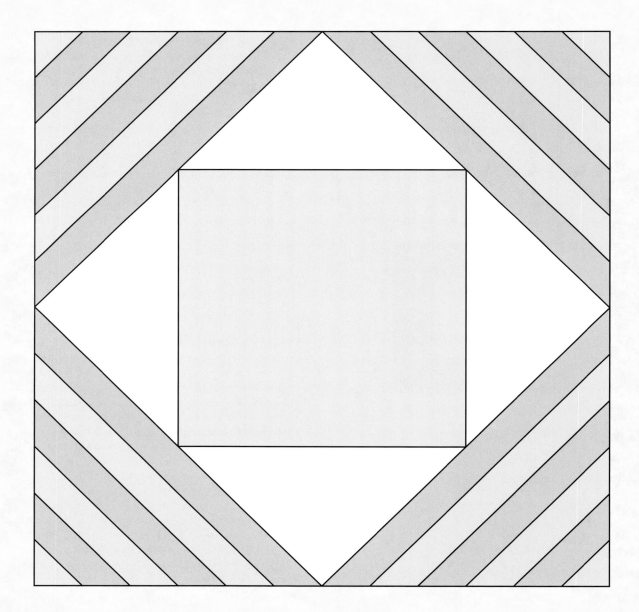

AULD LANG SYNE

Dear Wife,

Since writing, we have had a new accession to the beauties and pleasures of camp life. It is this: Some of the boys have been home on a French and came back bringing fiddles with them, and now it is fiddle-diddle continually, and now, while I am writing by candlelight, some are fiddling, some dancing, some are singing to the tune of Auld Lang Syne, and some are reading, and if I was to note down a few of the expressions that come to my ears, it would be more shocking than interesting to you, so I forbear.

Last Sunday, a couple of ladies came into our barrack with one of their husbands, a soldier. They had a baby with them. Should I be ashamed to say that it brought tears to me eyes to see it and think of the ones I left behind me? I am not. I had in my hands a little book, the temperance pledge, etc., with the names of the signers. The lady asked me if my name was in it, told her it was and showed it to her. She remarked that it was an awful comfort to the women to see their husbands' names there. I hope it will not be so to you, for it seems to me it must be dreadful to be so awful comfortable.

Mr. Palin has just come in and interrupted, bringing your letter and sugar, etc.

I am perplexed and know not what to say. I fear I could not get leave of absence on any pretext whatever, but will see tomorrow. I am sorry and much disappointed that Emma hasn't got her shoes. Mr. Palin also brought the most abusive letter from Mr. Hornick than I ever saw. Mr. Palin says he was to leave money with Lydia Arm for her to get a pair of shoes for Emma and send them to her, but she had moved and hadn't time to find her. My candle is down, and I must close.

From your affectionate husband,

David Coon

P.S. I have not received any pay or bounty yet. I will send a little money. Write often if it is but little, and let me know how you get along. I hope to hear that the children are better. I am much better than when I last wrote. I think if you could box up about 50 pounds or so of sugar, small cakes, and send here, I could sell it well and send back the money. If you should send any sugar, put on a card directed the same as you direct to me, and put in a bottle of molasses, well-corked.

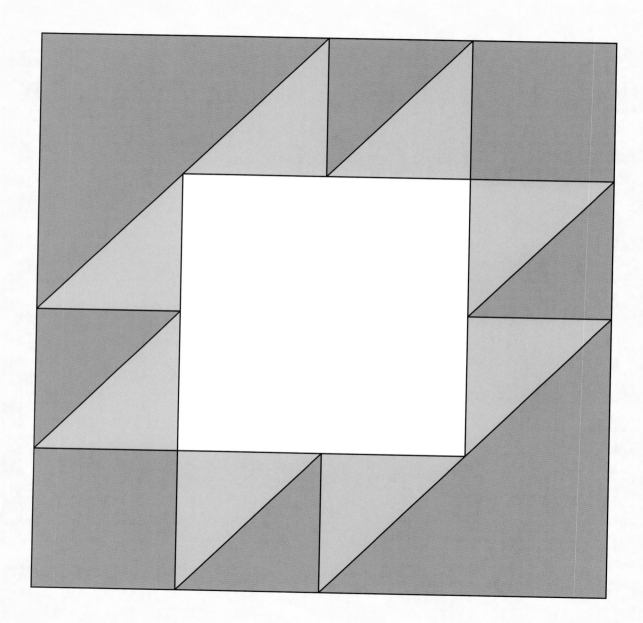

DRAWING FOR OUR CLOTHES

March 23, 1864

Dear Wife and Children,

Yours of the 21st has just come to hand, and I was very glad to hear from you again, as I had a good deal of anxiety on account of the children. I hope that Emma will soon be better. It will be quite a joke on Charley if that report is true. Mr. Dunlap did not know whether he would be able to pay any money down or not. I received a line from Mr. Clark and answered it, and also wrote Mr. Hornick and told him that when I got some money I would sent $15 to you for him to pay for the cow, or if he would pay you $5 for wintering, he could take the cow back. I don't expect he will do either nor don't care, but at any rate, don't let him have the cow until you have the greenback, or you may tell him it is your cow and he can't have her at all, but if he doesn't pay and take her right away, don't let him have her. I am glad Emma has got her shoes. They are French calf and cost $18.

We drew our clothes Saturday, and if you ever saw a little boy with his first pants with pockets in, you can guess how we felt and acted. I drew a woolen blanket and an India rubber one, a pair of pants, a dress coat, a blouse, two shirts, two pairs of drawers, one pair of shoes and one pair of socks. I drew a very nice coat, and it fits very nice. Our caps we have not got yet. I took a French Monday afternoon and went to Rutland. It is about 16 miles. Stayed overnight, came back early in morning, arrived about noon. Might just as well have stayed another day, but didn't like to run the risk. There have been three died out of our company, two in hospital and one home on a French, which makes it bad for his folks, as he is considered a deserter and forfeits his bounty and all.

I wrote you on Feb. 28, again March 2nd and 3rd, 11th and the 16th. The last one had a $2 bill in. I wish when you write you would acknowledge each one you get so that I shall know if you get them. I had to write this with a pencil for want of ink. I send a little present for Flora. This seems to be the fifth one that I have written you, but must stop.

Yours affectionately,

D. Coon

P. S. 24th. It must be about a month since I left home. We have to drill now every day. I am detailed to carry water again today. We have to carry it about 80 rods; four of us carry it 24 hours. I haven't had to stand guard yet. Herman went home yesterday. (If you should hear that I cried like a baby to go home, you needn't believe it.) Dwight Barnard, to pay Mr. Luckey and I for getting him out of his scrape, reported that we cried like babies because we couldn't go with him. Mr. Luckey did try to get a furlough at that time, but he says he didn't cry. I hadn't any thoughts of trying to go at that time, but I did think it was rather hard that I couldn't go when the children were sick. I can't make myself think yet that I shall have to leave the state without going home.

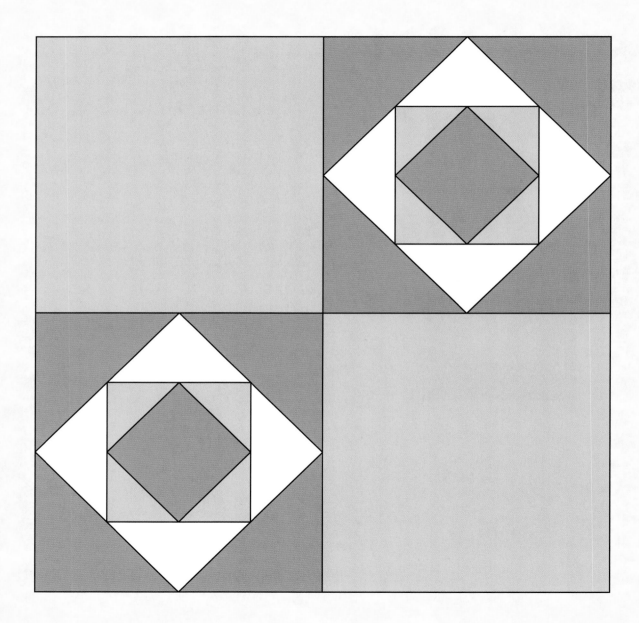

NOTHING LIKE AN AFFECTIONATE WIFE

Dear Wife and Children,

Mr. Vergin had letters from home today, by which I was very glad to learn that you were all getting better. I some expected to have got one from you, but did not. I have been very unwell since Sunday, and I'll tell you one thing, the camp is a miserable place to be sick. Boys that are sick here miss their mothers' care, and I learned long ago that there is nothing like an affectionate wife when I was sick, and can realize it now more than ever. There seems to be but little favor for the poor soldier, sick or well. I have concluded not to expect nor ask favors, and I have had occasion twice to stand for my rights since I have been here, once yesterday. If a person doesn't feel able to do duty, they must be examined by the surgeon in the morning and get excused by him, and unless he is excused by him, he must stand it, able or not, and it is sometimes represented by the petty officials that the person is shirking to get rid or work, etc., which perhaps is sometimes true, but my idea is that the doctor, if he knows anything, had ought to know the difference between a sick man and a well one. Well, Monday morning, I was excused by the assistant surgeon, and yesterday morning I was no better, and weaker, for I couldn't eat anything. I was examined and medicine prescribed, but not excused from drill. When the order was given to fall in for drill, I went to the orderly and told him that I wasn't able to drill. He couldn't help it; I had tried to get excused and couldn't, and his orders were strict. I then went to the captain. He couldn't excuse anyone and said that unless I could get excused in the morning, there was no help. I then turned and went right to the head surgeon, and in 5 minutes was back with a written order to have me excused. I had got the medicine prescribed and it lays on my shelf yet, for I thought if that was all the doctor knew, he might take his own medicine, and I borrowed some pills and took them. This morning he concluded to excuse me and prescribed some salts, a part of which I took, and I think tomorrow I shall not need to ask to be excused. Now I have no doubt but if I had drilled yesterday, it would have made me down sick. That little sugar you sent me has helped me a good deal, for when I felt as though I couldn't eat my rations, I have taken some of that and dissolved it and toasted a piece of bread and made out to eat some. Today I went up to Luman's and got some milk and made some porridge, and tonight I sat down to the table for the first time since Sunday morning.

From your affectionate husband and father,

David Coon

HOSPITAL ARRANGEMENTS

April 3, 1864

Dear Son,

Yours of the 27th I received on Friday the 1st. I have been quite unwell all of the week and am in rather different circumstances from what I was when I wrote last Thursday, which I suppose you have read. I was sent that afternoon here to help take care of the sick, and I scarcely feel able to take care of myself. You wrote that you were going to send some sugar. I went to the city yesterday but did not find it. I hope it was not sent, as I think I shall not now have time to attend to the selling of it. However, if it comes, I think I can sell it by the lot for 20 cents a pound, and I suppose it is worth more than that in Berlin.

Now, perhaps you would like to know something about hospital arrangements. This ward is a building about 100 feet long by 20 feet wide, with a row of bunks on each side, just near enough together for a person to go between them to attend to the sick, and then there is a few more down through the middle. I believe there are about 60 patients in this ward, and there are seven or eight wards in the whole hospital. They are not all as large as this.

There hasn't been a death in this ward for a week, but one morning there was one carried into the next ward from this ward, and died that day. There have been 56 deaths in the hospital within a month, and now, my boy, if you could just spend one day here, you could consider yourself a lucky boy to stay at home to take care of the place. There are some of the awful sights here that I ever saw. All of the measles and mumps cases are in this ward, besides some other cases, about 60 patients in all. Now wouldn't you think it a hard case to see a man sick and not able to sit up, and have a chain fast to his, foot attached to a ball of iron that would weigh 50 or 60 pounds. There are two such in this ward, and another one was sent back this morning to the bullpen.

Now I will tell you a circumstance that happened here about two weeks ago. One night, a man died and was laid out and carried to the dead house and put in a coffin. After a while the guard came running into the ward in a great fright, saying that that man was getting up and sure enough, so it was. They took him back, and he has since gone back to barracks. My boots are good. I will send them to you when I send my things home. I will write to Ma and Emma as soon as I get time.

Your affectionate father,

D. Coon

A Good Straw Bed

April 6, 1864

Dear Wife,

I started a letter directed to Herbert on Monday. I am getting better than I have been since I have been in here. I am kept pretty busy. I go to bed about 8 p.m. and sleep until 3 a.m., and then am pretty busy until about 2 p.m., and then have until about 5 to go out and look around or do what I please, so that three hours a day is about all the time I have.

A poor boy by the name of Alonzo Moore died here on Monday, a member of Company A. Two more died yesterday and two last night. There say there were 56 died in this hospital last month, and there have been over 20 since the first of the month. I don't know why they sent me here, but one thing I am satisfied of, and that is that I can do more good here than in any other place in camp; therefore, I am willing to be here. I have better fare than in the barrack. I have a good straw bed with a tick, a clean linen sheet, and we generally have first-rate bread with good butter and applesauce, but very poor tea and coffee and potatoes.

I look for a letter from you today. I suppose you had one from me about last Thursday. I wrote in that you had better not send any sugar for the reason I thought you had better not spare it, and I find it is cheaper here than in Berlin, and I feared I should not have time to peddle it out, etc. You wrote you expected to start it Wednesday, and I went over to the city Saturday but couldn't find it. If it should come, I will try peddling it out. If you haven't sent it, it will do just as well to sweeten custard with, and I am still in hopes to get a chance to come home and eat some yet before leaving the state. Our colonel has encouraged us to think all of the time that we should have furloughs, and he is going to do the best he can for us yet.

Another poor fellow died in here this afternoon. They are getting very strict about soldiers getting out without passes. I went out Saturday without one, but had one today. If I hadn't, I should have been brought in and put in the bullpen. Lots of them have been put in lately.

From your affectionate husband and father,

David Coon

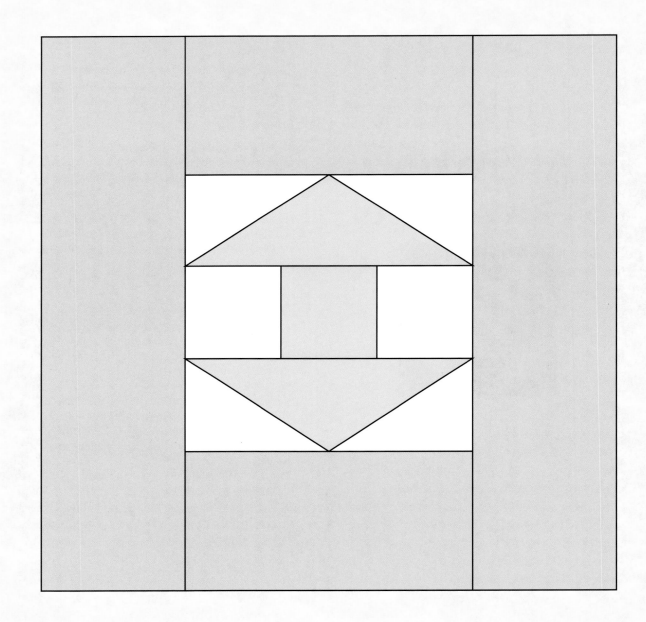

ANOTHER DEATH

April 16, 1864

Dear Wife,

I am still in the hospital, but the sick are getting thinned out, and there are but few dying to what there was. My own health is rather better. I suppose you would like to have sent the bottle of molasses if you had known of it. I suppose if I had stayed in the quarters, I should have had a chance to have you send something with the rest, but I guess I shall stand it.

I expected to have been paid off today but slipped up, but suppose it will come the first of the week to the tune of one month's pay and $60 on the bounty, $73 in all, and I wish you would send me the swampland certificate.

We have had all sorts of rumors about starting South, furloughs, but I believe that it is decided to let some of the sick go home, and furlough 15 out of each company next week for 12 days, but I don't see as it will help my case, for I am out of the control of the regiment while I am here, but I can't make it seem as if I should have to leave without going home. I have made another collar since I have been here, and there were about one-half dozen that I wanted to buy, and I finally concluded to take $2 for it, so you see, I make enough that way to pay for my apples.

It is shocking to see men lying at the point of death and hear them curse and blaspheme, and to hear nurses taking care of the sick curse and swear, but so it is, but I am thankful that it is not so with all. There was another one of Company A died this afternoon in another ward. I have been in the habit of going in to see him every day. I saw him this morning and thought he wouldn't live through the day. After I came back I called and found him dying. He had his senses perfectly and asked me if I didn't think he was most home. I told him I thought he was, and asked him how he felt about it. He said he felt all right, and was willing to die. I asked him if he had any fears. He said no, and I asked him why he was not afraid. He said because his trust was in God. I had to leave him and told him I would come in and see him again as soon as I could. He said perhaps he would be dead when I came back. It was an hour or so before I got a chance to go in, and they had just carried his corpse out.

Yours in haste,

David Coon

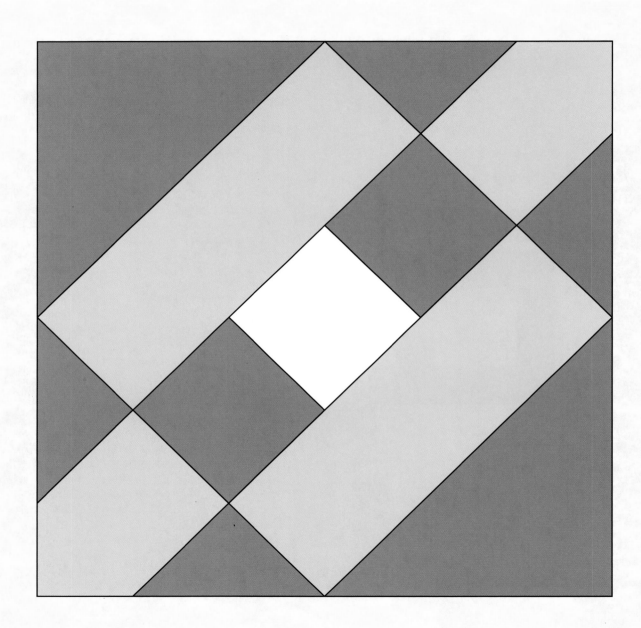

Writing Home on the Cars

May 13, 1864

Dear Wife and Children,

I shall try to pencil a few lines as the cars stop, as I have heard that we will not be allowed to write for a while after we get through. So if you do not get anything from me, you may know it is not my fault, and you will continue to write as often as you can, and direct to the Company and Regiment, Washington. I was quite disappointed in not getting a letter from you before I left camp, as I couldn't attend to that receipt. Now, if you did not send the receipt, I wish you would send it to the state treasurer. Simply write and say you were instructed by your husband to do so. If you wrote to Madison, Luman is to open the letter and take the paper and forward the letter to me.

We started Tuesday morning at 10 o'clock. I sent a letter to the office for you the same morning with a $10 greenback, which I hope you have received. We arrived in Chicago the same evening a little after dark, and after marching and countermarching around the streets for two or three hours, went to the Soldier's Home, and were treated to a first-rate supper, and started on after midnight. The next day about noon we passed through Fort Wayne, and about dark through Bucyrus.

Baltimore, May 14, 1864

We arrived here a little before daylight. We heard this morning that Gen. Lee is wounded. I have been quite unwell all of the way, besides troubled some with rheumatism, but I must stop and write particulars when I get through.

Yours affectionately,

David Coon

P.S. We expect to be in Washington before night.

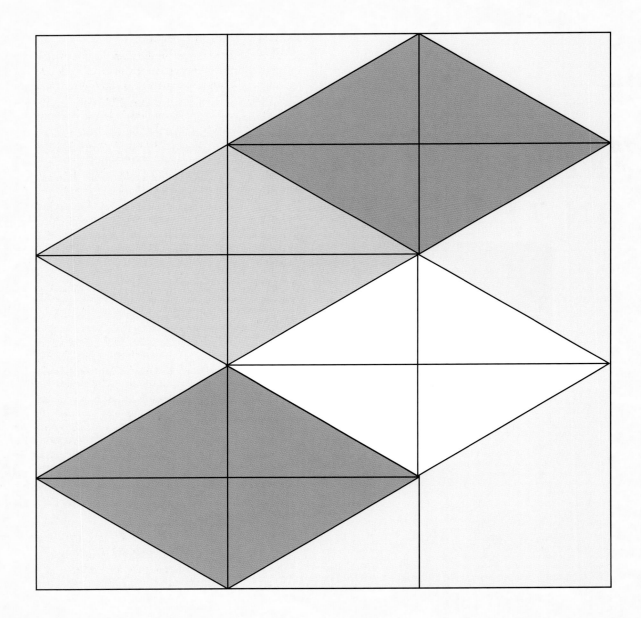

A LITTLE BROTH

May 26, 1864

My Dear Wife and Children,

I started a letter to you on the 24th. I sent it without finishing, and thinking that if you should get it before you get this you might be concerned about me, I therefore hasten to write again. I am now prepared to write more encouraging news, as I am now in better health than I have been for several weeks and have come to my appetite. About a week ago, I couldn't eat anything that I had or could get. I went out one evening to an encampment of artillery nearby, and picked up a fresh beef bone and scraped off a little meat and made a little broth, which tasted good, and did me a great deal of good. Oh, how much good it would have done me about those times if I could have been at home to have something that I could eat. Since then, we have drawn plenty of fresh beef, and all that I could eat was broth and coffee. I would have given anything for a cupful of Indian meal to make me a little gruel. I went to a house Sunday to try and get a little, which I might have done, but there were some officers there who drove me away without any.

The day before yesterday, as we lay behind some breastworks, I saw at a little distance some cavalry men with something in a bag that I thought might be meal that they had confiscated. I could not leave my place, so I sent a boy over to see if they would sell me some. They, like good fellows, sent word that it was flour, and they would not sell any, but if I was sick they would give me a cupful. I sent over my stew pan, and they sent it back full, about 2 pounds. I have made three meals out of it and have enough for about two more. I make it into minute pudding or pancake, and am getting stronger and can begin to relish my hardtack made into a stew with fresh beef, and my coffee goes pretty good.

We are having a pretty good time today lying in our tents. Some pickets skirmishing in hearing.

From your affectionate husband and father,

David Coon

FEMALE PRAYER MEETING

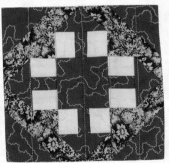

June 7, 1864

My Dearly Beloved Wife,

This morning I received two letters from home, May 18th and 26th. You write of troubles. I am truly sorry it is so, but you must keep up your spirits, and if you meet with troubles, just go and tell them to Jesus. Pray for yourselves and for me as I try to for you.

I am glad you have meetings and I wish you could have S.S. again. I wish when you go to the meeting you would take over those papers and books and give them to the children. Hadn't you better start a female prayer meeting, say once a week? It seems there is enough to pray for and need enough. What do you think of it?

Mother Clark I have written twice before since I left Washington. I shall expect a letter from home every week. This is the last writing materials I have. We have drawn pork rations once and fresh beef about every day, hardtack, coffee and sugar enough for three days at a time. We get along very well if we get a chance to cook meat and coffee, which we generally do. We are not having it very hard for a few days: picket duty and guarding our breastworks.

How are the grapevines and strawberries doing? Did any of the Tribune plants live? Well, Johnny, did you get the cup Pa sent you to drink your milk in? So, you would like to have Pa have some of your milk. Poor Pa doesn't see a bit of milk or butter or potatoes. So Mattie tried to write Pa a letter. Oh, how Pa would like to see and kiss you all.

Your affectionate husband and father,

D. Coon

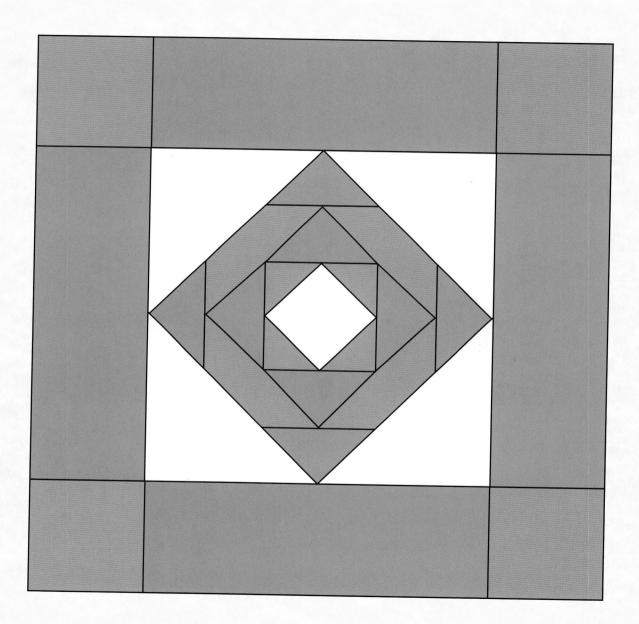

WHIZZING BULLETS

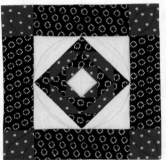

June 22, 1864

My Dear Wife and Children,

I started a letter to you the day before yesterday, 20th, and joined the regiment again yesterday morning. They had come to the conclusion that I had been taken prisoner by the Rebels. They said there had been a number of letters for me, which had been sent back to Washington; how many or what I could not find out.

I found the regiment had been in another fight and had lost, in killed and wounded, about 100, nine of Company A wounded and one killed. Dewey lost his left arm at the shoulder, and Upright was rather badly wounded in the last fight. Yesterday, soon after I came up, we started on a march of a few miles and are now entrenched again behind breastworks, only a few rods from the Rebel works, and as I write, the bullets are whizzing over my head, and I just heard a shell go over from our side to them. Yes, and there goes another. This morning, as I was digging on the breastwork, a bullet struck the bank close by the side of me (there goes another shell), and a few minutes after, a bullet passed me and struck a man of another regiment about a rod from me, mortally wounding him, I think. I have no doubt but it was aimed at me, as I was exposed at work. The Lord is able to preserve me, and in Him is my only trust for "Vain is the help of man."

Write again soon and often. You can't write too often. We are expecting another fight soon. The shells are flying over now pretty lively. Pray for me always. It is a comfort to get words of sympathy from family and friends in these trying times.

Ma, did you have any difficulty in drawing the money? I hope you got enough to make yourselves comfortable for a good while. If you have enough left, I wish you would pay Mr. Southwick, and I wish that cow was paid for. If Mr. Clark can't fix it so as to get his pay, I think it will be best to pay Hornick if he will take $20, and give a receipt in full, and if the lumber can be got down and the cash note for the fanning mill taken up, I should like it. Herbert, take good care of the fanning mill and all of the tools and utensils. Dig a well if you can, and get it curbed. Dig it in a dry time. I was glad to learn that you had some rain again. That sled timber you should have put in the corncrib or old stable. If you haven't done it, you had better soon.

Your affectionate husband and father,

D. Coon

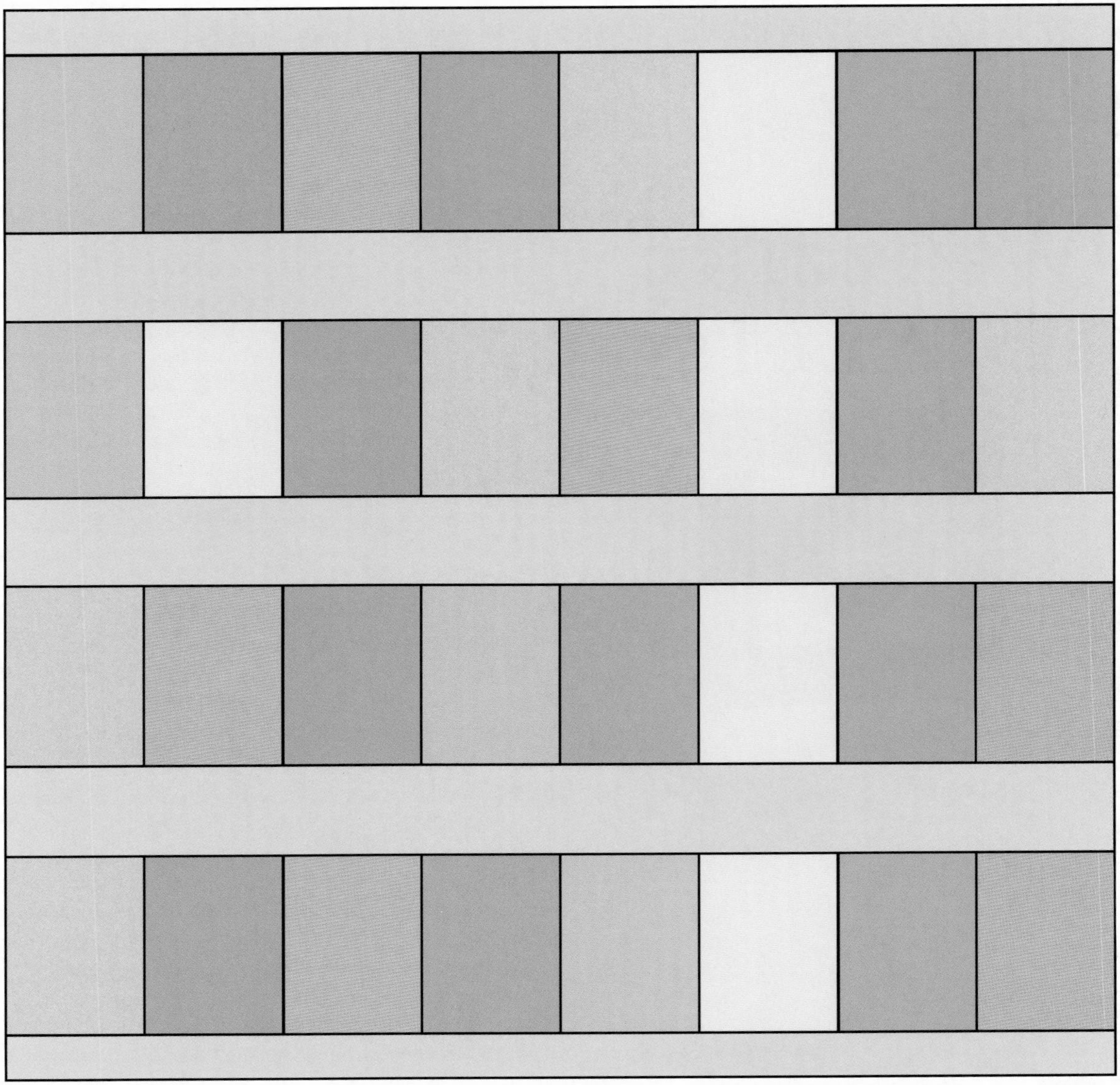

PROVISIONS

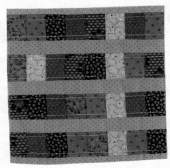

June 26, 1864

Dear Wife and Children,

I received a letter on the 21st, dated 9th, and one on the 25th dated 15th, and the one with Mary's is all from home, I think, since leaving Washington, though there were some that came when I was gone, as I wrote you, that were sent back to Washington, which I am afraid I shall never see. I started one to you on the 20th, and one on the 23rd. There seems to be quite a number that I have sent that you hadn't got at your last writing, but I think they will be around.

I am glad the heifers proved to be so good. What do you think I thought when you told about churning? Oh, that I had the buttermilk. We can get butter here for 75 cents a can of about a pound, cheese 50 or 60 cents a pound. So, Johnny would like to have Pa have some of the good things! My health is better and my appetite is very good, and I have plenty to eat, and all the coffee I want, which is a good deal this hot, dry weather. If I could exchange coffee and meat with you for a little butter, I would like it, for my rations are more than I can use. We draw potatoes and beans now pretty regularly, which I like pretty well with fresh beef and salt pork — more than I need — plenty of everything, only I could use more sugar just as well as not.

This last march I spoke of we only fell back from the front or fighting point about 2 miles, where we are resting. It is thought we are to go still further back for garrison duty, but we never know anything until after it happens. The 38th Regiment is not far from us, but I haven't seen them. I believe that and the 37th have fared about as we have.

Yesterday, slight near cakes, we moved back about 2 miles, and although the distance was so short, it was so hot that a good many were overcome with the heat. I would like if you would send me a Sentinel once in a while, and you could send me three or four Missionaries under a stamp.

Yours affectionately,

David Coon

P.S. You can send an envelope and a stamp. It may hasten answer.

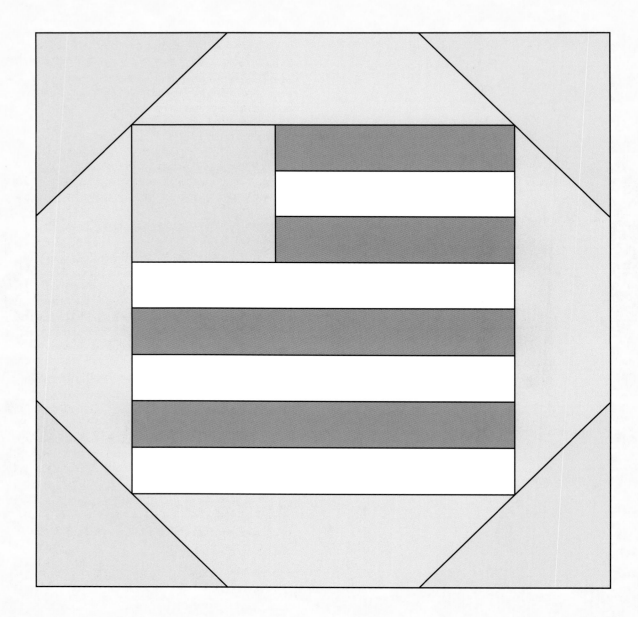

Changing Conditions

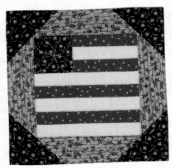

Aug. 22, 1864

My Dear Wife and Children,

I now seat myself on my knapsack to write on a drumhead with some ink that I made of pokeberries. As I suppose you will have received two pencil scribbles that I sent you last week before you get this, I will say that we stayed around near there where we had the fight on Sunday, the 14th, until Saturday, the 20th, and then started at dark on a march in the rain and had to go through the woods on the start, and oh, how dark, muddy and slippery it was.

We saw where a wagon and team had tipped over down a hill on going downhill to the river, and I don't know but more of them went over afterward, as it was a sideling place and very slippery. Well, we marched back on the same road that we marched when we were there a few weeks before. The night was cool, and the rain stopped soon after we started, and the moon came up so that it was not a bad night to travel, and we arrived back in our old camp yesterday morning at 9 o'clock, where we had spent so much time in cleaning it up and fixing shades, etc., that I couldn't get time to write to you, but oh, what a change! It had rained a good deal, and our sheds were all torn down, and the crotches and poles taken away, and also our bunks that we had fixed to sleep on, and the brush all scattered over the ground.

Well, we made a fire and got some breakfast. Fortunately, I had a little tea, which came in good after such a march. I had drawn three or four drawings from the Sanitary Commission, which was first-rate green tea.

We stayed there until 1 o'clock. I received your letter of the 10th inst. there, and was glad to hear from you again and that you were all getting better of your sickness, for it is hard to be sick, even at home. On looking at my memorandum, I see that yours was written the same day that I was cutting timber in the woods and dreaming about the pies and turnover, etc., that I wrote about. Well, I haven't tried my hand at making my turnover yet, as I haven't got any flour.

My health is not very good, but I don't feel quite so badly used up as when returning from the other raid. At 1 o'clock, we started on a march again and arrived here — 4 or 5 miles — a little before night. Got some supper and laid down in the pine woods and rested all night.

Your affectionate husband and father,

David Coon

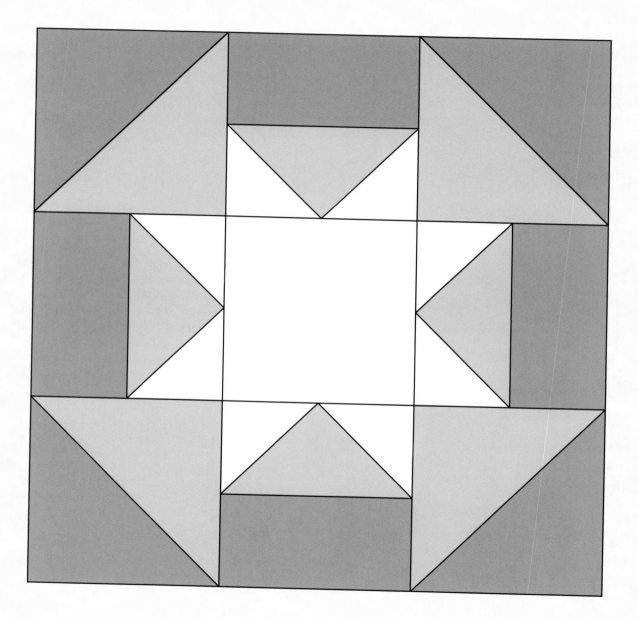

PRISONER OF WAR

Dear Wife and Children,

I write to inform you that, through the fortunes of war, I am a prisoner. In battle on the 25th inst., about our whole regiment was taken. I should think in order to get to this place from where we were taken we had to march 20 miles, and I can truly say that whatever treatment I may receive hereafter, I shall ever remember with gratitude the treatment received from the officers and guards who have had us in charge. Thus far I do not remember of hearing an order accompanied with a profane oath since I was taken, and in this respect, I think our men and officers would do well to take pattern. My health is very good. You will please write a few lines to let me know how you do. Your postmaster will inform you how to direct. We expect to go to Richmond tomorrow.

Your affectionate husband,

David Coon

P.S. W.W. Vergin is a prisoner, and Will Putnam is supposed to be safe by being in the rear sick. Keep up courage.

D.C.

David Read Evans Winn. David Read Evans Winn paper. Special Collections and Archives, Robert W. Woodruff Library, Emory University.

David Read Evans Winn

(July 5, 1831 - July 1, 1863)

David Read Evans Winn was born on July 5, 1831, in Camden, S.C. At the age of 4, he moved to Perry, Ga. He attended the Jefferson Medical College and started practice in Americus, Ga., at the age of 21. He was married to Frances Mary Dean in 1854, and they had two children, Cooper David and James Dean.

David mustered into service in Georgia on May 2, 1861, at the age of 29. He served with the 4th Georgia Regiment and soon moved up the ranks from lieutenant to captain to major to lieutenant colonel. He frequently wrote letters home to his wife, Frances, from battlefields in Georgia and Virginia. He often wrote about the separation from his family, and he was so eager to hear news from home about how his wife and children were doing.

He wrote most of his letters home from Camp Jackson, Va.; others were written from camps near Richmond, Va., and Fredericksburg, Va., as the troops advanced into battle. David fought in major battles in Virginia at Chancellorsville, Fredericksburg and Malvern Hill.

David's last letter home was written on June 9, 1863, while he was in Fredericksburg. All he knew was that he was going to go into battle. On July 1, 1863, David Read Evans Winn, 32, was killed in action in one of the first charges at the battle of Gettysburg.

A tribute offered for David Read Evans Winn and Col. Samuel P. Lumpkin, who was mortally wounded at the battle of Gettysburg, reads: "And though in a war of great magnitude in which many noble men have fallen, 'tis no disrespect to the dead, nor reproach to the living, to select from the former such men as Lumpkin and Winn, and make their memories be especial object of our care, affection and example. We sympathize deeply with the bereaved families of our lamented comrades in their great loss."

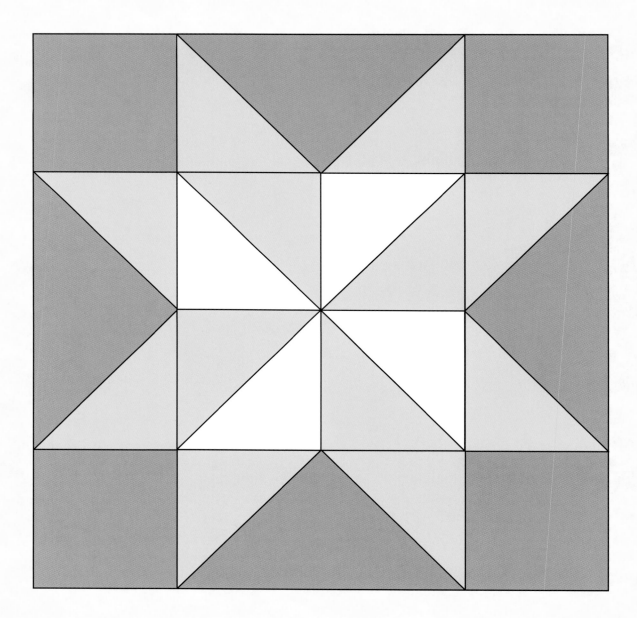

INCOMPETENT OFFICERS

April 30, 1861

My Dear Wife,

In the midst of the utmost confusion and bustle, beating of drums, bands of music and military parades, I take advantage of almost the first leisure moment of daylight that I have had since I have been in this place to write to you. But for the consideration that I have left home a devoted and much-neglected — still loving — wife and darling children, possibly forever, I would be comfortable. We are quartered in a good dwelling house, furnished by Col. Clanton (who, by the way, has just sent us in a box of cheese, a barrel of bread, 42 dozen nicely boiled hams, etc.)

Our company is very orderly and fast becoming disciplined — all cheerful and much-pleased with the other companies composing our regiment. We are not as well pleased, however, with the officers who received us here on behalf of the State. They seem to us either to be incompetent or to have sadly neglected their duty in preparing equipments. They are extremely anxious to get us off to Richmond half equipped, but we, with the officers of several other companies of our regiment, have resolved not to be mustered into service until we are equipped fully. The Sumter Light Guards have attracted universal attention and even admiration among 12 or 14 companies now rendezvoused here. Whenever we are on the streets, whether in company or scattered about singly, the ladies greet us with bouquets, etc. I enclose you a card which I received yesterday accompanying about one-half bushel of biscuits, corn bread, light bread, pickles, two big splendidly roasted chickens, with magnificent bowl of gravy, etc. What do you think of that?

We are constantly engaged, having no time even to read tactics. We are invited to parade with a volunteer regiment of Augusta today. We are obliged to decline, because we have not yet drawn our guns. Earnestly praying for your's and my boys' happiness and welfare, temporal and eternal, and with love to all.

I am your affectionate husband,

David

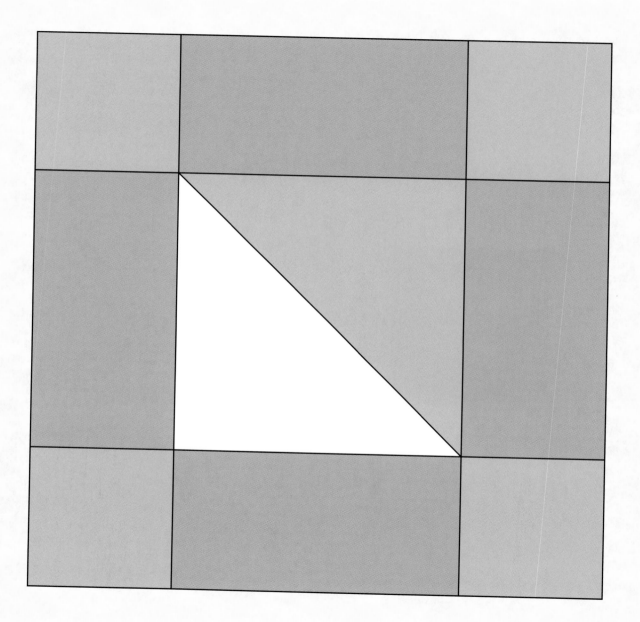

My Greatest Trial

May 16, 1861

My Dear Wife,

I received your very kind letter yesterday and was truly rejoiced to learn that you and our dear children were fortunate enough to escape being on the cars when the accident occurred above Americus. Truly it must have been providential, and we ought to be, and I hope are, extremely thankful.

I am grieved to see that you are distressing yourself about me. Again, it ought greatly to comfort you that I got off from home so early, for any that may have to go hereafter are pledged for three years of the war. I cannot get home, if alive, at the end of one year. If the war does not come upon soon, we may meet much earlier.

Your fears of my overworking myself are perfectly groundless. I am growing fat on high living and regular exercise. Just take as good care of yourself as I am taking — and propose to take — of myself, and I am sure that I shall be delighted by meeting you a stout, healthy woman on my return. Take good care of poor little Copper and Dean. The impossibility of seeing you and them constitutes my greatest trial; the hope of early restoration to my dear family — my greatest consolation.

We are still at the navy yard, somewhat more pleasantly quartered than when I wrote you last, in consequence of the removal of four companies out of our house. The life in camp — imagined from holiday encampments, etc. — has lost considerably its pleasantness, although we have not yet encountered the roar of cannon and whistling of bullets. The uniform round of duty is becoming wearisome, and the men gladly greet an order for extra work, even though it be to build embankments, dig ditches or mount cannon — harder work than any of them have ever been used to. My position is comparatively a pleasant one. Without the responsibility of the captain, I am relieved from all work, except drilling the men and such like duty.

Kiss my boys and receive the devotion of your affectionate husband.

David

I could scarcely scribble this out, writing as I am on a single sheet of paper on a board.

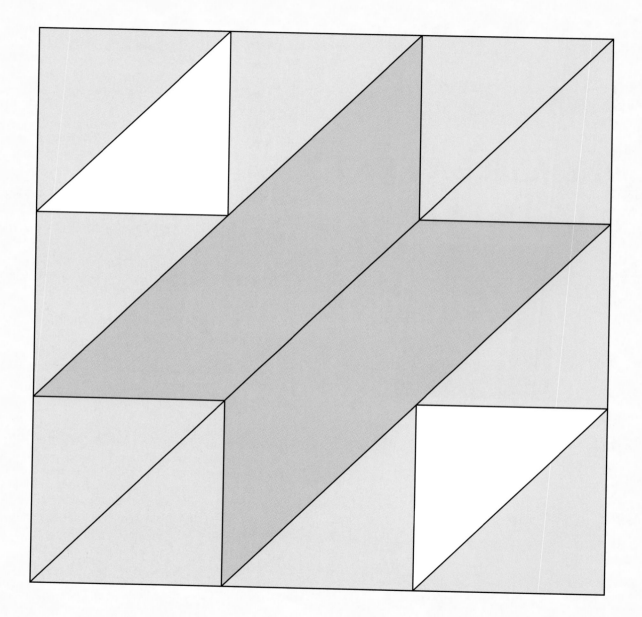

CITY LIGHT GUARDS

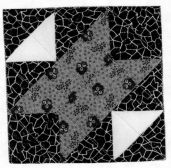

My Dear Wife,

On yesterday, we were waked at daylight with orders to move immediately to regimental camping grounds where the whole regiment could be assembled together and thoroughly formed, preparatory to moving to some point nearer the seat of war. We encamped upon a clover field, in which the clover was a foot high, and I have slept more sweetly than I have since I have been in Virginia, for hereto for I have slept upon the softer side of a hard floor.

I had just received your letter, my dear wife, of the 14th. I am surprised that you have not heard from me oftener, for I have written about every other day since I reached this place. True, I wrote some of my letters to Americus, thinking you had gone home. I hope that by this time, they have been forwarded to you. I regret greatly, dear Fan, that you continue to trouble yourself so much about your unworthy husband. Do, for my sake, cheer up and take care of yourself, assured that I am doing all that I can to be comfortable. For fear that you may wait to hear of my next destination before you write again, I will right here say that all letters directed to me at Portsmouth will be forwarded promptly to whatever place we may be sent.

Today, Peyton Colquitt's company, the City Light Guards, had the honor of crippling very badly a ship belonging to the U.S. that had attacked a small battery that was being erected by the Virginians about 8 miles down the river, near the camp at which Major Hardman's battalion was stationed. They have begun the fight there again this Tuesday morning, as every moment or two the roar of cannon greets our ears. We are preparing to march at 5 minutes' notice. Whether we will get it or not remains to be seen. The last few days have been extremely unpleasant, rainy and cold. Nevertheless, my health is excellent. I hope that your own health and spirits may be revived by this time. Take care of yourself. Give my love to all.

Embrace my babies, and be assured of the devoted love of your affectionate husband.

David

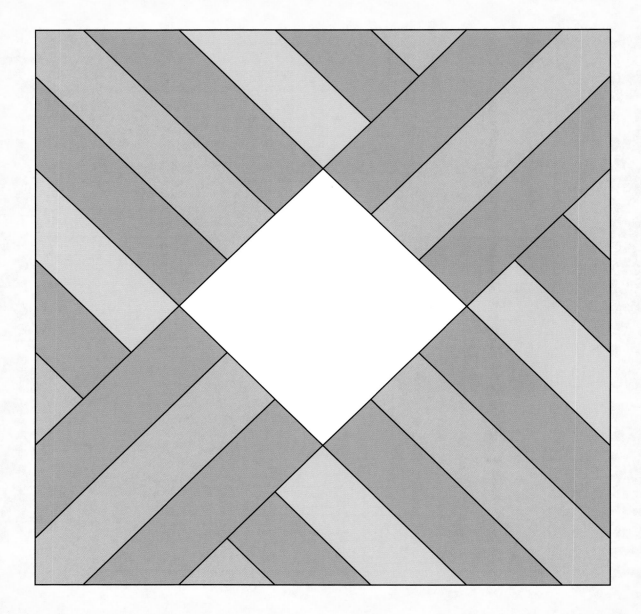

PIG POINT

My Dear Wife,

I have not written for several days for the reasons that I am 15 miles from the post office and communication is rare and news rarer. One day last week, I wrote to someone in Americus, from whom I received a letter, an account of a battle which I witnessed. 'Twas at Pig Point.

We are drilled by old Capt. Pegram, an old naval officer and an excellent man. On yesterday, I worked my men for him until dark and came home by a road of 2 miles, crossing a large creek on logs in the night. Today, I am resting. Since beginning this letter, a terrible but brief battle has been fought across the water. We were able to see the flashing of guns and hear the roar of musketry. All is now quiet over there, but from what we saw, we think the Federal troops were driven to Fortress Monroe, certainly toward it. This whole country is getting filled with troops, and I cannot help thinking we will soon whip the abolitionist from Virginia soil.

Andrew Hill is sick with the measles but is doing very well. He desires that his (sweetheart) may know it and that she be told not to come on here until he writes to her. He will write to her himself tomorrow. I shall do all I can to make him comfortable. Say hi to Miss Becca; I regret very much that she exhibited so little feeling at parting with me. I had expected that she would have at least turned her cheek to me, but was, as you know, disappointed — truly disappointed. But as she regrets her failure to do this much, I must forgive her and claim on my return to Americus so much the more cordial greeting.

This is written very hastily at midnight to be taken by Mr. Jackson, who has just been summoned home to see his father die. Remember me affectionately to Mrs. Hill, Miss Becca and the family, to Dr. Cooper and family, to Mr. Granberry and to all friends.

Embrace my dear children, and praying for yours devotedly.

David

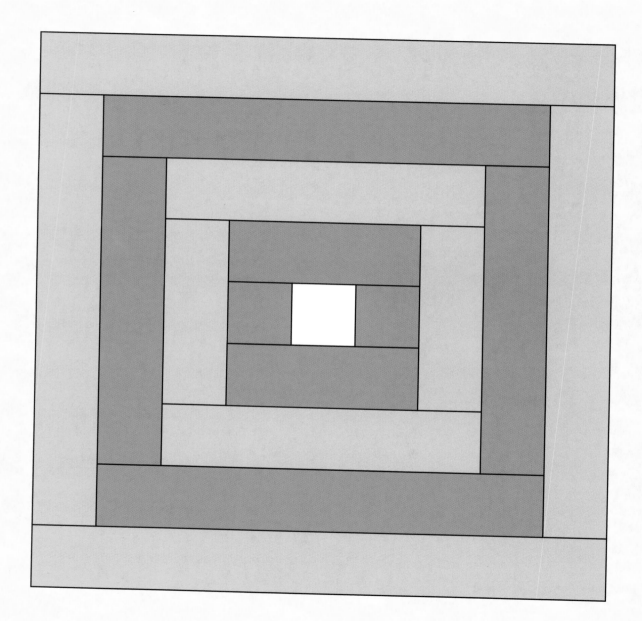

AMERICUS SOLDIERS RELIEF SOCIETY

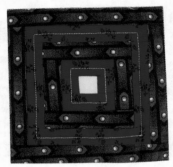

My Dear Wife,

Again, I have an opportunity of sending direct to you a letter. While I may write you a longer letter then I wrote by Coker, I will not promise to make it any more interesting. (I'm afraid pencil will rub out, and it is very difficult to write with greasy ink.)

I was very much gratified, indeed, to learn that matters were getting along so well, that occupation, even laborious, was agreeable to you. Before I received your letter, I had learned from the newspapers of your election to the honorable position of officer in the Soldiers Relief Society. I am certain that the ladies of Americus, who may be at work for our company, are wasting their time and goods, for nearly all of our men are now provided with more clothes than they can possibly carry in case they should have to move. It is true that there are hundreds of soldiers from Georgia to whom such Society may render great aid through Governor Brown. Still, I do not mean to say that our men will not need your aid before they get back to Americus, for they do wear out and ruin clothes in the camp faster than children do at home.

Before this, you have heard that we may have been in hearing of a fight for nearly a week and have been fast growing indifferent to the issue of war or peace, prepared in mind for either emergency. And while in full hearing of the enemies' music and in full sight of them, we are 7 miles from them, as the river was between us. From everything that has transpired up to the present time, we have no cause to apprehend much danger from the scoundrels. They don't fight well.

I am delighted to learn of Deanie's rapid progress to manhood and truly believe that Cooper and he will make no ordinary figures in the world if they live to adult age. I feel very much indebted to Miss Becca for her kind note and for her kindness in taking care of you. I can never repay her, for I do feel that she is a protection for you. Give her my love and kiss her for me.

With earnest prayer for health and happiness of my dear wife and children, your affectionate husband,

David

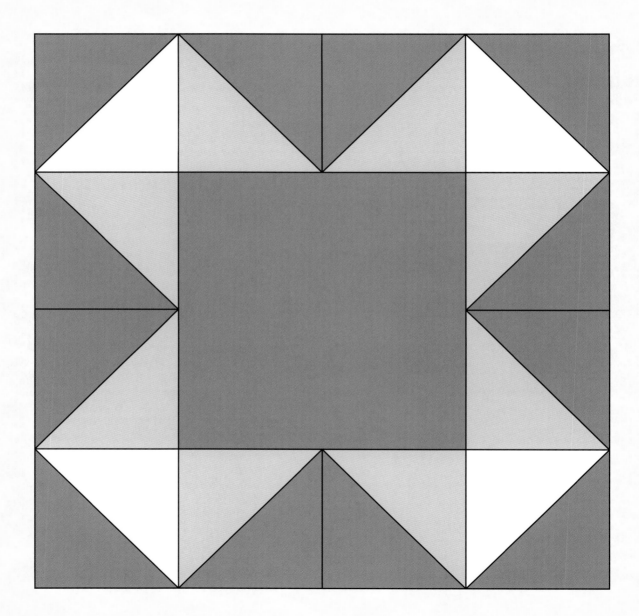

INFERNALLY UNGRATEFUL

My Dear Fan,

Two of our men leave for home this evening and have given me 15 minutes in which to write you. I regret that I'm not in better hands and have not better news to communicate.

I am physicianing in spite of myself, and I am worn out at it. My position is a wretched one. I cannot refuse to wait on the sick of our company, and yet the very wretches write home and complain here to the captain that I don't attend to them. These complaints are so infernally ungrateful that I am trying to get out of our company into one where I know and care for no one.

Poor John Foster will almost certainly die. I had been yielding my tent, cot and even bedclothing to the sick of our company until I caught a severe cold and had to refuse to do so further. Just about the time John took sick, and as I declined surrendering my tent, etc., they sent for another doctor. I'm now attending him, with Mrs. Andrews Hills' aid, and he is in the captain's tent, but I have scarcely a hope of his recovery. Typhoid fever is his trouble. Everything that can be will be done for him. The ladies on the ground are extra kind and attentive to him.

I expect Mr. Johnson, who left here when we were apprehending an early attack, has somewhat frightened you all by his ideas of our danger. It is all past now. The large fleet, which was threatening us is gone, and we are left as far as we can see to spend an idle winter. My ink is greasy, and Mr. Ransom is in a stew to leave. Can you make me two or three pairs of drawers?

That God will protect you and our boys is the prayer of your devoted husband.

David

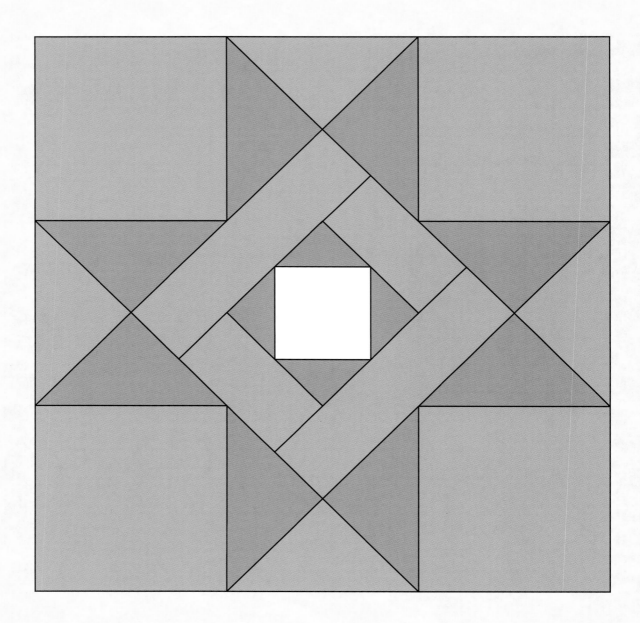

WRETCHEDLY COLD WEATHER

December 5, 1861

My Dear Wife,

With fingers nearly frozen, I attempt a hurried letter to you this morning simply because Capt. S. goes home today, and I am in command of the men from each company to build picket houses and sentry boxes, and they are now waiting for me to set them to work.

For two or three days past, we have had some wretchedly cold weather from which our sentries have suffered worse than anyone else, of course, because of their exposure to snow and sleet. This has made it absolutely necessary that my work should be quickly done. We that have been permitted to remain in our tents have gotten along much better than we expected. Our winter quarters have just begun, as we have had to suspend work on them for want of tools and materials. They will probably be finished by Christmas. By the way, what are you doing for wood during the cold weather?

Our soldiering here consists still in eating, drilling, working, sleeping and watching the enemy at a distance. It is getting very monotonous and wearisome. You asked me if it is probable that we will be disbanded soon. I think it is very probable. Everybody talks about it and the reason why it should be is a good one. There are a great many troops in camp who are enlisted for the war, and the government cannot arm them, and certainly would do right to give them preference over those in but for a few months. If the proposition is made to our regiment to re-enlist or be disbanded, many will enlist again immediately, but most would return home for a while first, and a few would remain there until forced to enlist again. For myself, I am in for the war, but of course, would make a short visit home.

I got a letter from Peg the other day. She was well and contented. Her letter contained a message from Cousin Mattie complaining of your not having her very kind letter of invitation received when I was at home. I am very sorry you have not answered it, and hope you will delay no longer in doing so. Earnestly hoping that you and our dear boys are well and getting along well, I am in great haste.

Your devoted husband,

David

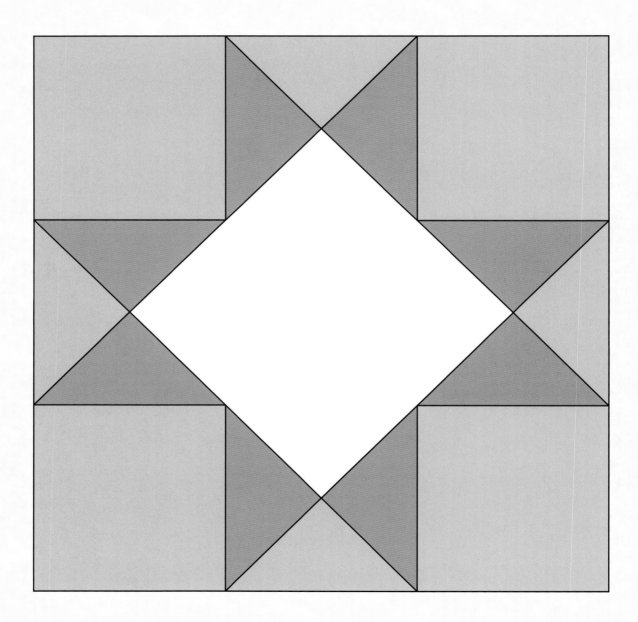

SUSPENSION OF FURLOUGHS

Jan. 16, 1862

After waiting impatiently for nearly three weeks, I received your short letter of the 10th today. You were so tardy in writing that I feared that your father might be dangerously ill, and the impression was strengthened by Peg writing to me that from your letter to her, the same impression had been made on her. This caused me to telegraph to Jack Jones the other day. From him I have received no answer.

I'm glad that your letter relieves me by the information that your father is recovering. At one time last week I thought I might visit you during this week, as orders were published at dress parade, Saturday evening, that the prohibition of furloughs was removed, and leave of absence would be granted to one officer and four privates of each company.

But, alas, on Monday morning, orders were received suspending all furloughs for officers and noncommissioned officers, and allowing them only to privates. Why this was done, I do not know; so it is. I'm glad to learn that Charlie has been up to see your father and has gotten your business in some shape, and I hope and believe that he will manage it as satisfactorily as time and circumstances will permit.

In regard to the letter which I sent him, it was sealed, and if open when he received it, I have no doubt that the thought was with that infamous Yankee humbug Spaulding's prepared glue.

I wish I could be at his wedding, but almost certainly cannot. Is the time fixed, and will you attend? You must, if possible, and give me a full account of the affair and description of our new sister. Kiss her for me, etc. In regard to the photograph — say to Becca — she certainly shall have one. I have had to get more taken for home folks; I will send them to you for distribution. Remember me affectionately to Miss Becca and Jim and all my friends. To my little Cooper, say that Father wants to see his little soldier very much and wants to find a good boy when he sees him. Kiss him and Deanie.

With love to all. I am yours devotedly.

David

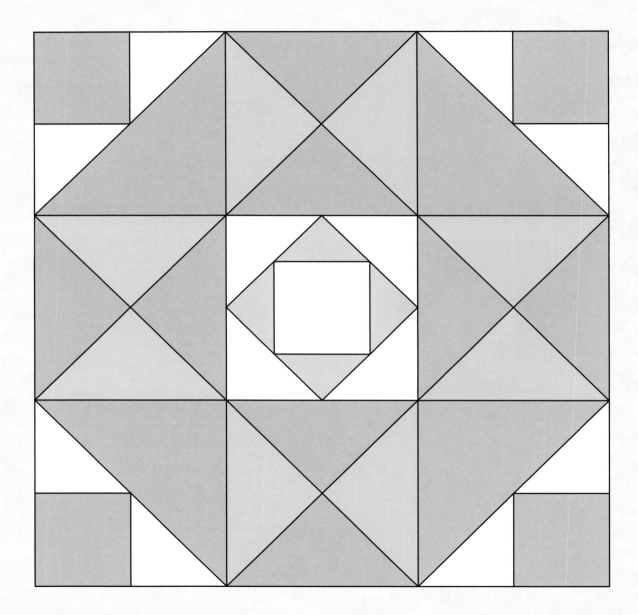

ROANOKE ISLAND

My Wife,

I came to town today on business and was met by the most distressing intelligence from North Carolina that the Yankees were landing troops at Roanoke Island. Tonight, the worst of our apprehensions have been realized. The Federalists have captured Roanoke and all our forces after a most murderous fight.

Our Gen. Blanchard has just told me that our regiment will remain in its present position, while five companies of the 3rd Volunteers will be sent with the North Carolina regiment station near us to the scene of the battle. Thus, we will be left at a secure position, for I have no apprehension of an attack at our point, while I have no doubt that the railroad below us will be attempted to be seized by the Federalists. In this event, communications between us will be temporarily suspended. This causes me to take this immediate opportunity of writing to you. Is it for the last time? My wife, I will not believe it. Do not think that I would distress you by writing at all, except to present any gloomy anticipation that you might create for yourself from newspaper reports of our present position. This has made me show you the dark side at once. Yet, we may never again meet.

Disease carries off thousands. Our regiment has already lost more men by this cause than any other which may have been in battle, lost by bullets. I am enlisted for the war, and firmly believe that the prayers of my dear wife and friends will prevail to preserve me through it. I cannot now give you an idea of when I will visit you. Furloughs are again refused. The events of which you will be acquainted by the newspapers will determine the matter.

I am compelled to write hastily because of the lateness of the hour and the duty of informing Capt. Johnson, who is at home, of the state of affairs. Remember me most affectionately to your father's family.

Embrace my dear children and believe me, your devoted husband,

David

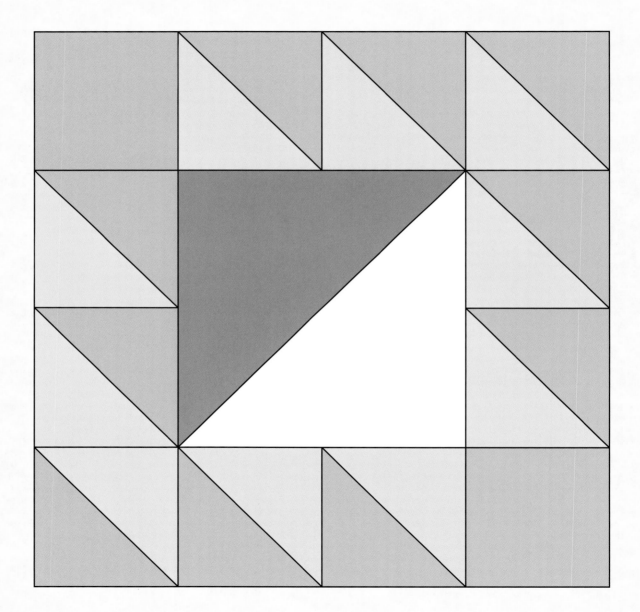

SECOND TERM

Feb. 21, 1862

My Dear Wife,

I received your affectionate letter yesterday and am glad to learn that you are struggling so nobly to sustain yourself under your present severe trials. Indeed, I am very proud of my little wife and only pray that I may be enabled to exhibit my appreciation of her after this war is over by a life of devotion. My dear Fannie, I know that yours is a hard lot and that you bear with Christian fortitude, but I know not how to repair it. I do most sincerely believe that I can best serve myself, yourself, my country, our children and our God by remaining in the field. But when I get into service for the second term, I will certainly be more prudent in my expenditures, and you and my dear children shall not suffer while I have an arm to raise.

I cannot tell you at what time I may be able to visit you. Be assured that it will be at the first possible moment permitted. Capt. Johnson is looking for today or tomorrow, being a little hurried by the bad news which reached him from this part of the world. Under ordinary circumstances I could get a furlough upon his return, but now it is absurd to think of such a thing. This state of affairs will not exist longer than a continuance of the present excitement. If we do not surely have stirring times, we will have extremely idle ones. What our chances of a fight may be, we can only judge from the proximity and declared purpose of the enemies.

I am very sorry indeed to learn of your father's still-failing health and hope that you may be unnecessarily apprehensive in regard to his feebleness. And Aunt Polly is with you? Give her my love — I would love very much to see her. Indeed, I am getting thoroughly homesick, and above all earthly things, would consider even a short visit to those I love the greatest privilege.

Enclosed I send you $50, all I can get now. Remember me affectionately to your father, mother and family and all inquiring friends. To yourself, my dear wife, and our darling children, I send greeting of my whole heart. God bless and keep you.

Your affectionate husband,

David

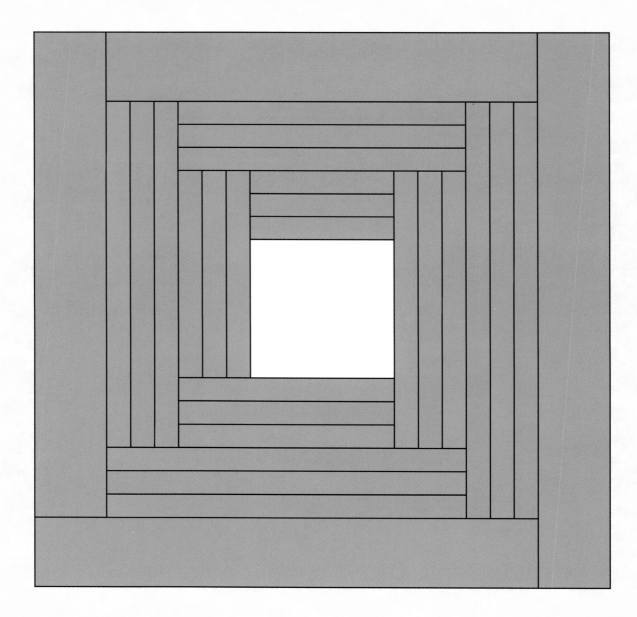

My Application

March 22, 1863

My Dear Wife,

Gen. Lee is a polite man and never keeps people waiting. Notwithstanding this, I have not heard one word from my application for a leave of absence sent up to him 10 or 12 days ago. I'm consequently left to conclude that he has thrown it into his fireplace, or some kind friend (as Gen. Rhodes), has not permitted it to go to him; ordinarily it takes but three or four days for paper to go up and be returned. Unfortunately, I cannot send up another application under the hypothesis of this one being lost, for Gen. Jackson has ordered that no more applications for leave of absence shall be sent up.

You can now judge of my prospects of an early visit home. Furloughs have been hitherto so easily obtained that I can scarcely think of my failure with any degree of patience. I shall attempt to console Dr. Cooper when I feel assured of getting leave myself. As I feel now, I should be tempted to knock down anybody that might offer me such sympathy. I'm homesick; I yearn to visit my wife and boys.

I was glad to learn that poor little Deanie was recovered from his mumps and hope that nothing worse may befall him in the way of sickness. Of course I'm satisfied with your sale of the carriage. It would doubtless have been ruined by the time you might get ready to use it. I think, however, from what I have heard from others, that David Hill cheated you in the price as much as he did me in the price of my horse. I am told that a set of carriage harnesses alone is worth $300 to $400. In regard to the piano, I would be pleased for you to make the purchase. But why did you give up buying Cousin Tom's? When you do buy, let it be a good one. Poor property is high at any price.

I am glad that you have visited Aunt Louisa and hope that you will have frequent opportunities at meeting her and cousin Fannie. Give my love to them all.

Kiss my boys for me and believe me your devoted husband.

David

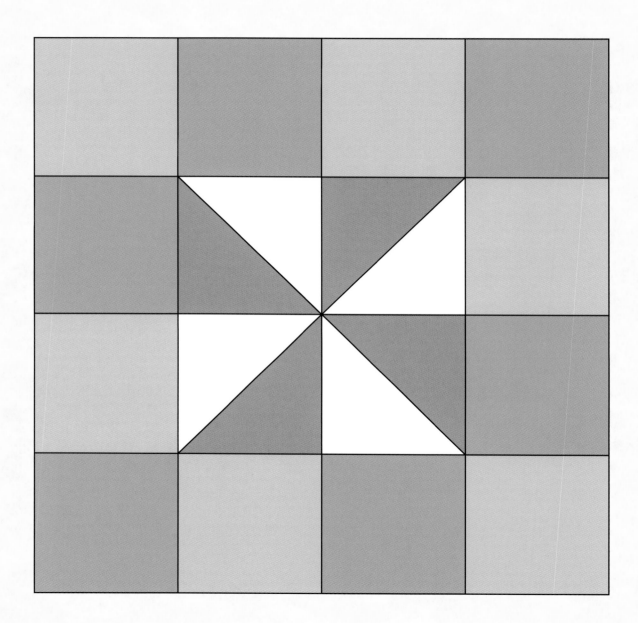

ANOTHER BATTLE

My Darling Fan,

I'm sitting in a very pretty grove about 2½ miles from the town of Culpepper, awaiting orders to march towards the enemy, my ears being constantly greeted by the music of artillery from a Cavalry fight now going on in front of us.

I do not know our participation in this difficulty. Certainly it is, however, that in a very short time this army will be engaged in another battle. Nothing can avert it. I presume that will result as others in which we have been engaged, that is, I believe that we will whip the Yankees, with a loss of many valuable lives and the permanent maiming of many others. Without speculation upon the consequences, I can only add that if I am left "to tell the tale," I'll take the first opportunity of informing you of the issue.

I was highly gratified by receiving your last dear letter on the very day on which I sent off my last and left our camping place. I am sincerely grateful that you are still preserved in health and my boys are equally favored. I do pray that this blessing may long be continued and that many days happiness with my beloved family are yet in store for me.

I'm happy to say that our new major was induced to decline his place by my threatening him to write to the secretary of war, informing him of the major's incompetence, etc. Since then, Jeff Davis has made Capt. Willis — the man I wanted — major, and we are getting on very smoothly, so you need have no fear of my having to resign and be a private for the reason I'm having a poor major. Indeed, you judged me rightly when you supposed I had written hastily.

I have not heard one word from Houston since I left home. What is the matter down there? Has Peg gone up yet? I hope not, but that she will be permitted to stay most of her time with you. Orders have come to be ready to move, so goodbye. Bless and kiss my sons for me. Remember me kindly to our friends, and believe me with prayer for your happiness and preservation.

Your devoted husband,

David

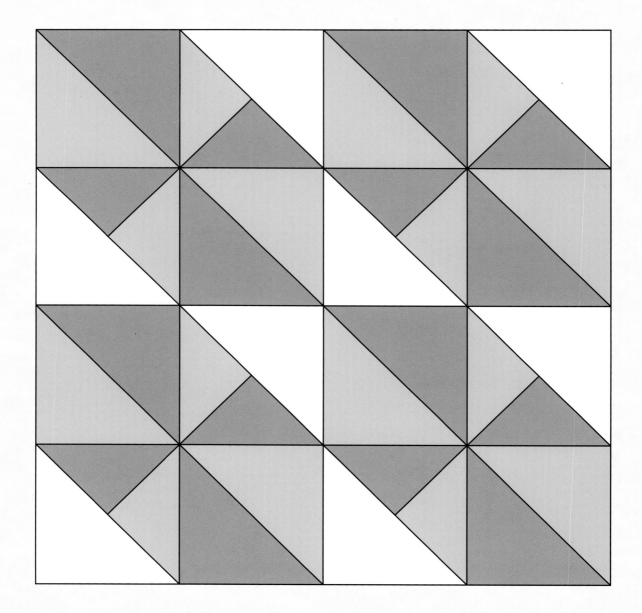

SINCERE SYMPATHY AND CONDOLENCE

Nov. 3, 1863
Headquarters Dole's Brigade
Mrs. Fannie Winn
Americus, Ga.

Madam,

As secretary of a meeting of the field and staff officers of this brigade convened to offer a tribute of respects to the memories of Lt. Col. David Winn, 4th Georgia regiment, and Col. S.P. Lumpkin, 44th Georgia regiment, it is made my duty to forward to you a copy of the proceedings which you will please find enclosed.

Having been intimately associated with Col. Winn, members of the same mess, occupying the same tent, it was my privilege to know him well and love him truly. And, while his frank and affable manner, his war and loyal impulses, his devotion to truth and right, no less than his heightened chivalry and sublime heroism, had endeared him to all, and yet only those who knew him intimately could fully know his worth or appreciate his loss. With the assurance of my sincere sympathy and condolence, I am very respectful.

F.T. Snead

Samuel Zinser. Photograph courtesy of Special Collection Center,
Bradley University Library.

Samuel Clement Zinser

(Aug. 20, 1836 - Oct. 15, 1908)

Samuel Clement Zinser was born Aug. 20, 1836, in Fairfield County, Ohio, one of seven sons and five daughters of Jacob and Elizabeth Zinser.

In 1851, when Samuel was 15, the Zinser family moved to Washington, Ill., where he began the trade of harness making. He courted Elizabeth Means, the daughter of Joseph Means and Sarah Oriel, who had moved from Kentucky to Illinois when she was a young girl.

It was on Aug. 16, 1861, at the age of 24, that Samuel enlisted in the Company B, 47th Illinois Infantry, for three years of service. He fought in many battles, such as Vicksburg, Tiptonville, Corinth, Mechanicsburg and Richmond.

Throughout his time in the service, Samuel wrote letters home to Elizabeth, which he viewed as a privilege. "Although we are separated by hill and dale and have not the power, or in other words, the satisfaction of conversing in a verbal form, yet it is a cheering thought to me to think that we have a medium by which we can talk together and exchange thoughts at times; were it not for this privilege. Oh! How dreary and lonesome this world would be to me and my present situation," he wrote on Oct. 13, 1861.

Samuel was discharged from the service on Oct. 11, 1864, and he mustered out as a corporal. On May 16, 1865, Samuel Zinser and Elizabeth Means were married. They had one child, Harry L. Zinser. Samuel went into the hardware business and also served as an alderman of Washington, Ill., for many years. Samuel Zinser died at the age of 72 on Oct. 15, 1908.

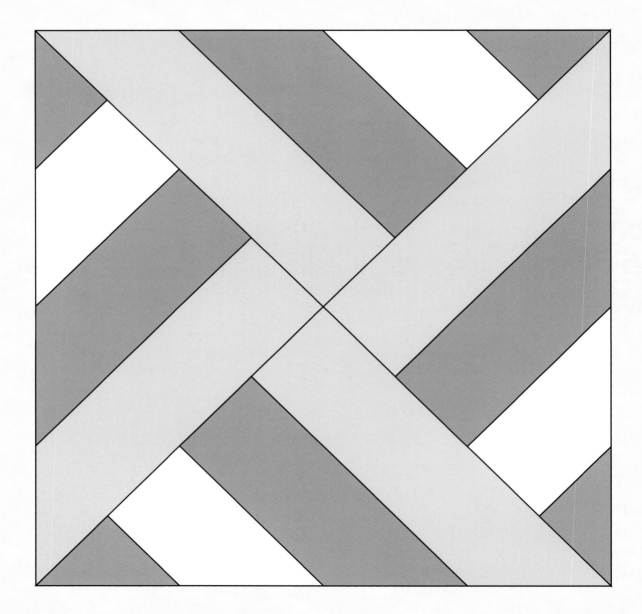

HISTORY OF TRAVEL

My Dear Friend Lizzie,

Although you did not ask me to write to you at any time, I have no reason to believe that a few lines from your humble friend would not be appreciated by you. On the contrary, I believe that it will bring an answer in due time; my faith is unwavering in that respect and shall be, until otherwise informed by you.

I will now give you a little history of our travels since yesterday until today about 2 o'clock, when we arrived here in Camp Benton almost wearied out, having marched about 5 miles.

You can well imagine how we look after marching all the way from a river through a perfect fog of dust and having traveled from the time we started until we arrived here without any rest, the cars being crowded so full, and the seats but of little account for resting purposes. We arrived at Alton this morning at 6. This was an interesting trip to me, it being the first time I ever rode on a boat in my life. It was truly a grand sight to me to see that, or in other words, glide along down the grand stream, the Mississippi, sometimes termed the father of waters; and had not my thoughts wandered back to home and friends, it would have truly been interesting to me. But as the boat was gliding along silently and everything seemed hushed in silence save the rustling of the waves, which achieved to and fro and seemingly groaned under the heavy burden they had to sustain, my thoughts naturally wandered back to Washington, and being Sabbath morning, I imagined you were going to church, and for a moment I could hardly realize the situation, and as I was thus meditating, a tear silently started, and I found that I had almost allowed myself to weep. I then tried to banish such thoughts, thinking it did not become a soldier to weep, but this I could not well do, the scene of Saturday morning being so vivid in my mind to be so easily forgotten. I thought that I could brave almost anything, but when friend Charles informed me that you where there and wished to see me, I could not altogether command presence of mind at the time. I must confess, the train, you will remember, had started before I knew you were there. I had been looking for you on the other side all the time; I would have given anything, it seems to me, to have the train stopped a few minutes longer.

All the boys are well and in good spirits in our company. I will close by soliciting an answer from you, and giving you my best respects to you, and also to Rebecca, and in short, all inquiring friends.

Samuel Zinser

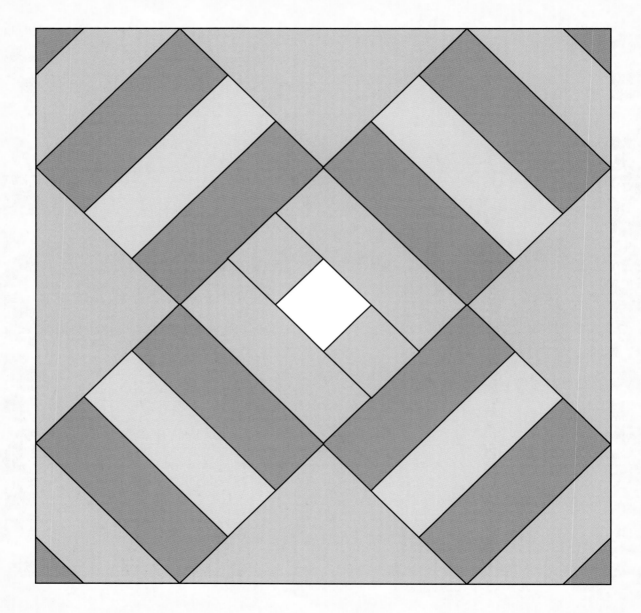

GUARDIAN
ANGEL

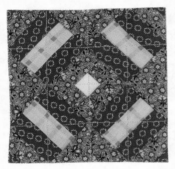

Sept. 29, 1861

Much-Esteemed Friend Lizzie,

Your kind favor was received, and you cannot calculate the amount of pleasure it gave me to hear from one I esteem so highly as I do the one that was the originator of the manuscript. It is the first that I ever received from you, and should it in the province of God prove to be the last, it shall be as a guardian angel to the last moment of my life come that hour when it may, either on the battlefield in the defense of my country and its liberties, or elsewhere; it shall be sacred as long as the memory shall last.

I'm sorry that I caused you unpleasant feelings by stating in my last that you had not particularly asked me to write to you, and I would recall it were it in my power, for I did not intend to wound your feelings. I assume you rather, would I, not have written at all than to cause you such feelings. You will please forget it and remember that our friendship is unbroken, and what affords me the most pleasure is to be assured that it never has been entirely extinct, although in a dormant state for a while, as it were.

You said something about being sad and lonely; could I but say anything to cheer that heart of yours, it would be a healing balm for my own, but I do not know what to say in the way of consoling you that would be of any consequence, as I am lonely myself at times and would be all the time, should I allow my thoughts to wander back home and to that parlor where I have passed so many happy moments, and so lately, too. I frequently meditate and wonder whether I shall have the privilege ever, to visit you again. I have strong hopes that such will be the case; although the future looks dark and gloomy, and tempestuous waves of disunion threaten the destruction of our once tranquil and happy government, yet let us trust in Him who ruleth the destinies of nations, that He will not forsake those who are engaged in the righteous cause.

Our regiment is under marching orders and expects to leave tomorrow for parts unknown to me; when you write, direct your letters here, as all letters are sent after all us. The boys are all tolerably well, with the exception of the few who are in the hospital.

No more at present, but will remain your devoted friend,

Samuel Zinser

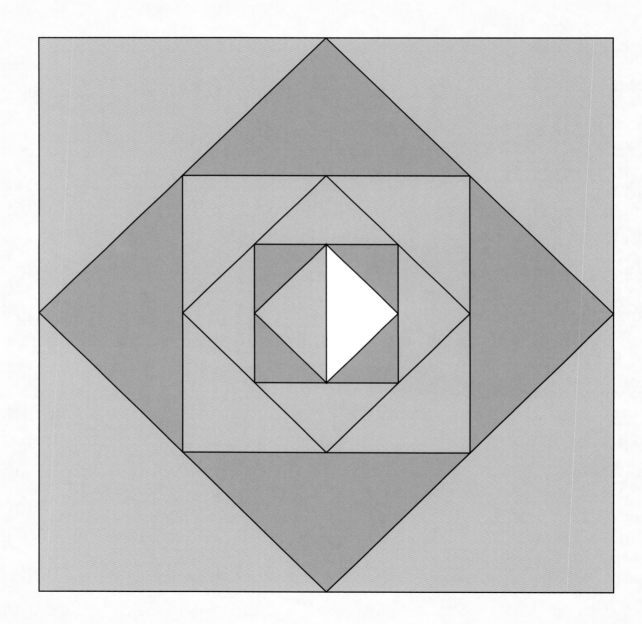

Exchange Thoughts

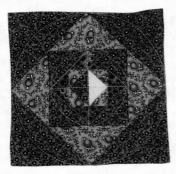

Oct. 13, 1861

Ms. Lizzie Means, Much-Esteemed Friend,

Yours of the 4th was received and perused with an incalculable amount of satisfaction. Although we are separated by hill and dale and have not the power, or in other words, the satisfaction of conversing in a verbal form, yet it is a cheering thought to me to think that we have a medium by which we can talk together and exchange thoughts at times; were it not for this privilege. Oh! How dreary and lonesome this world would be to me and my present situation. This is the Sabbath eve, and I fancy I see you sitting in one of the pews in church; I wish that I could for a moment look in and recognize those familiar faces with whom I have met so often. But, alas! That time has vanished like a dream, and when I shall again enjoy that privilege is only known to Him who guided the destinies of nations and manages the affairs of men in His own way and for the best.

I will now give you a brief history of our travels from St. Louis here. We started from there on the 9th in the afternoon, about 2 o'clock, and arrived here that night at 2. We remained in the cars the balance of the night waiting for further orders.

We went to our campground and worked all day without anything to eat. By evening, we had our tents erected and had the satisfaction of crawling into them with wet clothes and wet blankets, to pass away the night as best we could. It was amusing to see the long faces, and frequent sighs that passed from some. Undoubtedly, they were sighs for home and friends. I thought I could read the thoughts of those faces. I think they thought a soldier's life is truly a hard life. Perhaps you will say that I judged others by myself; well, I shall not dispute your word if you do, as I have tried arguing with you before and always get beat and have therefore concluded to argue only with those who are not any better at it than I am. I, however, anticipated such things and therefore was not disappointed. I knew that a soldier's life was one that afforded but little what we might term physical comfort, but this is not what the true soldier looks at; it is the welfare of his country, for which he is ready to sacrifice his life, fortune and sacred honor.

You wrote that your letters were not interesting. Please, Lizzie, let me be the judge of that.

No more at present, but remain your true and sincere friend,

Samuel Zinser

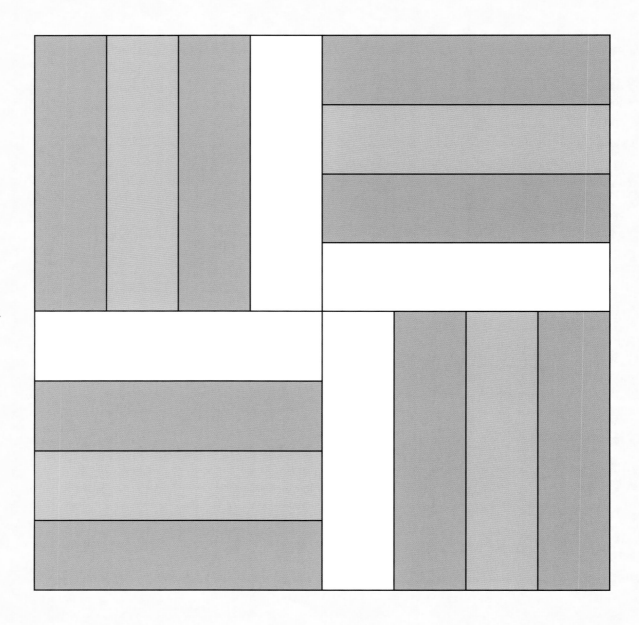

LONESOME PLACE

Ms. Lizzie Means, Kind Friend,

Yours of Nov. 1 was received, and never was I so gratified, it seems to me, on receiving a letter. Evening after evening I would go to camp for a letter from the worthiest of all of my correspondents, but none would I receive. I had almost concluded that you had dropped your humble correspondent, when to my unbounded satisfaction one evening, this spell was broken; I was informed that there was a letter for me. I was not very long, I assure, in learning its contents.

We are still here in this lonesome place, nothing of importance transpiring, save the monotonous routine of duties of camp life. The health of the regiment is not very flattering just at this time. According to report yesterday morning, the sick list in the 47th was as follows: 37 in regimental hospital, about 50 in the general hospital here in Jefferson City, and 60 in quarters. There are some at St. Louis that we left there when we came away from there; the number I cannot state, as there have been some returning all the time. Company B has but three at general hospital and perhaps 10 or 12 that are well in quarters, none dangerously ill. However, Capt. Miles is still sick, and it will be some time before he will be able for duty. Company A and B were on a scouting expedition; they returned last Friday, bringing some 30 prisoners with them. They said that is not hard, considering the hardships they necessarily had to go through.

Ms. Lizzie, your speaking of the weddings that had taken place in Washington and your commenting on the subject of patriotism met with my hearty approval. I, too, think that the brides nor the bridegrooms would not have had a very deep interest in the welfare of our country's good. I admire your patriotism; such a zeal for the maintenance of the glorious Stars and Stripes is worthy of imitation; and he that is so fortunate as to dare claim the affections as noble of heart as that may well be proud of it. I congratulate the individual, whoever he may be, that shall become the subject of the affections of the one I will not name again.

I will close by giving you my best wishes, hoping that our friendship may extend to the end of time.

From your friend,

Samuel Zinser

INDICATIONS

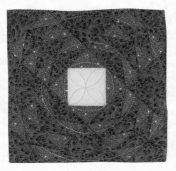

Dec. 7, 1861

Ms. Lizzie, Highly Esteemed Friend,

Yours of the 14th of November was received and perused with great satisfaction, as your letters always are. I must confess that I have not been as punctual this time in answering yours as I should like to have been. I have but little time of late that I can call my own; you will please pardon the delay this time, and I would try to be more punctual in the future. Although many miles intervene, and hills and dales separate us so that we cannot enjoy each other's society, yet we can mutually talk with our friends; not with the same satisfaction, of course, but still it is a privilege incalculable.

You were correctly informed with regard to our colonel not granting any more furloughs. It is, however, not his fault, as it was an order issued from the War Department at Washington City. You stated that you thought that the Colonel might grant me one anyhow; if reports be true, I want no furlough.

Owing to the desire of mailing this letter today before the mail goes out, I must be rather brief this time — I have nothing new with regard to war matters that you have not already seen in the papers.

The indications are in our favor everywhere, by land and sea, if accounts be true. May the Ruler of the universe so direct those who are in the command of our armies as to crush this rebellion from the Atlantic to the Pacific, from the Gulf of Mexico to the northern boundaries of the United States, and may peace and quietude again return to our borders. I close by wishing you a happy time. If you have any sleigh rides and parties in Washington, I hope they will be merry ones, if I can't be there. I congratulate you on receiving Mrs. Hormish for a neighbor; she is a particular friend of mine, you know.

No more at present; hoping to hear from you soon.

I remain your sincere friend,

Samuel Zinser

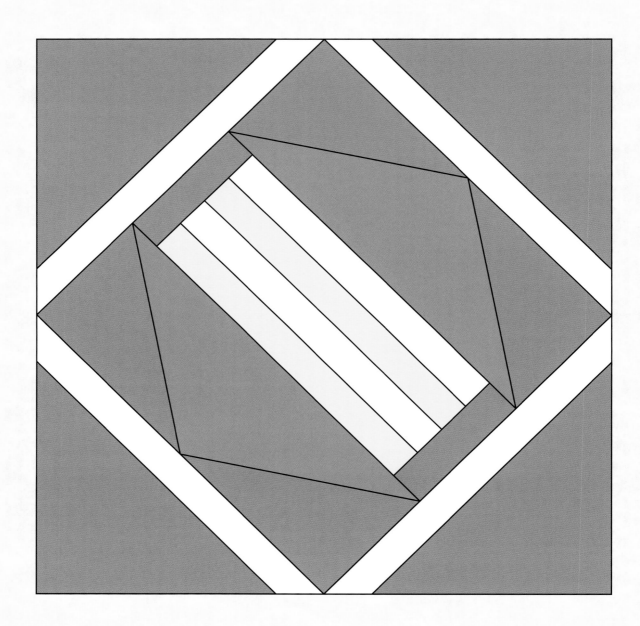

LOVESICK

Dec. 20, 1861

Ms. Lizzie Means, Kind Friend,

I received your interesting letter that was mailed at Eureka and have seated myself by a box to answer your kind favor and at the same time inform you that the gallant 47th takes its line of march tomorrow morning at 7 o'clock; whether, the future will reveal. This superstition is, however, that we will go up the Missouri River 55 miles to a place called Otterville. This was rather unexpected to us, as we had made up our minds that we had to remain in Jefferson all winter. We received intelligence today at 1 o'clock.

I have been helping Mr. Brown pack the medicines this afternoon. We finished a few minutes ago, and it is now perhaps 11 o'clock, and the rest have all retired. I feel somewhat fatigued, besides having a severe headache proceeding from a cold that I have had for a fortnight or more. I do not feel that interest in writing I have felt on other occasions. But I must have more, from the simple fact that I should not have written tonight were it not to the one whom I address. I will not complain of being sick, as there are so many in that list now, and if I should say that I was sick, you might think perhaps that Col. Miles' statement was true. You did not state what he said, but I have heard of it since I have received yours. I shall not deny the charge, but I will say that if the colonel has nothing else to do than to tell such stuff as that, he had better not say anything at all.

There is one thing certain: If I am lovesick, I have been able to perform duty every day since I left Washington and have not been obliged to make an application for a leave of absence in order to save me from the fatality of that disease. As he has taken the liberty to specify a complaint for me without any evidence, I presume he will allow me the same privilege. My opinion is that he was a little troubled with nostalgia.

But I must close for this time. You will please excuse the crook of strokes of my pen and promiscuous arrangement of words. We have to leave about 50 sick here in charge of the chaplain of our regiment, who says he will not leave our boys in the hands of strangers. I close by wishing you a Merry Christmas, and, if in the province of Him who ruleth the destinies of nations, this should be the last of your humble correspondent, I hope you will not have it to say that I was not faithful to my country's cause.

I am your humble and sincere friend,

Samuel Zinser

MANY FOND RECOLLECTIONS

Jan. 10, 1862

Miss Lizzie, Kind Friend,

Your very interesting epistle of the 30th of December was perused with unbounded satisfaction. I must confess that I have been some what dilatory in answering, however, not without a cause. At the time of the reception of yours, I received a letter from Jefferson City from the surgeon of our regiment requesting me to come to Jefferson immediately to make out a quarterly report of the sick, which was somewhat intricate and consequently kept me employed several days. I returned from there on the 8th. Joseph is there now and has been for some two weeks sick, not confined to his couch, however; you need not be uneasy. He has a good place where he stops and receives the best of medical attention. His illness, I think, is merely the effects of a bad cold. He was fast recovering while I was there, and the day I left, he told me he felt perfectly well with exception of weakness and thought he would be able to join us in a few days. Undoubtedly, he has apprised you of his illness ere this.

The cake that you sent I received. Many thanks to its kind donor. It was not only excellent quality, but was also the means of awakening many fond recollections of the past, thoughts that shall be sacred in the tablet of my memory until the last moment of my life. Your humble correspondent acknowledges the utter incapability of acknowledging the kindness bestowed as its merits, but hopes the few plain, blunt words will at least be sufficient to merit acceptance. I do not desire to return until the Stars and Stripes float again over every foot of American soil and peace and tranquility is proclaimed throughout our borders. You certainly can't have a very exalted opinion of my taste, should I acknowledge that I enjoy a soldier's life better than a quiet home circle or the pleasures of visiting the one addressed. But, I hasten to a close. There is nothing unusual in the way of war news. We do not expect to remain here long; where we will go, of course, we do not know. The weather is somewhat severe now.

No more at present, but soliciting an answer soon and wishing you life's choicest blessings.

I remain your humble friend,

Samuel Zinser

IMAGINARY FEELING

March 10, 1862

Esteemed Friend Lizzie:

When last I wrote to you, we were at Commerce. Whether you ever received the communication or not, I cannot tell, as I have not received anything from you since I left Jefferson. No doubt you have written, but on account of our moving all the time here late, we have not been able to receive any mail matter; neither have we been able to send any unless we sent it by a private conveyance to some point where it will be out of reach of Secesh. As I have a chance to send this by one of our men who is going home, I thought I would improve the opportunity so as to let you know that we are still alive. No doubt you will have learned ere this, through the medium of the papers, somewhere near where we are, or at least that we were destined for some point on the Mississippi River.

The imaginary feeling of the battlefield has at last become a reality. Although the 47th has not been into an engagement yet, they can testify that they have seen in part what a battlefield is, or at least tell what the feeling is to be shot at. As regards myself, my feelings were altogether different from what I had expected they would be. I always thought that by the time I could see the shells flying that I would feel like retreating, but I had no such feelings, and in fact, I felt more unconcerned with regard to danger than I did when I was 50 miles from the expected place of battle. While I could see the shells flying in the air, I felt like marching right to the scene of action.

Many more items I would like to mention, but I will have to let this suffice for the present.

Wishing you health and happiness, I remain your devoted friend,

Samuel Zinser

P.S. Direct to St. Louis regiment and it will follow us. I have not received a scratch of a pen from Washington since I left Jefferson. It would indeed be a treat to hear from there, especially from the one addressed; nothing would be more appreciated. Written in great haste, which you will readily perceive.

DANGEROUS DUTY

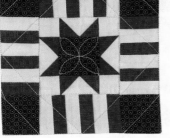

May 26, 1862

Kind Friend,

My letter will be brief this time, as I have nothing of importance to write at this time. I have news of which you are informed from time to time through the papers and consequently could not interest you, as it would be merely a repetition.

With regards to matters here, nothing of importance has transpired since I wrote to you, outside of activity preparations being made to resist an attack from the enemy, should they see fit to do so, which I do not think it all likely. Should they, however, they will certainly meet with a warm reception. They are doubtless going to act on the defensive this time. When we are going to move again, of course, we do not know, nor can we form any conclusions from the signs of the times. This is only known to our generals. Occasional skirmishing is going on with the pickets, and now and then, we capture some of them. We have been on picket duty since we have been here. This is a dangerous duty to perform, as the Rebels frequently advance on our pickets secretly and try to shoot them. Such is the treacherous and dastardly conduct of the Rebels, violating the code of all civilized warfare and adopting that of the savages.

While I'm thus writing, I cannot help reflect the sentiment contained in your last letter — how uncertain is life. The weight of this saying, or in other words, the proof, is certainly more significant with a soldier than the civilian at his or her quiet home, or at least should be so, as he takes his life as if it were in his hands. Yet strange as it may seem, the soldier seems to be but little concerned about the matter. Too much is this the case when we consider the justness of That Being to whom we owe our existence and who justly requires us to live in accordance with His divine law or never behold His face and peace. It may seem rather strange to you to hear as much the subject of Christianity from any, as I have never said more on this perhaps than I ever did before, but the reason I have not said more heretofore is not because I have not been a firm believer in it. My convictions have always been that I was too negligent in this matter. Little as I may have said on the subject, I always appreciated its worth when spoken of by others. In conclusion, let me add and that the kind admonitions given by you in your last shall be sacred to my memory. The sentiments uttered are worthy of being written in letters of gold.

Hoping that this may find you enjoying all the blessings of this life to its fullest extent,

Samuel Zinser

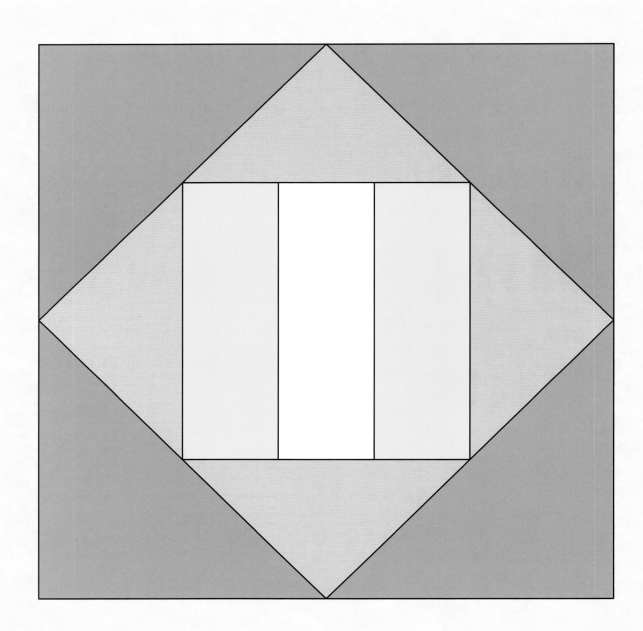

PRIVILEGE OF COMMUNICATION

Feb. 24, 1863

Dear Lizzie,

As I have leisure this beautiful afternoon, I will devote the precious moments in chatting with you.

This is a great pleasure to me, which, if I was deprived of, would render life dreary to me — yea, miserable. Although separated by hills and mountains, rivers and rivulets, thus preventing the exchange of thoughts and feelings verbally, alone whose bliss have no bounds could it be enjoyed, it is nevertheless a great satisfaction to have the privilege of communication at all.

Lizzie, I'll often wonder whether you do not grow tired at times in receiving a simple tokens of regard for me, a humble unpretending, character, not blessed or gifted in what the world calls great, such as professional or pecuniary endowments could give. I well know that you are worthy to move in this sphere and did not I know that true worth ought not to be judged by worldly renown and that you do not thus judge of true happiness, I might have reason to believe that you do not appreciate in me what I reason to believe that you do. Whether worthy of your esteem I will leave you to be the judge; hope I may always prove so. I state these facts because I think it would be wrong to deceive, and which I would not do through all my hopes should be blasted by acknowledging what I have, and should you see fit to erase me as a lover, you will at least esteem me for sincerity. No matter what my fortune may be in the future, the promotion of your happiness, fair one, shall be my inmost desire while the tide of life ebbs through my veins, though cast upon life's tempestuous waves to baffle against the surges to be encountered all along life's journey, forgotten by you. I should always cherish, in the tablet of my memory, a fond reflection of you.

The boys are all well as common. We live pretty well — have warm biscuits almost daily, butter, milk, etc. So our friends need not have uneasiness, you see, that we do not get enough to eat as it is frequently reported.

It is well and hearty — give my best regards to all. Tell Rebecca I would like to have another sing with her, and when we have a chance again, we will have you help us. No more at the present.

I remain yours as ever,

Samuel Zinser

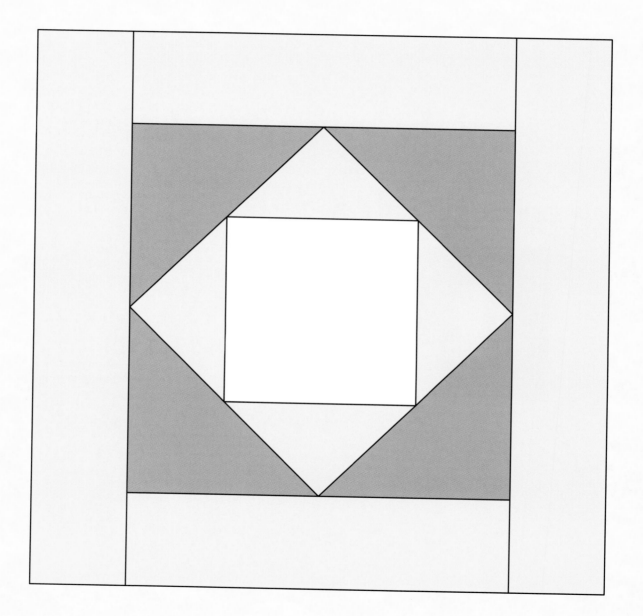

Queen of the West

Dear Lizzie,

This is a beautiful Sabbath morning and reminds me of thoughts of a May morning in Illinois, when all nature smiles, vegetation just putting forth, birds caroling and merrily skipping from branch to branch, making the air vocal with their music.

As I have just received yours through Joseph, and, to my surprise, learned that you have not received any of my letters since Jan. 6, I will write immediately, though this may serve the same fate of those before, some half-dozen perhaps, that have not reached their destination — hope, however, this may prove more successful. I cannot account for it — others complain of the same thing.

News of the war matters are somewhat fluctuating. The report of the capture of the Queen of the West in Red River seems to be confirmed; this was unfortunate to the gallant crew, but we hope that the Indianola who was sent in pursuit will recapture her.

Matters at Vicksburg are still undetermined as to the time of the final contest. A general attack, in which I feel sanguine of ultimate success, seems imminent. Much depends on this; if we are successful at Vicksburg, the rebellion will have received a blow in its vital parts from which it may not recover. Yet, we will have much to do, even then if they feel so disposed; they can and no doubt will annoy us as long as they can. If we could secure the leaders, it would be over; the Rebels' soldiery express themselves willing to come back in the Union, if we can believe their own men's account. Your speaking of sympathizing Rebels at home and in a manner you speak of them meets my hearty approbation. Persons in Northland with Secesh proclivities are most detestable of all, but I will not, however express myself; they are too contemptible. A day of retribution is coming.

The health of the camp is good — but a small percent compared with other regiments are sick. We had one death the other day, which was very sudden, considering the disease typhoid fever. He was sick but two days, I think; this was the first in a long time. I will close, as I have written you but a few days since, which I hope you have received. I hope, at least, you will receive some of them. As you have not received any for so long, I expect you will get quite a lot when they do come, so it will take quite a while for you to read and to answer them all.

No more at present, but remain yours as ever and solicit an answer soon,

Samuel Zinser

Richard H. Adams Jr. Photograph courtesy of
Virginia Military Institute Archives.

Richard H. Adams Jr. in later years. Photograph
courtesy of Virginia Military Institute Archives.

Richard H. Adams Jr.

(April 21, 1842 - Oct. 8, 1896)

Richard H. Adams Jr. was born in Marengo, Ala., on April 21, 1842, a son of Richard Henry Adams and Anna Carter Harrison. In May 1861, Richard was mustered into the Company D, Alabama Infantry Regiment.

Richard was serving as a staff officer when he was captured in Nashville, Tenn. During that time, Richard wrote approximately 47 letters home. He also wrote four different diaries while serving with his regiment and in prison. For almost two years, Richard was moved around to various prisons as a prisoner of war, often thinking he was going to exchanged and released. Most of his correspondence was written from prisons at Johnson Island, Point Lookout, Morris Island, Hilton Head and Fort Delaware Prison.

Some of the letters that Richard wrote during the Civil War were sent home to his sweetheart, Lottie Putnam, who may have been his cousin. His letters were very passionate, such as this excerpt from an April 24, 1864 letter: "Ah, well do I remember our first meeting, that day I walked you from the ambulance to the house, where we stopped on that trip, which brought such sunshine to my young heart that was then somewhat unhappy. The sweet whisper of love was first awakened in my breast, and I now love you with a love as sincere and ardent and as devoted as ever filled the breast of man. And now I ask: Am I loved in return? I tremble for your answer."

In June 1865, Richard H. Adams Jr. finally was released from prison. He returned home and married Lottie Putnam. He spent the years after the war working as an engineer and postmaster in Radford, Va. Richard died at the age of 54 on Oct. 8, 1896.

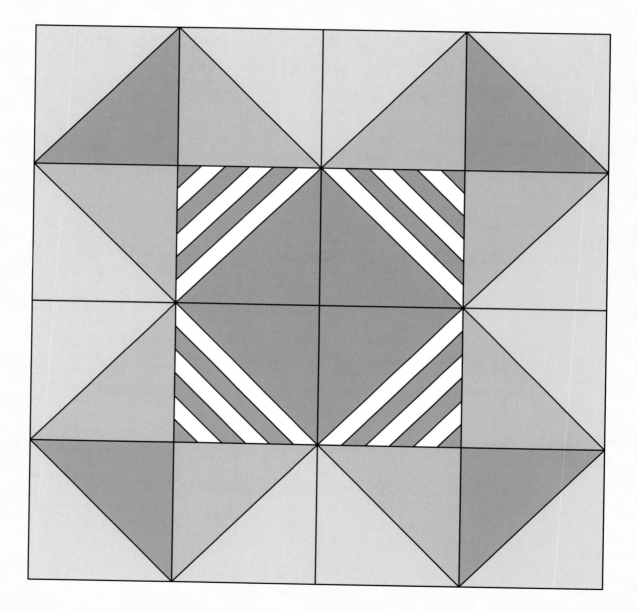

FIRST AND ALWAYS

Nov. 13, 1863

Dear Friend,

You did me great injustice in a letter to Dick Lacy by saying that as soon as I left Nashville, I had forgotten you. What reason have you for accusing me so unjustly? The only reason I could discover is that I had not written to any of the ladies of the "Tea Party." Hear me before you condemn me. Soon after I reached this place, I wrote to Miss McGamock, and a few days afterward, I addressed four pages to the little one whom I now have the honor of addressing. Am I to be accused of forgetting such friends when the mails are to be blamed? I don't think, my amicable little friend, you can in the goodness of your heart accuse me of forgetfulness now when I wrote you such a long letter. I was so willing to write another when I heard you had not received it. You ought to know me better; instead of "out of sight, out of mind," as you have said, you are first and always in my thoughts.

Does my little friend ever look back upon the past and cast a kindly recollection on the attentive Teasley? I hear that you're having a gay time, first in the country and then in the city. How often do you speak of the lisping captain to your friends and say, "I wish he was here?" You must know that you have Dick Lacy a willing captive also; the struggle will be a desperate and interesting one to "lookers on." I want to be "our special artists" and make sketches. The first scene on a boat is on the river, the captain having a good time and receiving considerable encouragement with poor Dick looking on, wishing for some friend to introduce him. I must see it, for I know Lacy to be a brave and dashing soldier in such a cause.

You told Dick Lacy to write to you for what he wanted. I now ask of you ladies to send us a box by express. You can put in it a ham, sausages and some butter, for they won't spoil on the way. Lacy requests me to remind you of the smoking tobacco he wrote to you of. I will remind you and the other ladies of the photographs you promised me. I was sorry you and your friend were disappointed when you went to see us; let me know who she is. I will write to Miss Julia in a few days.

Lt. Lovejoy, alias Lovey, joins Lacy and me in kindest regards to yourself and the other ladies.

Your friend,

Richard Adams

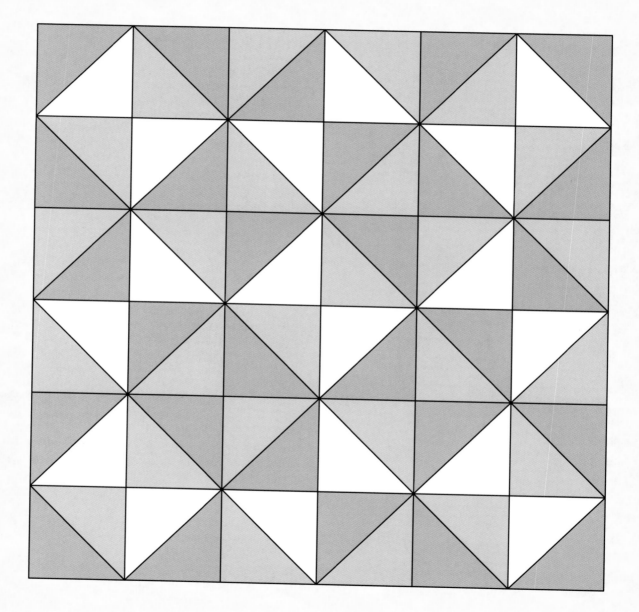

A BETTER CORRESPONDENT

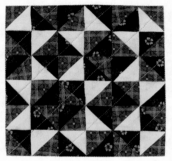

Jan. 1, 1864

Dear Friend,

I've heard, my dear little friend, that it is customary for one to visit all his friends on the first of every year whom he wishes to visit throughout the year. I regret very much that circumstances are such that I cannot pay you a visit, so I send my letter as a substitute. I suggest a correspondence instead of visits, as the latter is entirely out of my power to fulfill, but I can't say that I wish to correspond throughout the year if I have to remain at my present headquarters to carry it on, although that would be a great inducement for me to remain. But as long as I remain here, I have resolved I will be a better correspondent than I have been heretofore. I know you think I treated you badly in letting your last letter remain nearly two weeks unanswered. How has my little friend spent her Christmas? I hope very pleasantly. I well know she thought of her friends on Johnson Island who were living on "pork and beans." I often wished they were with her or with the "loved ones at home." Now, which did you wish? But anyway, the Christmas passed off very pleasantly, although the weather was so disagreeable. I had one glass of eggnog Christmas Day, so, you see, we live in something of a state of civilization and have not forgotten the proper respect that is due to that day. Late in the evening, I visited a friend who gave me a drink of splendid whiskey, or a splendid drink of whiskey, I forgot which. And, to Miss Lottie and the rest of the "Tea Party," I drank.

I'm sorry to inform you that our friend, Dick Lacy, is sick again, but I expect he will again "be up and doing" very soon, as he is improving very fast. Lovey and I are his nurses; if Lovey was a lady, he would be a second Florence Nightingale — "a dear little fellow" (as you ladies would say) he is.

I had another letter from home yesterday, also, one for my brother in Gen. Lee's Army. I never knew really how to appreciate a letter from home before I received a letter in prison. Of course, they hope soon to meet their "dear boy" in Dixie, but I am very much afraid it will be a long time before I am able to relieve all the anxiety they feel about me. My brother gave me more news, as he spoke of a certain "little one" of home you have heard me speak when on that famous trip over Sand Mountain.

Lt. Lacy and Lovey join me in love to yourself and the other ladies. Please send us some stamps, as they are hard to get here.

Your sincere friend,

Dick Adams Jr.

CIRCUMSTANCES ARE SUCH

My Dear Little Friend,

You will see from the heading of this that I have arrived safely at Point Lookout, and I consider it a duty incumbent on me to write immediately to my dear little friend and let her know my whereabouts.

I would have written the day I left Johnson Island, but there was such a stir and such excitement that I could not "compose my nerves sufficiently" to do so. I know our friend Dick Lacy would let you know all. I feel almost lost without him, as he has been my constant companion for so long. Do you not feel sorry for us? I hope, however, if we are so unfortunate as to be long in prison that we will again be able to be together again. I hear there is hope for an exchange. God grant that may be so, but I will regret exceedingly that "circumstances are such" that I will not be able to receive any more of those sweet little letters from my little friend. But, I hope that it will not be long before I am able to hold a verbal correspondence with you.

This is the first time that I ever considered myself fortunate in having a name commencing with A; we were sent off alphabetically. I have several friends among the number, and I am very pleased with my new place of sojourn. We are much better treated and have more privileges than we did at Johnson Island. My spirits are the same, I think a little improved. I never could see the use in being low spirited; no matter how hard someone's conditions might be, a low-spirited man is the murder of his own happiness. I am limited to one page.

As ever, your sincere friend,

Richard Adams Jr.

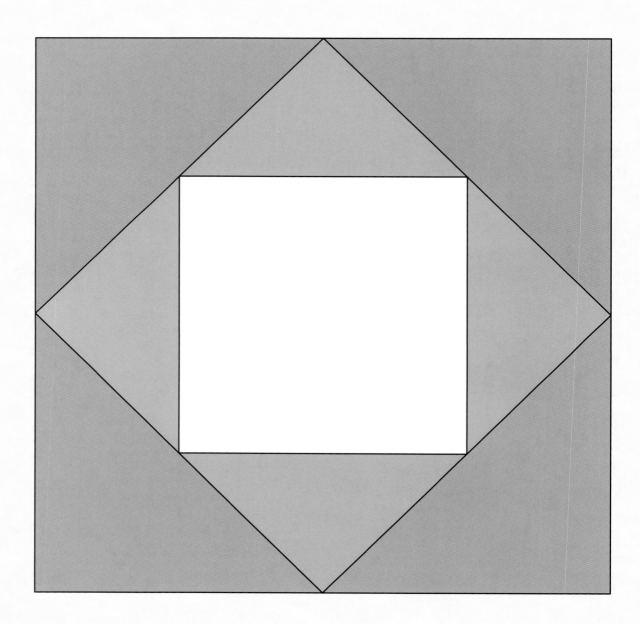

SWEET PLEASURE

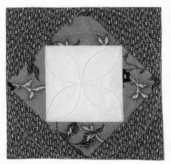

I have replied to your last letter twice, my dearest little friend. It is not your innocent scoldings that cause me to write this, but it is such a sweet pleasure to write to such dear little friends, and also think I will have a second pleasure in a reply to it that only characterizes the sweet disposition of the writer. I like for you to quarrel with me. There is so much of that disposition shown in it. You try to appear mad, but that innocence will show itself in all your attempts at madness. As you think you offend me by such innocent madness, I propose a truce to all disagreements, and let us write to each other as good children, for we are strong friends and hope that we will soon meet in "Dixie" and cultivate that friendship begun under such happy auspices.

My friendship for my dear little friend is as near the "we plus ultra" state as friendship can be, but she has treated me badly in not sending that long-promised photograph, which she knew I would value so highly and would add so much to cheer me in my unhappy condition, like that little sprig of cedar that was given to me descending Sand Mountain on a long-to-be-remembered expedition. I promised in my last to send you mine and now send it enclosed, but a miserable affair. I may never get yours, but if you are informed of my departure before you send it, be sure and carry one through for me.

How often do you hear from Dick? Miss Emma in her last says he writes in very low spirits. I hope you have not been quarreling with him, for he cannot stand it like your "Humble Servant." Where will you be in Dixie? Tell me your P.O. in your next letter. What is "Sis Jule" going to do? Shall I not have the pleasure of seeing her also? I expect the tea party will yet be complete in "Dixie." Love to her and Mrs. McG.

Sincerely your friend,

Dick Adams Jr.

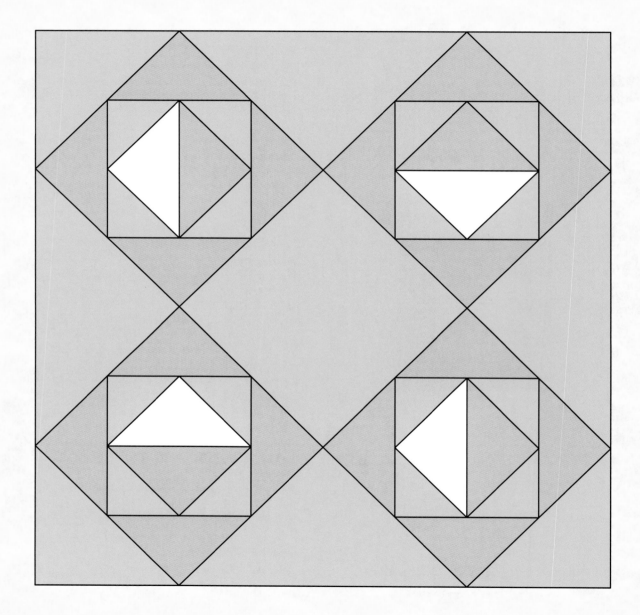

Long-Promised Photograph

April 24, 1864

Dearest Little Friend,

You have doubtless experienced the delight of one who has for some time looked forward to a promised joy or for some scene that said person values more than life itself even, so you can imagine mine when your two sweet missives were handed to me today, and that long-promised photograph was found enclosed in one of them. It brought a new era.

As I mentioned in a former letter, you must be aware that the sun sheds but a sickly light within prison walls, but now that day so long hidden from my vision has caused the most brilliant light to shine, not only within our prison, but upon my heart, which it seems has so long been shut out from sunshine. Like yourself, I take a "sweet glance" and then "on" with the letter.

You speak of our friendship and hope, my dearest friend, that it may be lasting. You must be aware from my actions always toward you and from the tone of my letters — although we have had some childish and innocent little quarrels — that you possess something far more pure and holy than my friendship. Friendship is like a drop to the sea as to explaining my feelings toward you.

Ah, well do I remember our first meeting, that day I walked you from the ambulance to the house, where we stopped on that trip, which brought such sunshine to my young heart that was then somewhat unhappy. The sweet whisper of love was first awakened in my breast, and I now love you with a love as sincere and ardent and as devoted as ever filled the breast of man. And now I ask: Am I loved in return? I tremble for your answer.

I hope you will not think I have spoken too freely. Why keep it forever hidden within my breast? Man was made to love. Sorry indeed am I to learn that you despaired of that anticipated visit to the "sweet sunny South." You will know that your little friend would run to your rescue if you really needed it and brave death itself for you. Still, he hopes to meet you soon in Dixie.

Why ask if you will be remembered when I return to Dixie? You might as well ask the sun, when he sinks behind the western horizon, if he rises in the morning. Yes, as long as life lasts, you will be remembered with feelings warm and true. I hope for an immediate reply to this. I will be true to my promise in writing. We are now in tents, and it is raining, which is the reason why I have made such a miserable scratch of this.

Sincerely and devotedly yours,

Richard Adams

Sweet and Gentle Disposition

May 5, 1864

My Dearest Friend,

You see that I am determined you shall once be satisfied with my writing, and now write this, my fourth letter, since I received your last. I suggest a new arrangement: You write to me every Wednesday, and I to you every Sunday, and I also promise an extra letter now and then, as I am only limited to one page, to make us even. You see, I am willing to do my part, but the quality is so far inferior to yours that I am almost ashamed to offer many in exchange for one of your sweet letters. I know you will agree to the arrangement, so we will proceed immediately with that.

But what will we do for quarreling if our correspondence goes on smoothly? Do you think that made the correspondence more interesting? I like for you to quarrel with me; you try to appear mad, but your sweet and gentle disposition would not allow it, and it was done in such an innocent and unoffending manner. Do not think that my seeming negligence was intended to provoke you to anger and harsh words, for I have proved to you that I was innocent of all the charges you brought against me.

Of "our friends," I hear from my old Mess frequently, and his head is above water. You cannot imagine with what anxiety I'm awaiting your answer to a question I asked in my first to you since I received yours. It seems as though my future life depends upon it, which it does to a great degree. I have often imagined that I've possessed that feeling toward others. But until that meeting with that "dearest little friend" of mine, it was a stranger to my breast, which has now grown to its highest pitch. Do you not think that little friend of mine knew she possessed a great influence over my heart? I would write to her fully and clearly, but circumstances prevent.

Sincerely and devotedly yours,

Richard Adams

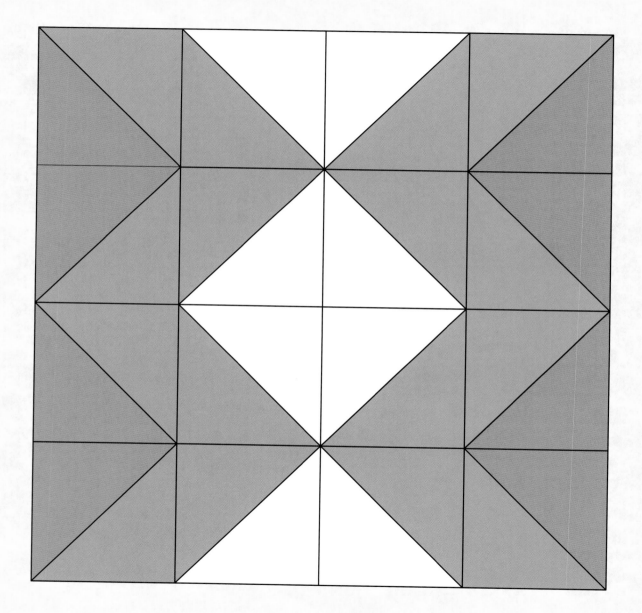

Numerous Excuses

May 29, 1864

My Dear Cousin,

During the past week I have awaited this day, Sunday, almost as anxiously as I have an answer to the many letters I have written you since I received one from you. I must say you have treated me shamefully, for it has been over a month since I received your last. You know in my last, I promised to write to you every Sunday if you would write to me every Wednesday. I am certain you will agree to the arrangement, which is the reason I write this, my sixth letter since I have received one from you. Every day I go to the mail and listen anxiously for my name to be called and hope that it will be from my dearest little cousin, but I am every day disappointed. I cannot stand disappointment and give numerous excuses to myself for you, such as my little cousin has gone south, and perhaps she is offended with my compassionate letter. But as I told you once before, every word of it comes from the bottom of my heart that beats only for my dear little friend of Sand Mountain.

Since I last wrote to you, I have been trying to get sick, but my spirits will not allow it, and I am again indulging in my childish amusements. The sunny air of spring, as warm and glowing as the generous and innocent heart of my little friend, has also cheered me and reminded me of that winning disposition of the "little" friend I so dearly love. Be sure and write every Wednesday. I told you in my last you were limited to one page here often, so you can afford to write one page every week.

Yours with much love,

Richard Adams Jr.

If you write more than one page, I will not receive it.

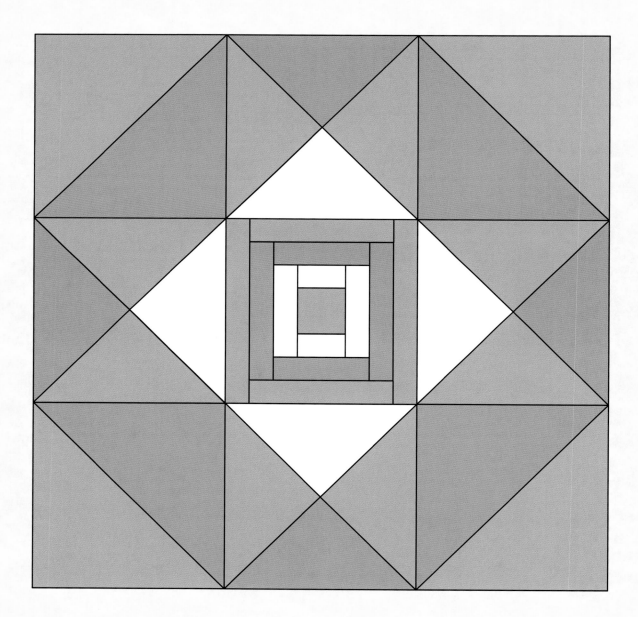

THE STRONGEST EMOTIONS

June 5, 1864

Another Sunday, another letter to my dear Cousin. A day or two since I received yours of the 25th of May, the first I have received from you since your enclosing your photograph.

You say my letters are a mystery, speak of my pretended love, asked me about a "black-eyed beauty" and say that you are certain I am not in earnest. I cannot understand why you look upon them as a mystery, for you must have known that "little" friend of mine possessed a wonderful influence over my heart, and after I have declared that heart all my "little" friend, you accuse me of not being in earnest. Why not tell me at once all and decide for me my fate and future happiness? But you know best. I beseech you to consider well.

I have often imagined I loved, but God being my witness, I will take an oath that my "little" friend is the only one who ever really possessed my heart, all and all. When I was taking that moonlight stroll with her on Sand Mountain, it was in a fit of almost madness that I told her of an imaginary being, for as I have said before, when I first met her, the sweet whisper of love was first awakened in my breast. I then thought she treated me with the greatest indifference (as she had cause to do, for she did not know who or what I was.) I attempted to drive the feeling from my breast by substituting an imaginary paragon for that little friend. I expected the next time I saw her, if ever, she would have forgotten there was such as one in the "land of the living" as Dick. On seeing her again in Nashville, the feeling was uppermost. I thought it was only madness to think of it (as it has turned out) that her affections were elsewhere. And when that photograph was sent, the strongest emotions of love arrived within my heart. I determined then to declare all, and now she will discard all that love. I was really happy in my hopes, although I had never taught myself to believe my love would be reciprocated. I am now prepared for the worst, but she has given me some room for hope as she said she will answer my question when we meet in Dixie. When, oh when, will it be? Night after night, when wrapped in my war-worn blanket on the soft side of a plank, which constitutes my tent floor, I have asked myself that question. Dick has been very sick, but improving. Thanks for one page; it is all I will be allowed to receive. Do you still intend to go South?

As ever, sincerely and devotedly yours,

Richard Adams Jr.

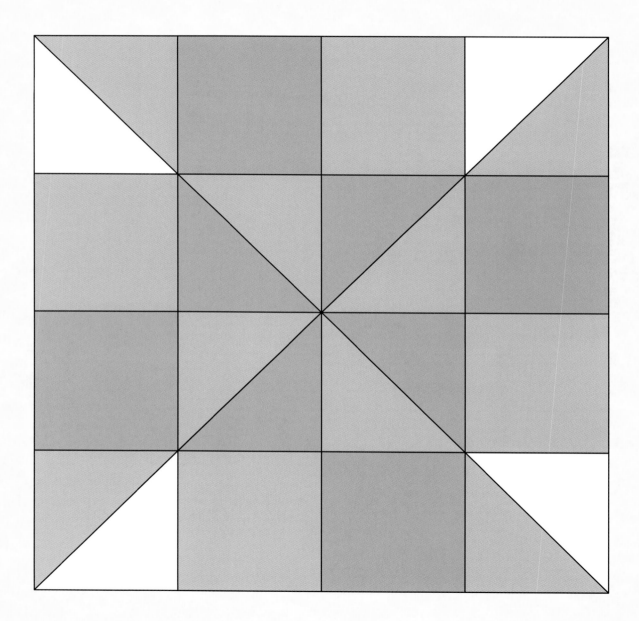

ANOTHER PRISON

June 26, 1864

My Dear Cousin,

Today is Sunday, and you see, although I am fatigued and mourned by my removal to another prison, I have not forgotten my duty. I landed at this, my "new home," yesterday after a very disagreeable trip for three days, partly over the waters of the Chesapeake, partly over the broad Atlantic, and partly over the waters of the Delaware Bay, without sleep in an oven of a vessel. I can assure you that Richard does not feel like himself, and had he a friend whom he could trust and had not passed through the same tiresome trip, I should call him to my aid...

The temptation is so great, and I am such a man of my word, that although I find great trouble in keeping my eyes open, I take great pleasure in writing my thoughts to my little cousin instead of being launched into a sea of repose to indulge in dreams of her, Sand Mountain and my happy past, when I was free as the unfounded wind. Dick is still as true and devoted to my little friend as when he first wrote to her from Point Lookout, trusting his secret to her; is she convinced of his sincerity yet? He thought of her often while he was in the hatch of the ship, where a breath of air never stirred, in her Mountain home, and looked forward with pleasant anticipations for the many missives she promised to shower upon him on your return from your "annual retreat."

You can write as formally as at Johnson Island and when I first went to Point Lookout. I am limited still to one page. I must beg my dear little cousin to excuse this apology for a letter. Please send me some stamps.

Sincerely and devotedly yours,

Richard Adams Jr.

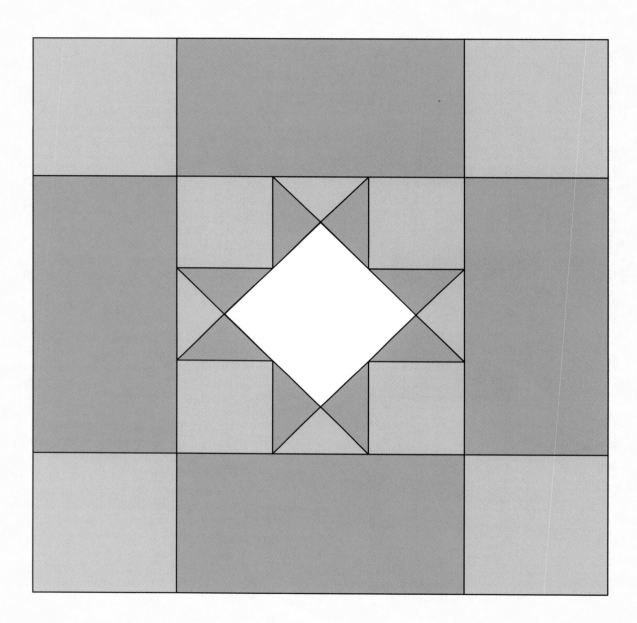

BRIGHTER FUTURE

Having just returned from hearing a good sermon, I am reminded of my promise and what is due my dear little cousin on this holy day.

Since I last wrote to you, I have received two letters from you, dated 19 and 22nd of June, forwarded from Point Lookout. I was almost tempted to answer them immediately, but must be faithful to the letter as to my promise. In one of your letters, you accuse me of not writing regularly since I promised you. I have not known a Sunday to pass unless I mailed a letter to you. Yes, a soft answer turneth away wrath.

Truly as you say, some of the "Tea Party" met by chance. May or may not that chance meeting result in the happiness of Dick, who always looks forward to such a brighter future? Ask my little friend for me; does she really believe yet Dick is not in earnest? I think I now understand her; poor fellow, it hurt him very much to think she would accuse him so unjustly of flirtation. One of your letters to me in reference to it and him caused his boyish heart to beat high and the more hopeful, but the one of later date accused him as before said, and you wanted to see from the tone of his letters if he was speaking truly. I know Sis knew it, and she would also fight for him.

You say you cannot understand why Dick acknowledges such a sacred thing to Miss L., who is unworthy of it all. I do not agree with you. I think she is. It is infidelity against love to think she would love anyone unless she was perfect, in his opinion. He told me he loves her for her virtues, and for her faults he loves her more. I understand your strategy; thank Sis for her affirmative answer, but above all, thank my sweet little friend for seconding the motion. Since I arrived here, I have met my most intimate friend, Lt. Carlson, who supplies the peace of Dick at Johnson Island. He sends his love to my little cousin and with me. Hope soon to meet Miss L. in Dixie. I hope soon to meet her and to know that Dick is the fortunate one to possess her heart. Love to Sis. Thanks for the tobacco, but it has not yet come to hand.

Sincerely and devoted,

Richard Adams Jr.

Excuse this. I write in great haste.

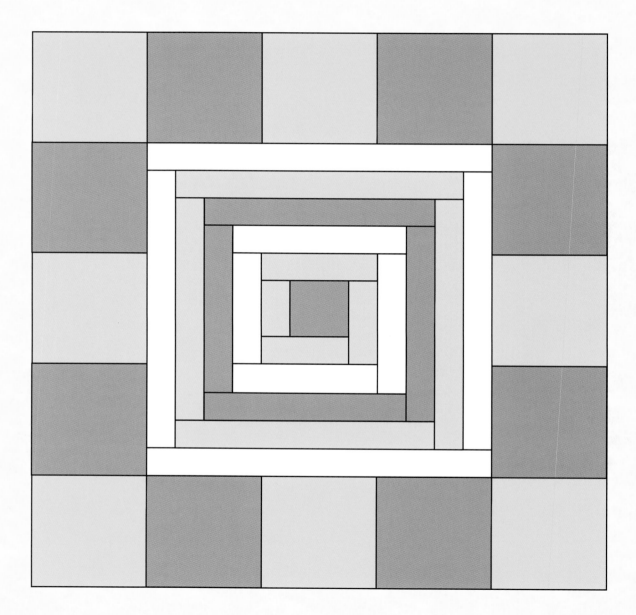

STILL PRISONERS

Sept. 11, 1864

You will see, my dear cousin, I am again on "Terra Firma," but still a prisoner and under very trying circumstances in sight of Charleston, the smoking and under the range of the "Rebel" guns and of the steeples of the churches, in which there are so many "rebellious spirits" at this time, oh divine worship.

You see, I have not forgotten my duty and sweetest pleasure to write to you every Sunday, nor did I forget you while in all my fog at sea, for I wrote you a long letter. Then, we expected to be exchanged as soon as we reached this place, but, for some reason not known to us, we are still prisoners. I am still the hopeful and cheerful being you have always known. We may be here for some time, and we may be exchanged very soon. So, you must write just as soon as you receive this, for you know what a great source of pleasure and comfort your sweet letters are to your prisoner cousin.

Tell my little friend, Birdie, she in all her innocence and loveliness, was not for one moment forgotten, and as soon as I land in Dixie, it shall be my first duty to write to her and yourself... Her devoted admirer told me today he hopes soon to meet her in the sweet, sunny South. My trip from Fort Delaware for the first was much pleasanter than I expected, for I had cabin passage, but all the while we were laying off Hilton Head and Charleston. It was very disagreeable, but still I preferred being on the transport for as long as we were on it. There was a hope of an immediate exchange. I was sorry I did remain long enough to receive the box you sent me, but willingly, I went and would leave everything and give out everything and you know what for an exchange, and that I pleaded as hard for one certain young lady would not believe I was in earnest and really needed it. That is in my estimation for such a priceless gift, and I was such a happy prisoner in possessing it. I would not lose it for the world and all its riches. Tell Sis I wrote to her in one of my letters to you while I was being rocked in the "cradle of the deep." She must write to me by fear of truce. Lt. Robinson promised to write and tell you all about me.

Devotedly,

Richard Adams Jr.

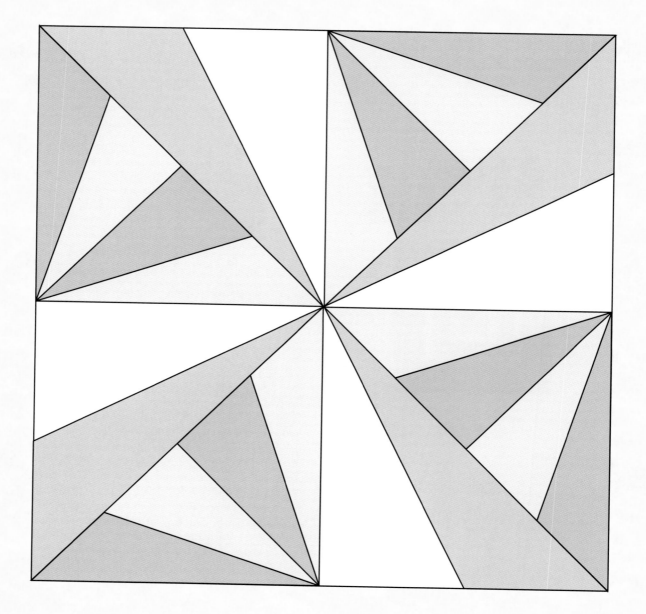

THOSE TWO LETTERS

Nov. 30, 1864

Imagine my delight a day or two since, my dearest Cousin, when two of your sweet missives were handed. Just think: I have spent four long, weary months of imprisonment without a line from my "little Cousin." The only one so near and dear to me within the lines and in one of your letters you say, "perhaps you have learned to forget."

Hard, hard indeed, but I must say I thought the same of my "little Cousin," that she took pity on me while I was a prisoner in a strange land, and as I was so near my Southern home with some chance for exchange, she would cease to cast her bright sunbeams toward my gloomy pathway. Sadness for the first time has possession of me, but as you say, that cloud, like clouds before the sun, was soon dispersed by those two letters. I was happy to know there were no grounds for my thoughts. I also received a sweet sisterly from Sis, dated since you left. She speaks of having received two of my letters to you, so you see, I have been true to my promises and have written every week.

Now, let me give you a small piece of advice. Do not be so hasty to condemn one, but always wait a little while and hear before you condemn. I have just learned it by experience, and so you have, but I have found it hard to make my Little Cousin acknowledge she is in the wrong when she is. It is the reason I write it now. At first, I was wondering why one of your letters was postmarked Louisville, but on reading it, I was happy to know Birdie would be in the land of the free before I would, perhaps. I trust she will not have to count many hours, and I promise I will write to her as often as a letter can go and as long letters as prison regulations will allow.

I am sorry, indeed, I was not present to receive that letter, but it will be safe until I arrive. You must tell Birdie to write to Mother and tell her I have been a good boy since. I have been exiled and I have not been sick, as she thinks. She thinks because I was once quartered in Hammond, I had a dangerous spell of sickness and I would not write about it.

I can assure you, Dick is as true and devoted to Birdie as man can be. Tell her I take good care of him, and he stands his imprisonment like a man. I would like to play escort again, but circumstances will not permit it. Love to Sis, who will forward this to you, for I do not know where to place you in.

Sincerely and devotedly,

Richard Adams Jr.

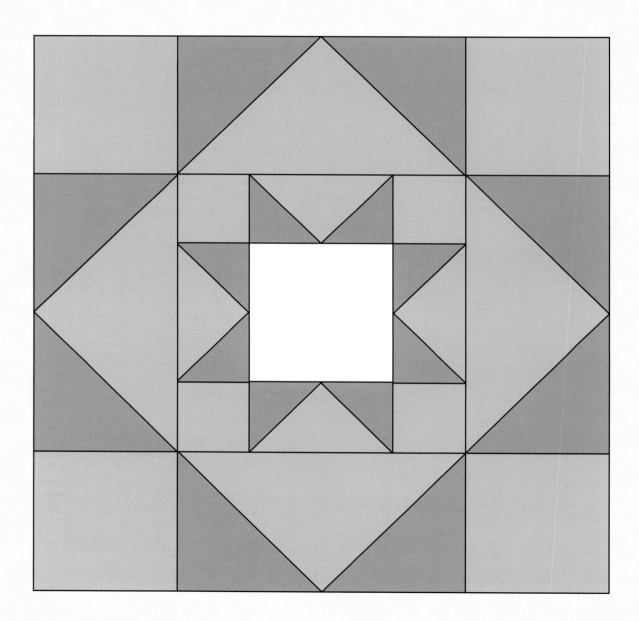

Always Hopeful and Cheerful

Yours of the 22nd of November from V., my Dearest Cousin, came to my hands today. You can well imagine the pleasure the sight of that well-known handwriting afforded me. Can it be that my "Little Cousin" is in the sweet, sunny South and I am still a prisoner? Yes, my eyes do not deceive me, and I sincerely hope it will not be long ere I clasp her hand again in the "happy land" as in the days of yore.

Since I read your letter, I have caught myself again and again putting on the "airs" of an escort. It would have been the height of my ambition to have played an escort again, but alas! "How the mighty have fallen!"

You must write to my mother and tell her what a good Little Cousin you have been since my imprisonment, and what a good boy I have been and have not been sick and would not let her know it as she thinks. If I am so fortunate as to be exchanged, you know my final effort will be to get a furlough and visit my dearest Birdie. You must tell her to write as before, and I will do the same. I saw Lt. Robinson's name among a lot of exchanged prisoners who arrived in Richmond. Yes Lt. C. is a "dear little fellow about 6 feet, 2." One of the noblest-hearted boys living, he is one of the dearest friends of your devoted admirers and very much like him in disposition: always hopeful and cheerful when everything seems "dark and dreary." In other words, they are both men and can stare fate in the face.

I received a letter from Sis the same day I received your two, and answered yours and hers and also wrote to Miss Ida, apologizing with all due submission for being such a diligent correspondent, telling her I was severely reprimanded by "your ladyship" and made numerous promises for the future, but it seems she will not receive them, as Gen. Hood is around Nashville. Give me an account of your trip.

Always your attached Cousin,

Richard Adams Jr.

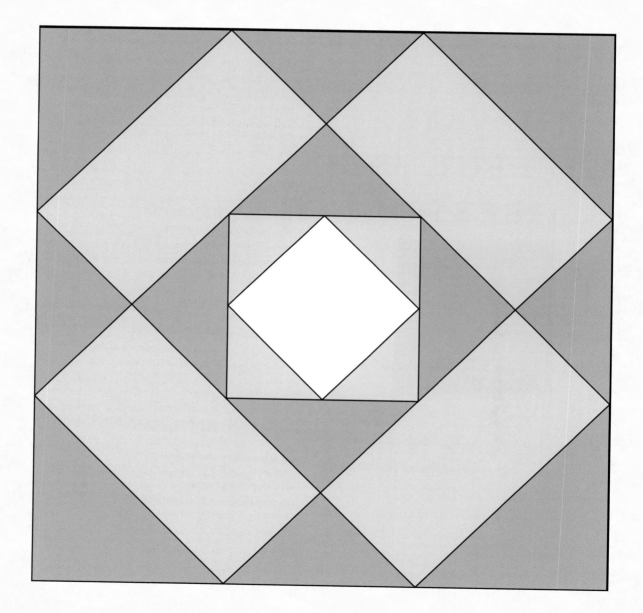

ANGEL VISITS

April 26, 1865

I wrote you some time ago, my Dearest Cousin. Since that time, we have not been allowed to receive or write until a few days ago. Yesterday, I had a letter from Miss Julie, saying three of my letters to you have been forwarded from N. to her, which she had forwarded to you. You will understand why my letters heretofore have been like "Angel visits," although I have tried to make them otherwise.

I trust some little Angel has been guarding my Little Cousin while one who has been happy is more than happy to be her protector has been a captive. I have thought of you continually since the late, sad news from Gen. Lee's Army reached me; it falls heavily on me, and you must know it depressed even my spirits at first, but I am not to be kept down. I shall hope, for it is by hope I have lived for the past 20 months, and not until I know everything has failed and it is useless to indulge longer in hope will I dash the "forlorn hope" with little discretion against the fortifications of fate. If the prisoner is ever so fortunate as to be released, Birdie will see he has been as true to her as to the cause. That hope, with the thought that she is true to me, is my only support. Whenever my spirits began to flag, "Richard is himself again" by glancing at a slip of Mrs. Craddock's letters sent me by Miss Julia, saying "Birdie has a great many admirers but her heart is still, too, to her prison friend and lover." I then have a "heart for every fate."

Give me an account of your late travels and such as the "gay times" you have been having since in A. Miss Julia keeps me posted, I have been longing for a letter from you, for it has been an age since I heard from you and the other dear ones. Have you paid that promised visit to mother? You must know how anxious I am about you and them. I want to direct this to N., as Mrs. McE. has gone home and will forward to you. Love to all.

Yours devotedly,

Richard Adams Jr.

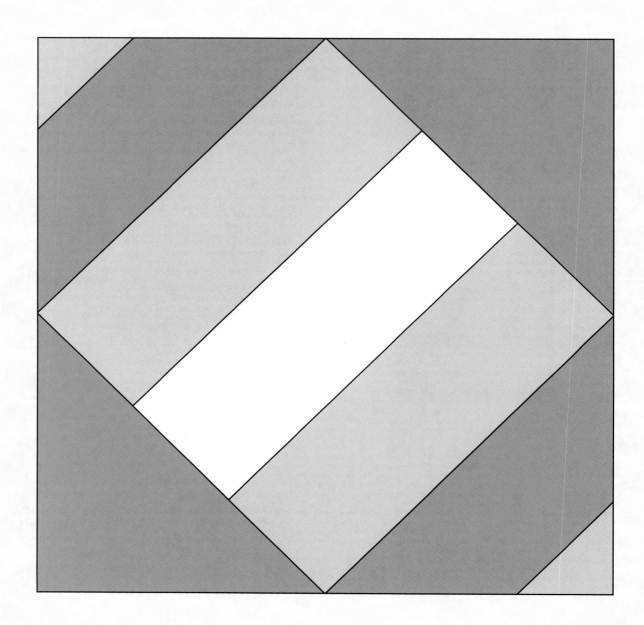

At Last A Free Man

Here I am, at last a free man at my dear old home, surrounded by all the dear ones. I am really a happy man, but you will know, my dearest one, that happiness will not be complete until I can claim you as my own, dearest Birdie. Of course, I have visited all my relatives and first of all, my "little sister cousin." She was very happy to see her "pet cousin," as she said, and commenced her questions very soon about "Miss Lottie," and is very anxious to form your acquaintance. Although she says she feels as though she had known you as a very dear friend for the interest you have taken in me. I saw your two letters to her; by across questioning, she tried to find out the secret (like that generality of Lady is a great deal of curiosity), but I suppose she was thinking of my future welfare and happiness, for she said she knew she would love Miss Lottie dearly as a cousin. I know Miss Lottie would love the dear "little girl" as such. I had written that note to be sent by return train to Artesia the morning I left you, but saw no one home I thought I could trust it with. So, I thought I would wait until Sunday and write you that long letter I promised. I was really ashamed that I was compelled to show so little gallantry and leave you to wait for your train, but saw you were in good hands and felt that I could trust you. Although I flatter myself, I would have made a more gallant escort, much truer than when I was your "military escort."

I will write to you as soon as I can pay you that visit. I do not know whether postal arrangements are well-enough made to take this to you, but as I have never broken a promise made you, I will visit you. Just from church saw all the young ladies of the neighborhood except "our friend," Miss Augusta Du Bose, who was on a visit in another neighborhood. She has lost four brothers since the war and several other families in this once-gay neighborhood have "vacant chairs." It makes me very sad in visiting very old friends.

I would really be one of the happiest man in the South now were you mine or were I conversing with you tonight about this subject nearest my heart, but I trust we will have but very little more talking to do but to act. I regret very much I did not see Mr. Putnam while I was in Nashville and have a little conversation with him. I suspect he thinks rather strangely of it, that I cannot be as I see her as I ought to be, as our acquaintance has been so short, but I know my heart and you, Miss Lottie, acknowledged you were convinced of my sincerity. I think we know each other, but we will say nothing more about such things now. Soon, we will meet in Nashville and arrange all. Mother was very sorry you did not receive her letter in answer to yours and pay her visit. She sends her love. Lizzie says "be sure and give my love to Miss Lottie and tell her I will write to her very soon."

Yours devotedly,

Richard Adams Jr.

P.S. I scarcely know what I have written. I beg of you to excuse this, my first from home after release, as you must know my feelings. Although this is a most pleasant duty, yet I am almost wild with joy and not accustomed to writing like a free man. Goodbye.

HOME SWEET HOME

July 15, 1865

You have, no doubt, received my first written from "home sweet home," and I am so anxiously awaiting an answer. I think it was to prove that anxiety by a few lines to my dearest one. Let me now congratulate you on your arrival home. I could not do so in my last, as you had not then arrived, but now you, like myself, are surrounded by all the dear ones at home with the exception of C. You cannot claim Miss C. as belonging to your home, as you all have given her away. I fell in love with her at Mrs. McE.'s nearly as much so as with the "little fair-haired sister." My older brother has arrived here a few days ago with his bride from Mobile, so we cannot call our domicile a bachelor's hall any longer. I sometimes think it a great pity to break up the ease of comfort of the "establishment," but it is said "everything happens for the best." Therefore, I do not cry when I think of days gone by, which passed so pleasantly at that place. Perhaps a pleasure found in those days was only imaginary, and the smiles of one of the fairest may produce a new charm; at any rate, there will be a nice little housekeeper.

I have often thought that Miss Lottie would think of that place when I am the fortunate and happy one you know. I doubt no one until I have the best reason in the world for doing so. I am certain from what Miss Lottie told me in Columbus that I am fortunate enough to possess a great treasure (her love). Everything is being rapidly arranged now, and I can soon pay you that promised visit. I can do nothing until that is arranged; as soon as I start, I will telegraph you from the nearest place to let you know I am en route.

I attended a party in the neighborhood in which Miss Taylor lives a few nights ago. Her remark to me at first was "is that Miss Lottie Putnam a lovely character." I told her I knew her very slightly. She laughed very mischievously and said ,"I know all about you, Sis." I had nothing more to say until she asked when you were to live in this portion of the world. Smart young lady, is she not?

I hope you have a gay and pleasant time since you arrived at home.

All of my relatives are very curious to find out something about that letter "a young lady from Tennessee wrote my mother." They are always informed; that is my business. I have told Lizzie all I could. Do you object? I hope not. She always keeps my secrets. I have written in great haste, as I will have an opportunity to send this when the mails are in "running order."

Ever, yours devotedly,

Richard Adams Jr.

P.S. Direct hereafter to Uniontown, Perry Company, Alabama. I am no longer in idle man in a few days at my father's house, but a "country farmer," a working free man.

David Bailey Freeman

(May 1, 1851-June 18, 1929)

Written by Alan Freeman

David Bailey Freeman, the son of Beverly Allen Freeman, a lawyer, and Mary Ann Reynolds Murray, was born May 1st, 1851, in Ellijay, Gilmer County, Georgia and was reared in middle Georgia and Gordon County. David's brother Madison Montgomery Freeman (1840-1869) was crippled with White Swelling (now known as phlebitis) but was a member of the Fulton Blues and full of military spirit. He was elected Lieutenant and was uncertain if he could serve due to his disease. He asked his mother to allow David to go to camp with him as his aid. David was the tender age of 10 years old, one month before his 11th birthday. So they headed into Camp Felton, near Cartersville. There, was organized Smith's Legion, comprised of an infantry battalion and a Calvary battalion. David was offered position as a "Marker" for the Calvary, and with his mother's and brother's consent, he enlisted in the 6th Georgia Calvary Company D. David's father had passed away when David was only four years old.

David wrote his recollections after the war and wrote: We took our sleeps in the woods well away from the roads and were four days on our way. We were fired on several times and narrowly escaped being captured or killed. At Cumberland gap we were halted by guards, to whom we told our story of special service, but as we had no official papers and they would not let us pass. We moved back well out of sight and awaited some wagons we knew. Those of Colonel Maddox's Regiment came along. We were allowed to hide, each, in a wagon, with horse tied behind, thus we evaded the guards, finding our command over the mountain.

David served two years; and then the last two years of the Civil War. He was self-proclaimed to be the youngest confederate soldier, but with no other contenders, was given the title. In his later years, David was active in his newspaper he was a politician, and was active in the United Confederate Veterans, and a friend to other veterans, helping them with their veteran affairs and their pension problems. He had been awarded rank of lieutenant in the Civil War, however with the U.C.V., he earned the title and rank of "General."

Late on the evening of June 18th, 1929, at the age of 77, General David Bailey Freeman, the Civil War's youngest confederate soldier, quietly and peacefully died of a heart attack in his apartment in Atlanta, Georgia. He had been ill for several days, and had just returned from a Confederate Veterans Reunion in North Carolina just 10 days earlier. Many of the obituaries named David as "General Freeman", and all pointed to his youthful service to the Confederate States of America.

David Bailey Freeman. Photograph
Courtesy of Alan Freeman.

David Bailey Freeman. Photograph
Courtesy of Alan Freeman.

Robert W. Bennett

(Dec. 25, 1844 - Oct. 27, 1864)

Written by Megan Taylor Harding

Robert W. Bennett was born on Christmas day 1844 to Henry Innes and Sarah Witham Bennett in Mechanicsburg, Ind.

Henry, who served as a justice of the peace in his township for 16 years, was a devout Christian who spent a lot of time studying scripture. When asked in 1861 to deliver a speech to gain recruits for the Civil War in 1861, Henry eagerly agreed. His moving speech prompted many young men to line up to join the service, but Henry was shocked when his eldest son, Robert, who was barely 18, was the first to mount the podium. As Robert signed up, his father wept. Before Robert departed for the front lines, Henry gave his son a cherished pocket Bible, which Robert probably carried over his heart.

Robert W. Bennett enlisted as a private in Company D 72nd Indiana volunteers, a scouting unit whose soldiers were mounted on horses and whose focus was to locate and harass the enemy. In one of the forays made by his regiment, now famous as Wilder's Brigade, Robert was captured and thrown into Andersonville prison. Here, all news of Robert ended until one of his gaunt and sickly friends, Henry Nabes, showed up at Robert's father's doorstep to deliver a small pocket Bible. While in Andersonville prison, Robert and three of his comrades planned an escape and dug a narrow passage to tunnel out. When it appeared the time was right to leave, Robert was so weak from hunger and thirst that he knew that he would not make it or would be so slow he would risk his friends being recaptured.

Robert encouraged his friends to go ahead without him. He said he would pray for their escape and would do his best to hide the entrance to the tunnel. Robert passed his Bible to Henry Nabes and asked him deliver the Bible to his sister, Martha Catherine, saying she would miss him the most. Robert then dragged his body over the entrance to the passage, where he passed away. By the time the guards moved his body the next morning and discovered the tunnel, his friends were safely on their way to freedom.

The notice that later reached the family was that Robert had died of scurvy on Oct. 27, 1864. His sister, Mary Catherine Bennett Pavey, always cherished Robert's Bible, and it has been safely handed down in her family.

Robert W. Bennett.
Photograph
courtesy of Paul
Harding.

Martha Catherine
Bennett Pavey.
Photograph
courtesy of Paul
Harding.

UNION SOLDIER PATTERN

FOR MY LOVE

Finished size: 59" x 73". Pieced by Gay Bomers;
machine quilted by Tammy Finkler.

MATERIALS

· 3 yd. of fabric for border and binding
· 1 yd. of fabric for lattice strips
· 2¼ yd. of fabric for background and cornerstones
· Scraps of assorted fabrics to make 48 of your favorite blocks
· 4 yd. of fabric for backing
· 67" x 81" of batting
· General tools and supplies (listed in How to Use This Book)

CUTTING INSTRUCTIONS

From the cornerstone fabric, cut:
· 63 cornerstones (1½" x 1½")
From the lattice fabric, cut:
· 110 lattice strips (1½" x 6½")
From the inner border fabric, cut:
·2 border strips (43½" x 3½")
·2 border strips (61½" x 3½")
From the outer border fabric, cut:
·2 border strips (61½" x 6½")
·2 border strips (59½" x 6½")
From the backing fabric, cut:
· 2 strips (2 yd. x the width of the fabric)
· 8 binding strips (2" x the width of the fabric)

ASSEMBLY INSTRUCTIONS

1. Using various scraps, piece 48 of your favorite blocks.
Refer to Piecing the Blocks, page 8.

2. Assemble the pieced blocks, lattice and cornerstones into
seven rows of six blocks each. Refer to Assembling the Quilt,
page 9. The connecting rows will contain seven cornerstones
and six lattice strips.

3. Sew the inner border strips, 3½" x 43½" to the top and
bottom of the assembled blocks.

4. Sew the inner border strips, 3½" x 61½" to the sides of the
blocks of the assembled blocks.

5. Sew the outer border strips that measure 6½" x 61½" to
the sides of the assembled blocks.

6. Sew outer border strips, 6½" x 59½" to the top and
bottom of the assembled blocks.

7. Stitch together the two backing fabric strips. Trim the
sewn unit into a 67" x 81" rectangle.

8. Assemble the backing, batting and quilt top. Refer to
Adding the Backing, page 9.

9. Bind the quilt. Refer to Binding the Quilt, page 9.

Homeward Bound

Finished size: 37" x 37". Pieced and quilted by Christine Yeager.

Materials

· 1 yd. of fabric for border and binding
· ½ yd. of fabric for lattice strips
· ⅛ yd. of fabric for cornerstones
· 1 yd. of fabric for background
· Scraps of assorted fabrics to make blocks and appliqués
· 1¼ yd. of fabric for backing
· 45" x 45" of batting
· Soldier patterns on pages 271 and 273
· General tools and supplies (listed in How to Use This Book)

Cutting Instructions

From the cornerstone and lattice strips fabric cut:
   · 24 cornerstones (1½" x 1½")
   · 36 lattice strips (1 ½" x 6 ½")
From the background fabric for the appliqués, cut:
   · 1 square, 13½" x 13½"
From the border fabric, cut:
   · 2 border strips (4½" x 29½")
   · 2 border strips (4½" x 37½")
From backing fabric, cut:
   · 1 backing square (45" x 45")
From the binding fabric, cut:
   · 6 binding strips (2" wide x the length of the fabric)

Assembly Instructions

1. Assemble 12 of your favorite blocks using the various fabric scraps. Refer to Piecing the Blocks, page 8.

2. Appliqué the soldiers onto the background fabric. Refer to the instructions on page 287.

3. Assemble the blocks, lattice and cornerstones into two rows of four blocks each. Refer to Assembling the Quilt, page 9. The connecting rows will contain five cornerstones and four lattice strips. Also assemble two rows horizontally of two blocks each. They will be connected by one lattice strip between the rows and will have added to the outer side two lattice strips and one cornerstone.

4. Assemble the quilt so the 13½" x 13½" square is in the middle and the two rows of two blocks are each on each side; refer to the photograph for details. Next, add the sections of four blocks to the top and the bottom of your quilt.

5. Sew the border strips that measure 4½" x 29½" to the top and bottom of the assembled blocks.

6. Sew the border strips that measure 4½" x 37½" to the sides of the assembled blocks.

7. Assemble the backing, batting and quilt top. Refer to Adding the Backing, page 9.

8. Bind the quilt. Refer to Binding the Quilt, page 9.

CIVIL WAR SOLDIER QUILT

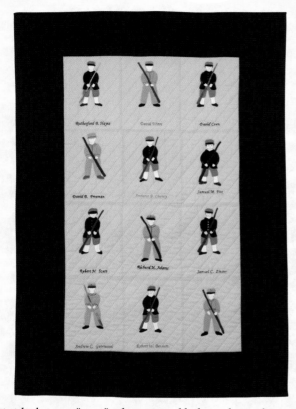

Finished size: 36" x 54". There are 12 blocks in this quilt — one to represent each soldier in the book and a blank one to which you can add your name or the name of a Civil War ancestor. A group of special ladies that I meet with on Tuesdays at the Attic Window Quilt Shop completed blocks for this quilt. The blocks were made by: Roberta Decker, Sally Johnson, Christine Yeager, Annette Hampton, Barbara David, Sue Steinhauer, Virginia Bergmans, Norma Zawistowski, Audrey Berkenpas, Suzanne Schultz, Bonnie Major and Pat Anisko. Assembled by Rosemary Youngs; machine quilted by Tammy Finkler.

MATERIALS
· 1 yd. of background fabric
· Scraps of assorted fabrics to make soldier appliqués
· 1½ yd. of border fabric
· 2¼ yd. of backing and binding fabric
· Black embroidery floss or black permanent ink fabric pen
· Embellishments as desired (optional)
· 45" x 62" of batting
· Soldier patterns on pages 271 and 273
· General tools and supplies (listed in How to Use This Book)

CUTTING INSTRUCTIONS
From the background fabric, cut:
· 12 blocks (8½" x 11")
From the border fabric, cut:
· 2 border strips (6½" x 42½")
· 2 border strips (6½" x 36½")
From the backing fabric, cut:
· 6 binding strips (2" wide x the width of the fabric)
· 1 rectangle 44" x 62"

ASSEMBLY INSTRUCTIONS
1. Using the soldier patterns to represent the soldiers featured in this book, appliqué one soldier on each of the 12 blocks. Follow the appliqué instructions on page 287.
2. Add the name of each Civil War soldier to each block. Use two strands of black embroidery floss to stitch each name, or use a permanent ink fabric pen to write each name. Add other embellishments, including the hair or facial features, as desired.
3. Assemble four rows of three blocks. Follow the instructions for Assembling the Quilt, page 9.
4. Sew the border strips that measure 6½" x 42½" to the sides of the quilt.
5. Sew the border strips that measure 6½" x 36½" to the top and bottom of the quilt.
6. Assemble the backing, batting and quilt top. Refer to Adding the Backing, page 9.
7. Bind the quilt. Refer to Binding the Quilt, page 9.

Civil War Table Runner

Finished size: 23" x 37". Machine pieced and machine quilted by Barbara David.

MATERIALS

· ¼ yd. of fabric for background
· ¾ yd. of fabric for borders and binding
· ¼ yd. of fabric for lattice strips
· ⅛ yd. of fabric for cornerstones
· Scraps of assorted fabrics to make blocks
· 1 yd. of backing fabric
· 31" x 44" of batting
·General tools and supplies (listed in How to Use This Book)

CUTTING INSTRUCTIONS

From the cornerstone fabric, cut:
  · 15 cornerstones (1½" x 1½")
From the lattice fabric, cut:
  · 22 lattice strips (1½" x 6½")
From the outer border fabric, cut:
  · 2 border strips (15½" x 4½")
  · 2 border strips (37½" x 4½")
From the backing fabric, cut:
  · 1 rectangle (31" x 44")
From the binding fabric, cut:
  · 4 binding strips (2" wide x the width of the fabric)

ASSEMBLY INSTRUCTIONS

1. Assemble eight of your favorite blocks using the various scraps of fabric. Refer to Piecing the Blocks, page 8.
2. Assemble the blocks, lattice and cornerstones into two rows of four blocks. Refer to Assembling the Quilt, page 9. The connecting rows will contain five cornerstones and five lattice strips.
3. Sew the border strips that measure 15½" x 4½" to the sides of the assembled blocks.
4. Sew the border strips that measure 37½" x 4½" to the top and bottom of the assembled blocks.
5. Assemble the backing, batting and quilt top. Refer to Adding the Backing, page 9.
6. Bind the quilt. Refer to Binding the Quilt, page 9.

WORDS OF LOVE IN TIMES OF WAR

Finished size: 34" x 41". Pieced and quilted by Dagmar Kessler.

MATERIALS

· 1 yd. of fabric for outer borders and binding
· ⅜ yd. of fabric for inner border
· ½ yd. of fabric for lattice strips
· ½ yd. of fabric for background and cornerstones
· Scraps of assorted fabrics to make blocks
· 1½ yd. of fabric for backing
· 42" x 49" of batting
· General tools and supplies (listed in How to Use This Book)

CUTTING INSTRUCTIONS

From the cornerstone fabric, cut:
· 20 cornerstones (1½" x 1½")
From the lattice fabric, cut:
· 31 lattice strips (1½" x 6½")
From the inner border fabric, cut:
· 2 border strips (22½" x 2½")
· 2 border strips (33½" x 2½")
From the outer border fabric, cut:
· 2 border strips (26½" x 4½")
· 2 border strips (41½" x 4½")
From the backing fabric, cut:
· 1 rectangle (42" x 49")
From the binding fabric, cut:
· 4 binding strips (2" wide x the width of the fabric)

ASSEMBLY INSTRUCTIONS

1. Assemble 12 of your favorite blocks. Refer to Piecing the Blocks, page 8.

2. Assemble the blocks, lattice and cornerstones into four rows of three blocks each. Refer to Assembling the Quilt, page 9. The connecting row will contain three lattice strips with four cornerstones.

3. Sew the inner border pieces that measure 22½" x 2½" to the top and bottom of the assembled blocks.

4. Sew the inner border pieces that measure 33½" x 2½" to the sides of the assembled blocks.

5. Sew the outer border pieces that measure 26½" x 4½" to the top and bottom of the assembled blocks.

6. Sew the outer border pieces that measure 41½" x 4½" to the sides of the assembled blocks.

7. Assemble the backing, batting and quilt top. Refer to Adding the Backing, page 9.

8. Bind the quilt. Refer to Binding the Quilt, page 9.

Home Warmer

Finished size: 41" x 41". Pieced and quilted by Carol Shultz, who made this especially for her daughter, Jennifer, for her new home.

Materials

· 1½ yd. of fabric for background, binding and borders
· ¼ yd. of fabric for lattices
· ⅛ yd. of fabric for cornerstones
· Scraps of assorted fabrics to make blocks
· 1½ yd. of fabric for backing
· 49" x 49" of batting
· General tools and supplies (listed in How to Use This Book)

Cutting Instructions

From the cornerstone fabric, cut:
· 25 cornerstones (1½" x 1½")
From the lattice fabric, cut:
· 40 lattice strips (1½" x 6½")
From the border fabric cut:
· 2 border strips (6½" x 29½")
· 2 border strips (6½" x 41½")
From the backing fabric, cut:
· 1 rectangle (44" x 49")
· 1 strip (5½" x 49")
From the binding fabric, cut:
· 4 binding strips (2" wide x the width of the fabric)

Assembly Instructions

1. Assemble 16 of your favorite blocks. Refer to Piecing the Blocks, page 8.
2. Assemble the blocks, lattice and cornerstones into four rows of four blocks each. Refer to Assembling the Quilt, page 9. The connecting rows will contain five cornerstones and four lattice strips.
3. Add the border strips that measure 6½" x 29½" to the sides of the assembled blocks.
4. Add the border strips that measure 6½" x 41½" to the top and bottom of the assembled blocks.
5. Sew the 5½" x 49" strip to one of the 44" sides of the backing rectangle to make a 49" x 49" square.
6. Assemble the backing, batting and quilt top. Refer to Adding the Backing, page 9.
7. Bind the quilt. Refer to Binding the Quilt, page 9.

STARS AND STRIPES TABLE RUNNER

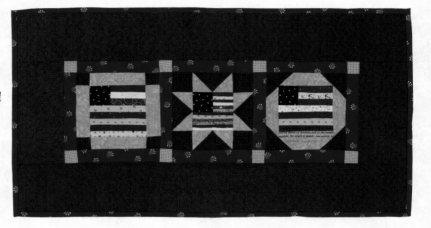

Finished size: 16" x 30". Pieced and quilted by Maureen Baly.

MATERIALS

· 1 yd. of fabric for background, borders, and binding
· ⅛ yd. of fabric for lattice strips
· ⅛ yd. of fabric for cornerstones
· Scraps of assorted fabrics to make blocks
· 1 yd. of fabric for backing
· 24" x 32" of batting
· General tools and supplies (listed in How to Use This Book)

CUTTING INSTRUCTIONS

From the cornerstone fabric, cut:
   · 8 cornerstones (1½" x 1½")
From the lattice fabric, cut:
   · 10 lattice strips (1½" x 6½")
From the outer border fabric, cut:
   · 2 border strips (8½" x 4½")
   · 2 border strips (30½" x 4½")
From the backing fabric, cut:
   · 1 rectangle (24" x 38")
From the binding fabric, cut:
   · 3 binding strips (2" wide x the width of the fabric)

ASSEMBLY INSTRUCTIONS

1. Assemble three of your favorite blocks using the various scraps. Refer to Piecing the Blocks, page 8.

2. Assemble the pieced blocks, lattice and cornerstones into one row of three blocks. Refer to Assembling the Quilt, page 9. The connecting rows will contain four cornerstones and four lattice strips.

3. Sew the border strips that measure 8½" x 4½" to the sides of the assembled blocks.

4. Sew the border strips that measure 30½" x 4½" to the top and bottom of the assembled blocks.

5. Assemble the backing, batting and quilt top. Refer to Adding the Backing, page 9.

6. Bind the quilt. Refer to Binding the Quilt, page 9.

ROSEMARY'S NINE BLOCK

Finished size: 28" x 28". Machine pieced and quilted by Margo Spencer.

MATERIALS
- ¾ yd. of fabric for borders and binding
- Scraps of assorted fabrics to make blocks
- ⅛ yd. of fabric for cornerstones
- ¼ yd. of fabric for lattice strips
- 1 yd. of fabric for backing
- 36" x 36" of batting
- General tools and supplies (listed in How to Use This Book)

CUTTING INSTRUCTIONS
From the border fabric, cut:
- 2 border strips (3½" x 22½")
- 2 border strips (3½" x 28½")

From the cornerstone fabric, cut:
- 16 squares (1½" x 1½")

From the lattice strips fabric, cut:
- 24 lattice strips (1½" x 6½")

From the backing fabric, cut:
- 1 panel (36" x 36")

From the binding fabric, cut:
- 4 strips (2" x the width of the fabric)

INSTRUCTIONS
1. Assemble nine of your favorite blocks. Refer to Piecing the Blocks, page 8.

2. Assemble the blocks, lattice and cornerstones into three rows of three blocks each. Refer to Assembling the Quilt, page 9. The connecting row will contain four cornerstones and three lattice strips.

3. Sew the border strips that measure 3½" x 22½" to the top and bottom of the assembled blocks.

4. Sew the border strips that measure 4½" x 28½" to the sides of the assembled blocks.

5. Assemble the backing, batting and quilt top. Refer to Adding the Backing, page 9.

6. Bind the quilt. Refer to Binding the Quilt, page 9.

Soldiers of the Civil War

Finished size: 41" x 62". Machine pieced and hand embroidered by Susan Zomberg; machine quilted by Tammy Finkler.

Materials

· 2½ yd. of fabric for borders, binding and ovals for soldiers
· ½ yd. of fabric for lattice strips
· ⅛ yd. of fabric for cornerstones
· 1 yd. of fabric for background
· Scraps of assorted fabrics to make blocks and appliqués
· 4 yd. of fabric for backing
· 49" x 71" batting
· Soldier patterns on pages 271 and 273
· General tools and supplies (listed in How to Use This Book)

Cutting Instructions

From the cornerstone and lattice strips fabric cut:
  · 38 cornerstones (1½" x 1½")
  · 67 lattice strips (1½" x 6½")
From the background fabric for the embroidered squares, cut:
  · 2 squares (13½" x 13½")
From the border fabric, cut:
  · 2 border strips (6½" x 50½")
  · 2 border strips (6½" x 41½")
  · 2 squares (13½" x 13½")
From backing fabric, cut
  · 2 rectangles (2 yd. x the width of the fabric)
From the binding fabric, cut:
  · 8 binding strips (2" x the width of the fabric)

Instructions

1. Assemble 20 of your favorite blocks using the various scraps of fabric. Refer to Piecing the Blocks, page 8.
2. Embroider the soldiers onto the background fabric, place the 13½" x 13½" border fabric over the soldiers. Appliqué the oval around the soldiers. Follow the appliqué instructions on page 287.
3. Assemble the blocks, lattice and cornerstones. Refer to Assembling the Quilt, page 9. Four of the connecting rows will contain eight cornerstones and seven lattice strips. Assemble three rows horizontally of two blocks each. Assemble the quilt with the 13½" x 13½" squares in the middle, with two rows of two blocks each on each side. Refer to the photograph. Next add the two rows of seven blocks each to the top and bottom of your quilt.
4. Sew the border strips that measure 6½" x 50½" to the top and bottom of the assembled blocks.
5. Sew the border strips that measure 6½" x 41½" to the sides of the assembled blocks.
6. Sew the two pieces of backing fabric together, and trim the unit to create a rectangle that measures 49" x 71".
7. Assemble the backing, batting and quilt top. Refer to Adding the Backing, page 9.
8. Bind the quilt. Refer to Binding the Quilt, page 9.

JoAnn's Civil War Table Runner

Finished size: 16" x 37". Pieced and hand quilted by JoAnn Fuhler.

MATERIALS

- 1 yd. of fabric for borders and binding
- ¼ yd. of fabric for background
- ⅛ yd. of fabric for lattice strips
- ⅛ yd. of fabric for cornerstones
- Scraps of assorted fabrics to make blocks
- ¾ yd. of fabric for backing
- 24" x 45" batting
- General tools and supplies (listed in How to Use This Book)

CUTTING INSTRUCTIONS

From the cornerstone fabric cut:
- 10 cornerstones (1½" x 1½")

From the lattice strip fabric cut:
- 13 lattice strips (1½" x 6½")

From the border fabric, cut:
- 2 border strips (4½" x 8½")
- 2 border strips (4½" x 37½")

From backing fabric, cut:
- 1 rectangle (24" x 45")

From the binding fabric, cut:
- 4 binding strips (2" x the width of the fabric)

INSTRUCTIONS

1. Assemble four of your favorite blocks using the various scraps of fabric. Refer to Piecing the Blocks, page 8.

2. Assemble the blocks, lattice and cornerstones into one row of four blocks. Refer to Assembling the Quilt, page 9. The connecting rows will contain eight cornerstones and seven lattice strips. The connecting rows will contain five cornerstones and five lattice strips.

3. Sew the border strips that measure 4½" x 8½" to the sides of the assembled blocks.

4. Sew the border strips that measure 4½" x 37½" to the top and bottom of the assembled blocks.

6. Assemble the backing, batting and quilt top. Refer to Adding the Backing, page 9.

7. Bind the quilt. Refer to Binding the Quilt, page 9.

CHOCOLATE AND RASPBERRIES

Finished size: 56" x 68". Machine pieced by Natalie Randall; machine quilted by Carol Huster.

MATERIALS

· 2½ yd. of fabric for borders and binding
· 1½ yd. of fabric for alternate squares
· 1½ yd. of fabric for inner border
· Scraps of assorted fabrics to make blocks
· ⅛ yd. of fabric for cornerstones
· ¼ yd. of fabric for lattice strips
· 4½ yd. of fabric for backing
· 64" x 76" of batting
· General tools and supplies (listed in How to Use This Book)

CUTTING INSTRUCTIONS

From the inner border fabric, cut:
· 2 border strips (1½" x 54½")
· 2 border strips (1½" x 44½")
From the outer border fabric, cut:
· 2 border strips (6½" x 58½")
· 2 border strips (6½" x 56½")
From the alternate square fabric, cut:
· 36 squares (6½" x 6½")
From the backing fabric, cut:
· 2 rectangles (76" x the width of the fabric)
From the binding fabric, cut:
· 4 strips (2" x the width of the fabric)

INSTRUCTIONS

1. Assemble 32 of your favorite blocks. Refer to Piecing the Blocks, page 8.

2. Assemble the blocks; alternate each pieced block with a plain block. Refer to Assembling the Quilt, page 9. You will assemble seven rows of nine blocks.

3. Sew the inner border strips that measure 1½" x 54½" to the sides of the assembled blocks.

4. Sew the inner border strips that measure 1½" x 44½" to the top and bottom of the assembled blocks.

5. Sew the outer border strips that measure 6½" x 58½" to the sides of the assembled blocks.

6. Sew the outer border strips that measure 6½" x 56½" to the top and bottom of the assembled blocks.

7. Sew the two pieces of backing fabric together; trim the unit to create a rectangle that measures 64" x 76".

8. Assemble the backing, batting and quilt top. Refer to Adding the Backing, page 9.

9. Bind the quilt. Refer to Binding the Quilt, page 9.

THE CIVIL WAR CHRISTMAS

Finished size: 50" x 64". Machine pieced and hand quilted by Mary Ellen Zeitz.

MATERIALS

· 2 yd. of fabric for outer border and binding
· ¾ yd. of fabric for lattice strips
· 2 yd. of fabric for first border
· 1½ yd. of fabric for background and cornerstones
· Scraps of assorted fabrics to make blocks
· 4 yd. of fabric for backing
· 56" x 70" of batting
· General tools and supplies (listed in How to Use This Book)

CUTTING INSTRUCTIONS

From the cornerstone fabric, cut:
· 48 cornerstones (1½" x 1½")
From the lattice fabric, cut:
· 82 lattice strips (1½" x 6½")
From the first border fabric, cut:
· 2 border strips (36½" x 1½")
· 2 border strips (52½" x 1½")
From the outer border fabric, cut:
· 2 border strips (38½" x 5½")
· 2 border strips (62½" x 5½")
From the backing fabric, cut:
· 2 rectangles (2 yd. x the width of the fabric)
From the backing fabric, cut:
· 8 binding strips (2" x the width of fabric)

INSTRUCTIONS

1. Assemble 35 of your favorite blocks. Refer to Piecing the Blocks, page 8.

2. Assemble the blocks, lattice and cornerstones into seven rows of five blocks each. Refer to Assembling the Quilt, page 9. The connecting rows will contain six cornerstones and five lattice strips.

3. Sew the first border strips that measure 1½" x 36½" to top and bottom of the assembled blocks.

4. Sew the first border strips that measure 1½" x 52½" to the sides of the assembled blocks.

5. Sew the outer border strips that measure 5½" x 38½" to top and bottom of the assembled blocks.

6. Sew the outer border strips that measure 5½" x 62½" to the sides of the assembled blocks.

7. Sew the two pieces of backing fabric together; trim the unit to create a rectangle that measures 58" x 72".

8. Assemble the backing, batting and quilt top. Refer to Adding the Backing, page 9.

9. Bind the quilt. Refer to Binding the Quilt, page 9.

The Civil War Heart of Love

Materials

- 12" x 12" scrap of fabric for background
- Scraps of assorted fabrics to make the heart
- Scraps of lace for trim
- Buttons or other embellishments (optional)
- Heart pattern
- General tools and supplies (listed in How to Use This Book)

Appliqué and Assembly Instructions

1. Enlarge the pattern by copying at 200%. Place a sheet of freezer paper over the pattern and trace around all of the shapes.

2. Cut out all of the freezer paper pattern shapes. Do not add a seam allowance.

3. Choose the fabrics you will use for each part of the heart. Set your iron to a no-steam setting. Iron a freezer-paper pattern piece to the right side of each corresponding fabric. Add a little less than ¼" seam allowance to all of the sides of each piece of fabric.

4. Piece together the heart.

5. Appliqué the heart to the background fabric. Use the needle to turn under the seam allowance on the first appliqué piece. Hold the piece down with your thumb, insert the needle into the back of the background fabric, and come up through the folded edge of the appliqué, near the spot your thumb is holding. The needle should be as close to the edge of the appliqué as possible. Insert the needle back into the background fabric, as close as possible to where the needle just came up, and take another stitch. Continue to stitch this way around the appliqué, placing stitches about ¹⁄₁₆" apart until you reach the starting point again.

6. Add embellishments, such as buttons, charms or lace, as desired.

CIVIL WAR HEART OF LOVE PATTERN
(Pattern at 50%. Copy at 200%)

Civil War
Soldiers Label

The Constitution and Union Forever

Finished size: 10" x 10". Made by Judy Day.

Materials

- 12" x 12" of fabric for the background
- Assorted fabrics for the appliqué pieces
- Fabric pens for the faces and/or signature
- Embroidery thread
- Freezer paper
- Matching sewing threads
- ½" sequin pins
- Soldier patterns on pages 271 and 273
- General tools and supplies (listed in How to Use This Book)

Appliqué and Assembly Instructions

1. Place a sheet of freezer paper over the pattern; trace around all of the shapes.

2. Carefully cut out each template on the lines you have drawn. Do not add a seam allowance.

3. Choose the fabrics you will use for each part of each soldier. Set your iron to a no-steam setting. Iron each freezer-paper pattern to the right side of the corresponding fabric.

4. Cut out all of the shapes, adding a little less than ¼" seam allowance around all of the sides.

5. Trace each soldier pattern onto the background fabric; be sure to center it on the panel.

6. Pin the first appliqué to the background; use ½" sequin pins.

7. Choose a color of thread that best matches the appliqué. Thread a hand sewing needle with an 18" length of this thread.

8. Pick up the background fabric, and use the needle to turn under the seam allowance on the first appliqué piece. Hold the piece down with your thumb, insert the needle into the back of the background fabric, and come up through the folded edge of the appliqué, near the spot your thumb is holding. The needle should be as close to the edge of the appliqué as possible. Insert the needle back into the background fabric, as close as possible to where the needle just came up, and take another stitch. Continue to stitch this way around the appliqué, placing stitches about ¹⁄₁₆" apart until you reach the starting point again.

9. Repeat Step 8 for all of the appliqué pieces.

10. Use the embroidery floss to stitch buttons or other details as desired on each appliqué.

11. Use a fabric pen to add a face to each soldier, and add your signature to the completed block.

Get the Complete Collection

THE AMISH CIRCLE QUILT
121 quilt block patterns that tell a story
by Rosemary Youngs

Inspired by heartwarming letters from a circle of Amish friends, this original circle quilt book takes you inside this treasured quilting tradition, and captures your heart and mind. The letters and 121 related quilt blocks tell the story of family and friends who come together to create a beautiful work of art. Step-by-step instructions guide you through your own Amish circle quilt, as well as eight smaller projects, such as a baby quilt, wall hanging, table runner and appliquéd aprons and bags. Features full-size color patterns.

Softcover • 8¼ x 10⅞ • 144 pages • 50+ color photos, 125+ illus.
Item# AMCQ • $24.99

THE CIVIL WAR DIARY QUILT
121 Stories and The Quilt Blocks They Inspired
By Rosemary Youngs

Bring the past alive with distinctive and exquisite quilt blocks that tell the stories of 10 women living and surviving the Civil War. Explore diary entries of each woman, plus instructions for 121 related quilt blocks. You'll meet a variety of women including a Michigan woman who took on the task of tending to her family's 160-acre farm while her husband was fighting the war, a 17 year-old who encountered the Union army as it trampled South Carolina, and a young bride who fled her home state of Tennessee to start a new life elsewhere.

Softcover • 8 x 8 • 288 pages • 121 color illustrations
Item# CWQD • $22.99

Quilt blocks in each book are interchangeable

krause publications
An imprint of F+W Publications, Inc.

P.O. Box 5009, Iola, WI 54945-5009
www.krausebooks.com